Digital Diasporas
Identity and Transnational Engagement

In the first full-length scholarly study of the increasingly important phenomenon of digital diasporas, Jennifer M. Brinkerhoff examines how immigrants who still feel a connection to their country of origin use the Internet. She argues that digital diasporas can ease security concerns in both the homeland and the host society, improve diaspora members' quality of life in the host society, and contribute to socioeconomic development in the homeland. Drawing on case studies of nine digital diaspora organizations, Brinkerhoff's research supplies new empirical material regarding digital diasporas and their potential security and development outcomes. She also explores their impact on identity negotiation, arguing that digital diasporas create communities and organizations that represent hybrid identities and encourage solidarity, identity, and material benefits among their members. The book explores these communities' implications for policy and practice.

Jennifer M. Brinkerhoff is an Associate Professor of Public Administration and International Affairs at the George Washington University. She holds a Ph.D. in public administration from the University of Southern California in Los Angeles and an MPA from the Monterey Institute of International Studies. She consults for multilateral development banks, bilateral assistance agencies, NGOs, and foundations. Combining her research with this work, she published *Partnership for International Development: Rhetoric or Results?* (2002), as well as three co-edited journal issues and more than forty-five articles and book chapters on topics ranging from evaluation to NGOs, failed states, governance, and diasporas. She is the editor of *Diasporas and Development: Exploring the Potential* (2008). She also completed an edited volume for the Asia Development Bank titled *Converting Migration Drains into Gains: Harnessing the Resources of Overseas Professionals* (2006), and she is the editor of the book series *Diasporas in World Politics*. She is the co-director and co-founder of GW's Diaspora Research Program, a multidisciplinary research program on diasporas, identity, policy, and development; she also co-founded the GW International NGO team and co-edited *NGOs and the Millennium Development Goals: Citizen Action to Reduce Poverty* (2007).

Digital Diasporas

Identity and
Transnational Engagement

JENNIFER M. BRINKERHOFF
George Washington University

CAMBRIDGE
UNIVERSITY PRESS

CAMBRIDGE UNIVERSITY PRESS
Cambridge, New York, Melbourne, Madrid, Cape Town, Singapore, São Paulo, Delhi

Cambridge University Press
32 Avenue of the Americas, New York, NY 10013-2473, USA

www.cambridge.org
Information on this title: www.cambridge.org/9780521741439

First published 2009

Printed in the United States of America

A catalog record for this publication is available from the British Library.

Library of Congress Cataloging in Publication Data

Brinkerhoff, Jennifer M., 1965–
Digital diasporas : Identity and transnational engagement / Jennifer M.
Brinkerhoff.
p. cm.
Includes bibliographical references and index.
ISBN 978-0-521-51784-3 (hardback) – ISBN 978-0-521-74143-9 (pbk.)
1. Immigrants – Computer network resources. 2. Internet – Social aspects.
I. Title.
JV6225.B75 2009
305.9'06912–dc22   2008643639

ISBN 978-0-521-51784-3 hardback
ISBN 978-0-521-74143-9 paperback

Contents

Tables and Figure

Acknowledgments

This project began with the notion of collaboration and in the immediate aftermath of September 11, 2001. My colleague, Lori Brainard, suggested it would be interesting to pursue a research project together. Our challenge was finding a hook that linked her expertise in online communities with my interest in international development. I am deeply indebted to Lori for exposing me to the wonders of communities in cyberspace, suggesting a collaboration in the first place, embracing such an unusual combination, and working with me on the first phase of the program. That phase was funded by the George Washington University Center for the Study of Globalization, to whom I also owe a debt of gratitude.

A large number of graduate research assistants helped along the way. In the first phase, in particular, these students sat through lengthy, mind-twisting meetings as Lori and I explored and communicated our evolving research methodology. Our team of students contributed their own thoughts, ideas, and experience and worked tirelessly to randomly select and analyze discussion threads, conduct link analyses, and transcribe interview tapes. I am grateful not only for all of these contributions, but also for their patience and perseverance as they were exposed to everything from sometimes esoteric and deeply religious thoughts to raunchy discussions replete with profanity. These are the many faces of people in cyberspace and together we met them all. Throughout the project our team of dedicated research assistants included: Tom Bryer, Andrew Edelson, Sarah Epps, Tara Hill, Dana Epstein, and Aliza Inbal Belman. I am particularly grateful to Tom

Bryer, who led our student team during the first phase; Tara Hill, who led the second phase and provided particularly insightful analyses of the two most contrasting cyber communities; and Aliza Inbal Belman, who in addition to putting up with the transcription seemed to enjoy the wonders of these inspiring people and ideas and who also suffered the incredibly mundane task of organizing my literature database.

Obviously, this project would not have been possible without the amazing individuals featured in these pages. I especially thank the founders of the organizations studied and all those whom we interviewed. Your commitment to your communities, to your identity, and to service will remain a source of inspiration for me for a long time to come. Thanks to Abdullah Qazi, Abdul Meraj, Tooba Mayel, Ferdous Hakim, Hassib Amiryar, Michael Meunier, Homira Nassery, George Andraws, Nermien Riad, Phoebe Pharag, the staff of Coptic Orphans in Cairo and the many volunteers and children of its Valuable Girl Project there, Bal Joshi, Robert Granger, Daniel Koch, Abdi Osman, and Dorjee Nudup.

The German Marshall Fund and the Rockefeller Foundation invited me to participate in the Bellagio Dialogue on Migration in the summer of 2006. They provided me two glorious weeks of interaction with a range of actors concerned with issues of migration and development, including scholars from a variety of disciplines, advocates and social workers for migrants in receiving countries, legislative assistants, government officials, and leaders of diaspora organizations. Not only did these discussions stimulate my thoughts and provide fodder for further inspiration, during my two-week stay I was gifted four full days in beautiful Bellagio fully dedicated to this project. These were among the most productive days throughout the project, and I thank the German Marshall Fund and the Rockefeller Foundation for this opportunity.

Mike Brown, Dean of the Elliott School of International Affairs at George Washington University, provided invaluable assistance in helping me to better recognize the contributions of this study.

Most especially, I thank my husband, Derick Brinkerhoff. Derick came up with the project's working title and clever acronym: Digital Diasporas, Identity, and International Policy Processes, or DIP squared (DIP^2). Beyond this creative contribution he is, as always, the most supportive husband a professional woman could ever hope for. And patient too – I thank him for putting up with my almost constant vocalized observations, confirming that identity is everywhere.

Digital Diasporas

Identity and Transnational Engagement

I

Introduction

The world after September 11, 2001, is a scary place. Many, already feeling powerless due to globalization, now feel even more vulnerable to factors beyond their control. From social, political, economic, and psychological points of view, current events and media reports lead us to fear "other" perhaps as never before. The result in some circles is a creeping xenophobia and general anxiety about the unknown. Two logical targets for this fear and insecurity are immigration, especially diasporas – immigrants who still feel a connection to their country of origin, and information technology (IT). Much has been written about them to inspire fear, including their links to terrorism.

A case in point is the 2008 United States Senate report, *Violent Islamist Extremism, The Internet, and the Homegrown Terrorist Threat*. Nonprofit and Muslim organizations greeted it with scathing criticism of its underlying assumptions about the Internet and immigrants, especially American Muslims; the American Civil Liberties Union (ACLU) railed against what it called proposed violations of freedom of speech. These groups argued that the narrow focus represented by the report will inspire fear, justify discrimination, and violate constitutional rights – all without necessarily preventing or protecting American citizens from homegrown terrorism. Citing the example of Timothy McVeigh – a native-born terrorist – the ACLU argued, "This narrow focus could cost us dearly in the future" (cited in OMB Watch 2008).

While policy efforts related to the report are underway, the data to support the connections between diasporas, the Internet, and terrorism remain sparse. The U.S. Senate report cites three examples of Internet-supported homegrown terrorism by immigrants but does not provide data beyond these anecdotes. It refers only (in an endnote) to the 2007 Pew Research Center survey of Muslim Americans, wherein 27% of those polled refused to state an opinion on Al-Qaeda and 5% viewed the organization favorably. Other research shows a significant increase (approximately threefold) in the number of websites linking diasporas and terrorism from September 11, 2001 to May 2002 (Brynen 2005). Neither of these data sets measures a connection between diasporas and actual terrorist activities or their use of the Internet and terrorist activities.

Writing about fear factors, and especially terrorism, is a growth industry. And, yes, individual diasporans may use the Internet to participate in violent and/or terrorist activities. But surely there must be different perspectives on these issues? Immigration, information technology, and their implications for society worldwide are complex phenomena. They deserve a nuanced investigation, a more holistic analysis, and a view to looking beyond gloom and doom to balance the scorecard on these realities, which, after all, are embedded features of the world today.

In this book, I analyze the impact of digital diasporas – diasporas organized on the Internet – in international affairs. These impacts include potential to foster democratic values, support integration in the host society, and contribute to security and socio-economic development in the homelands. I argue that migrant integration can be eased when diasporans (members of diasporas) have opportunities to express their hybrid identities (a sense of self that is neither wholly of the homeland nor exclusively reflective of the hostland) collectively. Such expression increasingly occurs through activities in support of the homeland. It is most supportive of peace and integration when it encompasses liberal values and other features consistent with an increasing identification with the adopted country. IT facilitates these agendas on a number of fronts. Digital diasporas use the Internet to negotiate their identity and promote solidarity; learn, explore, and enact democratic values; and mobilize to peacefully pursue policy influence, service objectives, and economic participation in the homeland.

How do communities of migrants become diaspora communities, that is, with identities that sustain at least psychological links to the homeland? How do these identities reflect the diaspora experience? How do they become transformed into something more than an identification with the homeland, yet not exclusively identified with the adopted country culture? And what are the implications of these hybrid identities for integration in the adopted society, and for policy and development influence vis-à-vis the homeland? How does information technology contribute to identity outcomes and their potential manifestation in the real world? This introductory chapter addresses why we should care about these questions, and reviews our current state of knowledge. I then introduce my own approach to this subject matter, and discuss the contributions and implications of this study. The next sections present the research design and provide an overview of the five home countries for the digital diaspora case studies. I close by presenting the structure of the book.

UNDERSTANDING MIGRATION AND INFORMATION TECHNOLOGY: THE IMPERATIVE

Diasporas have always been important actors in global and domestic affairs. As early as the fifteenth century, Chinese trade networks fostered important transnational economic benefits and the Chinese diaspora influenced – for better or for worse – the political, social, and economic systems in their adopted societies. More recently, the United States faced the challenge of integrating the Irish into American society at the turn of the twentieth century and later concerns regarding their support to the Irish Republican Army. Since the 1950s, the United States has provided organized support for the integration of the Cuban diaspora, while it hopes that some diaspora members will participate in, and possibly return to, a post-Castro Cuba.

Today, information and people cross international borders at speeds and in numbers unimagined previously. Together, migration and telecommunication advancements make diasporas all the more relevant to international affairs. The answer of why we should care about diasporas and the Internet revolves both around the risk factors and the great potential they hold for constructive political and socio-economic contributions. I begin with the former.

Diasporas and the Internet: Potential Security Implications

Some see the accelerated movement of people and information as cause for alarm, particularly after September 11, 2001. Globalization has enhanced economic and political interdependence and, at the same time, has afforded opportunities for some countries and communities to advance while leaving others behind. The resulting marginalization exacerbates the potential for conflict, nationally and internationally, on economic, political, and/or social grounds.[1] The first decade of the new millennium was fraught with conflict. Already in the 1990s, ethnic conflicts became much more numerous and severe (see Anderson 1999; Duffield 2001), in several cases spilling over into neighboring countries and international policy deliberations. Social tension leading to conflict inside nation-states is not new, though the consequences and potential for conflict escalation through external intervention have increased through globalization.

Organized diasporas may threaten global security (see Faist 2002; Weiner 1995). Several studies examine the role of organized diasporas in promoting policy and regime change in their home territories.[2] Some scholars describe the evolution of diasporas' relations vis-à-vis their homeland governments as moving "from victims to challengers" (see Cohen 1996). In situations of conflict, diaspora communities may raise money to support continuing warfare, promote public opinion and international interventions in support of their cause, and may prevent resolution, even when their compatriots are prepared to negotiate (Anderson 1999). The existence of diasporas may substantially increase the likelihood of conflict in their home countries (Collier and Hoeffler 2001). The instability diasporas generate within countries can have spillover effects with implications for global security.

---

[1] See Collier et al. (2003); Gissinger and Gleditch (1999); and Lake and Rothchild (1996).

[2] See, for example, Byman et al. (2001); King and Melvin (1999/2000); Shain (1999, 1994–1995).

Organized diasporas may use information technology to facilitate these agendas.

With the recent war on terrorism, even elective migration to industrialized countries has sparked new concerns ranging from the migration of terrorists to the harboring of terrorists by immigrant communities, the financial support of terrorist activities through charity foundations, and, finally, the recruitment of terrorists from within seemingly assimilated diasporas. These possibilities magnify the importance of socially and politically integrating migrants and refugees into receiving societies. In addition to economic challenges, immigrants face the socio-psychological challenges associated with negotiating their way through a new culture and embracing an altered identity, while still maintaining an identity associated with their culture of origin.[3] For many, integration is a stressful process culturally, socially, and economically (Nelson-Jones 2002).

The inability to integrate, or identity distress, may be associated with violence (Hernandez, Montgomery, and Kurtines 2006). The structure of violence encompasses exclusion, inequality, and indignity (Galtung 1996). Feelings of marginalization and social exclusion may lead to violent behavior and exacerbate existing conflict.[4] This linkage may be particularly salient for youth (Phillips and Pittman 2003). Those who lack a collective identity have been described as "psychologically desperate" and easy prey for terrorist organizations who seek to fill this psychological void (Taylor and Lewis 2004, 184). In other words, if they lack an existing sense of belonging, individuals become vulnerable to recruitment into whichever social structures can provide it, regardless of the purpose of these social structures (Brinkerhoff 2008a).

Conventional wisdom holds that IT, especially as it is applied transnationally, poses a threat to nation states' sovereignty and capacity to govern. IT has "exposed the porosity of geographic and political borders and the limited extent of any national jurisdiction" (Montgomery 2002, 26). Wilson's (1998) literature review found a significant degree of agreement that state sovereignty – and, arguably, capacity – is being

---

[3] Hermans and Kemper (1998); Lavie and Swedenberg (1996); Friedman (1994).

[4] See, for example, Barber (2001) on Palestinian youth and the Intifada; and Lemarchand (2000) on the conflict in the Great Lakes region of Africa.

eroded by IT, as a result of states' increasing inability to control information both within their borders, as well as at the supranational level.

Recent research on IT and terrorism confirms the Internet's enabling features for terrorist activities, including its ease of access, anonymity, and international character.[5] The Internet's speed and flexibility accelerates the global dissemination of ideas and agendas, and the absence of mediation enables the articulation of these without the review and fact checking of traditional media (Margulies 2004). Indeed, the Internet has become the principal platform for dissemination and recruitment for jihadist terrorist movements (see, for example, Awan 2007). Some have even claimed that IT highlights the marginalization resulting from globalization, promoting despair and hopelessness in the South, and thus contributing to the emergence of terrorism (Elnur 2003).

Diaspora groups may use the Internet not only to promote particular political agendas that may foment conflict in the homeland, but also to promote secessionist movements and civil war. Those opposed to their homeland government may "use the Internet to reach out to the international media to disseminate propaganda, recruit, train, and solicit funds and influence international public opinion, and, most importantly, to network with diasporas across the globe" (Tekwani 2003, 178). For example, Kashmiri militants fighting for independence from India maintain websites in Britain. Separatist groups similarly have used the Internet to advocate against the Indonesian government in East Timor and Papua New Guinea, with websites based in Portugal and New Zealand respectively; and against the government of Papua New Guinea, with a website hosted in Australia (Tekwani 2003).

Diasporas and the Internet: Potential Contributions

Diasporas' potential constructive contributions encompass policy influence supportive of liberal values, integration and conflict

---

[5] See Weimann (2006); Tsfati and Weimann (2002); and Lal (2002). See also the *Washington Post*'s series: August 7–9, 2005 (Coll and Glasser 2005; Whitlock 2005; Glasser and Coll 2005). These concerns were voiced before 9–11, see for example Whine (1999).

prevention, and socio-economic development, each of which may be facilitated by the Internet. Due to their attachments to the homeland and the ease of telecommunications, diasporas are increasingly apt to insert themselves into economic, political, and development processes vis-à-vis the homeland.

Diasporas have become essential to many national economic and political agendas. In several countries, diasporas contribute significant portions of their homeland's gross domestic products (GDPs). In 2006 (International Fund for Agricultural Development (IFAD) 2007), for example, in Latin America diasporas accounted for over 31% in Grenada, almost 25% in Honduras, and approximately 21% in Haiti. In Africa, diasporas accounted for almost 49% of GDP in Guinea-Bissau, 39% in Sao Tome and Principe, 38% in Eritrea, and over 34% in Cape Verde. In Asia diasporas contributed almost 37% of GDP in Tajikistan, over 34% in PDR of Laos, and over 31% in Kyrgyzstan. Almost 35% of the West Bank and Gaza Strip, and a little over 25% of Lebanon's GDP come from their diasporas. In Europe, over 31% of Moldova's, and almost 22% of Albania's GDP come from their diasporas. Globally economic remittance estimates now outpace official development assistance: $70 billion per year in 2004; and estimated at $125 billion in 2005, and $167 billion in 2006 (World Bank, 2004, 2005, 2006). Other estimates place 2006 global remittances at $300 billion, with most going to Asia (over $113 billion), followed by Latin America and the Caribbean (over $68 billion), Europe (over $50 billion), Africa (over $38 billion), and the Near East (over $29 billion) (IFAD 2007).

Diaspora homeland investment may be crucial to resource-strapped developing countries; their relatively weak institutions, political risks, or lower incomes may discourage the typical, nondiaspora foreign investor (Riddle, Brinkerhoff, and Nielsen 2008). First, diasporans may be more likely to invest in economies that others would consider high risk, simply because they have knowledge and relationship opportunities that other investors lack (see Gillespie et al. 1999; Gillespie, Sayre, and Riddle 2001). Second, they can combine this knowledge with the skills, knowledge, and networks they have cultivated abroad, yielding important synergistic advantages (Gillespie et al. 2001, 1999). In India's IT industry, diasporans played a significant role not only as direct investors (approximately 16% of foreign direct investment (FDI) to the sector) but as brokers of investment relationships, leading to the much-lauded success of India's IT industry (Margolis et al. 2004; Saxenian 2002a). Part of this success is attributed to the Indian diaspora's role in proposing and promoting necessary changes to the legal framework in order to improve the investment climate (Saxenian 2002b).[6]

Beyond economic contributions, developing countries can benefit from diasporans' skills transfer, and cultural and civic awareness/experience (Nyberg-Sorensen 2004). These contributions are particularly salient in countries suffering from brain drain in specific technical sectors, but also in countries seeking to advance their development more generally (see Wescott and Brinkerhoff 2006). Diasporans may repatriate for the purpose of capacity building, whether permanently or for short-term assignments. Experimentation with virtual return is also on the rise, whereby diasporans contribute knowledge and expertise and/or transfer knowledge through IT technologies and video conferencing. Examples include Dutch-Ghanaian doctors providing patient diagnosis to hospitals in Accra, and diasporan delivery of health policy analysis training by video conference in Ethiopia. Diasporans may also contribute to homeland development through employment in the development industry (see, for example, Brinkerhoff and Taddesse 2008).

Diasporas represent important opportunities for more formal development organizations (those funded through Official Development Assistance) to recruit expertise and solicit information for development programs; and disseminate information about priorities and programming, potentially reducing duplication and cross-purpose efforts (Brinkerhoff 2004). Diaspora philanthropy organizations can act as important intermediaries between these formal development actors, and diasporas and local communities, for example, identifying and communicating needs and priorities of local communities and soliciting funding and expertise for those from donor organizations, non-governmental organizations (NGOs), and diaspora members. Diaspora philanthropy organizations may also demonstrate innovative programs and approaches that can be replicated and/or used to

---

[6] Research on the most effective mechanisms and government promotion efforts targeting diasporas is still in its infancy. For path-breaking examples, see Riddle et al. (2008); Gillespie and Andriasova (2008); and Riddle and Marano (2008).

advocate for development industry administrative and programmatic reforms. These contributions are particularly salient to countries emerging from conflict, for example in Afghanistan (Brinkerhoff 2004) and Liberia (Lubkemann 2004).

On the political front, beyond promoting regime change in their home territories, diasporans have become important constituents and advocates for homeland governments. As of 2000, approximately eighty-nine countries allowed for dual citizenship or included migrants as official members of their political communities (Renshon 2000). The government of Mexico is a leader in terms of incorporating and seeking political support from its diaspora. Elected diasporans can serve in state parliaments. The Institute of Mexicans Abroad, housed in the Federal Secretariat of Foreign Relations, provides advocacy training to Mexican diaspora organizations and includes a Consultative Council of 105 elected representatives of immigrant groups in the United States and Canada (see Ayón 2006). According to Executive Director Carlos Gonzalez-Gutierrez organized diaspora visits include presentations on the government's policy agenda vis-à-vis the United States and training on how to lobby the U.S. government (personal communication).

Diasporas' political activities are likely to grow as they both benefit from and contribute to democratization. Democracy affords both a more conducive environment for diaspora political engagement from the hostland and more opportunities for influence in the homeland (Koslowski 2005). Policy influence in the homeland may support improved enabling environments for socio-economic development, as in the Indian IT sector, and/or it can be used to promote partisan platforms with arguable public benefit. Rather than alternatives (see Hirschman 1970), exit may be necessary for the exercise of voice (Birch 1975; qtd. in Koslowski 2005). Diasporas may have influence disproportionate to their numbers owing to knowledge, skills, and financial capital acquired in the host society, and through their influence on the host country's foreign policy vis-à-vis their homelands (Koslowski 2005, 11). Similarly, diaspora support to homeland political campaigns may disproportionately influence outcomes due to relative currency exchange rates.

Diasporas can both "humanize" and "Americanize" U.S. foreign policy, combating isolationist tendencies, and reflecting American values of freedom and democracy (Shain 1995, 1999). In the United States, diasporas elect or are pressured to adopt liberal values (Shain 1995, 1999). Their influence on host-country foreign policy – motivated by traditional cultural identity – is most effective when it corresponds with host-country national interest and values – their American identity (Shain 1999). The best known examples in the United States are the efforts of the Armenian and Israeli diasporas (see Shain and Barth 2003). Diaspora communities of identity are often explicitly maintained and mobilized for the purpose of influencing international public opinion and building political support for human rights and political freedoms, for example, groups of the Haitian, Tibetan, and Cuban diasporas (see Shain 1994-1995; see also Koslowski 2005).

Countering exclusive assumptions about their threat to state sovereignty, diasporas have potential to contribute to all three governance components: legitimacy, effectiveness, and security (Brinkerhoff 2007). They can act as an additional watchdog on homeland governments. Given their potential access, through networks on the ground, to local information on policy implementation, regulatory enforcement, and human rights abuses, diaspora organizations may be well-placed to play a monitoring role in support of good governance and donors' efforts to promote governance reforms (Brainard and Brinkerhoff 2006). Using IT, diasporas can facilitate communication channels in support of accountability and responsiveness to human rights concerns, enhancing governance legitimacy (Brinkerhoff 2005). By contributing to the provision of public goods and technical assistance/capacity building of government agencies, diasporas support governance effectiveness (Brinkerhoff 2004). Additionally, they may potentially prevent the participation of fellow diasporans in continuing or instigating renewed violence in the homeland (Brinkerhoff 2006a).

By fostering both bonding and bridging social capital, diaspora organizations can support integration and may prevent latent conflict from becoming manifest.[7] Bonding social capital emphasizes

---

[7] Conflict prevention aims not necessarily to eliminate the sources of latent conflict, but to reduce the likelihood that conflict will become manifest through violent action (see Leatherman et al. 1999).

dense social networks that can engender trust (Coleman 1988, 1990). It can counter the destabilizing forces of marginalization and provide a social safety net for group members (Gittel and Vidal 1998). This potentially raises the stakes for diasporas to engage in conflict – with bonding social capital based in the host country, there is more to lose.[8] Bridging social capital emphasizes heterogeneous networks, where members have greater opportunities to access information and understanding beyond their current intragroup resources (see Burt 2000). Diaspora organizations can foster bridging among diaspora subgroups and between the diaspora and the host country society. Through repeat interaction and the discovery of shared needs and interests, bridging social capital prevents the dehumanization of "other."[9]

In addition to its support for mobilization, especially for small, marginalized groups,[10] the Internet fosters community, solidarity, and liberal values. It provides forums for the exchange of ideas, debate, and the mobilization of opinion, potentially culminating in strong social bonds and relationships (Rheingold 1993).[11] Cyber-grass-roots organizations (CGOs), grassroots organizations existing only in cyberspace, can cultivate online communities that offer solidary benefits to members (Brainard and Brinkerhoff 2004), or associational advantages that flow from feeling connected to others and belonging to a community (Wilson 1995). IT may also promote cosmopolitanism, or "a universal moral code transcending state boundaries and state interests" (Jacobsen and Lawsen 1999, 205), which increasingly encompasses respect for human rights and democratic practices.[12] The Internet facilitates the expression of liberal values such as individualism and freedom of speech, either through anonymity or access

---

[8] Bonding social capital can only mitigate potential violence in this way if the bonding does not itself occur around separatist or violent identities and agendas.

[9] See, for example, Rubin, Pruitt, and Kim (1994); Northrup (1989).

[10] See, for example, Brainard and Siplon (2002a, 2002b); Ayres (1999); Bennett and Fielding (1999); Brophy and Halpin (1999); Wittig and Schmitz (1996).

[11] While some scholars remain concerned about the Internet's potential to foster increasing parochialism, where individuals can more easily selectively pursue information and interaction opportunities (Barber 1995; Elkins 1997), this may only occur when the range of communication remains small (Greig 2002).

[12] For further discussion of the role of information technology in promoting liberalization and democratization, see Kalathil and Boas (2003).

opportunity. In effect, it can become a test bed for experimenting with liberal values.

What Do We Know About Diasporas' Use of IT?

Given the obvious salience of diasporas and IT, what do we know about diasporas' use of IT? Digital diasporas are relatively recent phenomena, growing in tandem with the evolution of and access to Internet technology. Those who live in diaspora participate in physical diaspora communities, which are largely place-based. With the advent of IT, individuals within and across such communities can create additional, online communities, or they may simply use the Internet to pursue purposive objectives related to their homeland identity (e.g., philanthropy, news sources). As a tool for communication and community building among dispersed populations, the Internet is ideally suited for connecting diasporans who are geographically scattered and removed from their homeland. One would expect IT to have a significant impact on diaspora communities and their ability to mobilize for community building, economic, and political purposes. Indeed, the only major study to date of diasporas and media technology confirms that diasporas are frequently on the cutting edge of technology adoptions (Karim 2003a; see also Dahan and Sheffer 2001). IT leads to new diasporic identities with stronger ties within and among diaspora communities and with the homeland, leading Panagakos (2003) to argue that we are nearing the end of conventionally conceptualized ethnic group identity.

Despite the growing significance of this expanding phenomenon, none of the few existing studies analyze the connected processes through which diasporas use the Internet to establish communication networks, explore identity, and mobilize these to foster democratic values and contribute to security and socio-economic development in their homelands. This book is the first to examine digital diasporas' significance for international affairs.

Studies of diasporas have been intermittent. Diasporas were first comparatively analyzed in the late 1980s (Sheffer 1986b). However, scholars did not immediately build on this work, and in the 1990s the phenomenon of diasporas was reintroduced as if it were a new subject (Cohen 1997). The second significant study appeared at the end of that decade and comparatively analyzed diasporas' influence on U.S. foreign affairs (Shain 1999). The next full-length study of diasporas, which includes some comparative analysis, was published only recently, and focuses on diaspora politics (Sheffer 2006). Most studies still emphasize defining the nature of diasporas, and exploring their political and cultural implications, with little reference to policy and programmatic implications. Scholars are just beginning to turn their attention to the economic and development impacts of diasporas on their homelands (see Merz, Chen, and Geithner 2007; Saxenian 2006). These more recent efforts do not address the role of digital diasporas in these endeavors.

Scholars have not comparatively examined diasporas' use of the Internet to create online communities for exploring their identities and contemplating agendas vis-à-vis the homeland. Existing studies demonstrate that the Internet is increasingly instrumental to diasporas' ability to negotiate their identity and retain psychological links to the cultural identity of their homelands.[13] However, studies of digital diasporas thus far have focused on single case studies, often from an anthropological perspective, with little or no comparative analysis or discussion of policy implications.[14] The combination of diasporas and the Internet may be a useful resource in promoting peace and prosperity. Yet, a lack of understanding of the nature of these contributions, how to mobilize them, and the circumstances that are most likely to yield positive results hamper policymakers' ability to tap this expanding resource.

Digital Diasporas: Expanding our Learning Now and Into the Future

This book responds to this need. I develop an analytic framework that identifies several aspects of digital diaspora activities, highlighting their importance to global and national arenas. Digital diasporas can ease security concerns in both the homeland and host society,

---

[13] See, for example, Sökefeld (2002); Hozic (2001); Sapienza (2001); Lal (1999); Rai (1995).

[14] See, for example, Panagakos and Horst (2006); and selected chapters from Karim (2003b).

improve diasporans' quality of life in the host society, and contribute to socio-economic development for their families and compatriots in the homeland. The interactive components of the Internet enable the creation of cyber-communities that connect dispersed populations and provide solidarity among members. Members use discussion forums to disseminate information about the homeland faith and/or culture; to reinforce or recreate identity to make it more relevant and sustainable across generations in diaspora; and to connect to and participate in homeland relationships, festivals, and socio-economic development. Members' discussions reflect diasporas' embrace and experimentation with liberal values, which inform conflict mitigation, political agendas, and homeland socio-economic development contributions.

I analyze nine digital diaspora organizations from five primarily U.S.-based diasporas from: Afghanistan, Egypt (Egyptian Copts), Somalia, Nepal, and Tibet. I selected these cases to address: 1) the most important functions of digital diasporas: community building, norm development, and issue framing; and 2) their most important activities: fostering solidarity and hybrid identity (a sense of self that is neither wholly of the homeland nor exclusively reflective of the hostland), promoting cultural survival and religious identity among members, advancing socio-economic development and reconstruction in the homeland, and supporting human rights policy and preventing conflict escalation both within the diaspora and in the homeland. Through interviews and discussion thread analysis, I identify how members are creating self-regulating online communities and exploring issues of identity, sometimes testing the boundaries of community norms. I analyze how these communities frame issues for what is or is not acceptable to discuss and/or promote and how they incorporate liberal values into their discussions of identity as well as perceptions of the homeland and its future. Finally, I examine how digital diasporas contemplate and pursue interventions to assist the homeland.[15]

---

[15] Because communication between digital diaspora members takes place through instant messaging and private email to which I had no access, I was not able to assess the results of all of the interventions proposed in online discussions.

Diasporans have a choice about the types of communities they create and the types of purposive action they pursue, using the Internet or otherwise. Elsewhere I have more thoroughly discussed the factors that may lead individuals to direct their diaspora identity mobilization toward destructive (criminal and/or violent activities) versus constructive aims (well-intentioned activities that are noncriminal, nonviolent, and consistent with liberal values of human rights, including basic freedoms of speech, assembly, and self-determination) (Brinkerhoff 2008a). Diaspora communities are diverse. There are those who migrate with the sole intention of fomenting violence, just as there are those who will be recruited into such activities for reasons beyond the control of their families, communities, and public policy. My analysis suggests that rather than fear diasporans' use of the Internet and discourage homeland identity expression, host societies and governments should recognize how invaluable the advantages of the Internet are. In fostering identity expression and creating communities with solidary benefits, diasporas' use of the Internet can relieve identity stress, counter marginalization, and socialize individuals into adaptive normative systems, providing comfort to participants, and potentially preventing those vulnerable to recruitment into violent activities from pursuing that path.

This book makes several important contributions. First, it is the first full-length, scholarly study of the increasingly important phenomenon of digital diasporas. Second, it presents a broad comparative perspective on the subject. Third, it develops an analytical framework that outlines how digital diasporas function and identifies their most important potential impacts. Fourth, the case studies supply new empirical material that is both descriptive and analytic in terms of what digital diasporas are doing, how they are doing it, what their impacts are, and how they are influencing national and international affairs. Fifth, it provides a guiding framework for future research on this important subject. Finally, I develop several important policy implications.

Research Design

I present and analyze nine organizations from five primarily U.S.-based diasporas from Afghanistan, Egypt (Egyptian Copts), Somalia, Nepal,

TABLE 1-1. *Digital Diaspora Case Studies*

Diasporas	Policy Issues	Nature of State in Home Country	Ethnic/Religious	Organizations
Afghan-Americans	Development and reconstruction of Afghanistan	Failed; rebuilding	Tribal/clan diversity/conflict; Islamic identity	AfghanistanOnline Rebuild-Afghanistan Afghans4Tomorrow
Egyptian Copt-Americans	Cultural survival/religious identity; human rights policy; quality of life improvements	Semi-authoritarian	Ethnic homogeneity; Christian identity Ethnic cleavages in the homeland vis-à-vis the Muslim population	Mycopticchurch.com U.S. Copts Association (Copts.com) Coptic Orphans
Tibetan-Americans	Cultural survival; human rights, political freedom, sovereignty	Authoritarian/ repressive Parliamentary Democratic Government in exile	Ethnic homogeneity; Buddhist identity	TibetBoard
Somali-Americans	Prospects for peace in Somalia; conflict within the diaspora	Failed; civil war	Tribal/clan diversity/conflict; Islamic identity	SomaliNet
Nepali Diaspora	Identity maintenance, local economic development	Civil unrest; strained parliamentary democracy and constitutional monarchy	Primarily Hindu	Thamel.com

and Tibet. Table 1-1 summarizes these diasporas and organizations, their policy issues, and context. Together, the case studies explore solidarity and hybrid identity, socio-economic development and reconstruction, religious identity and human rights policy, and the prevention of conflict escalation. I identified each proposed website through a web search and selected it based on the liveliness of interactive components (extensive membership, volume of posts, and currency). All but three (Afghans4Tomorrow, Coptic Orphans, and Thamel.com) can be classified as CGOs, grassroots organizations existing primarily in cyberspace (Brainard and Brinkerhoff 2004).

Each case study is based on interviews with the founder(s), an analysis of at least three months of web-based discussion among members (where available), and a webpage link analysis. Non-CGO cases (i.e., those organizations with a physical presence) include interviews of additional staff, project reports and evaluations, and, in one instance, a project site visit and staff interviews in the homeland (Coptic Orphans, Cairo). I selected from the discussion forums threads for analysis based on the topic's relevance to the research questions. I analyzed webpages and their interactive components along two dimensions: the nature of the benefit gained from the member's participation (purposive, material, solidary, and cultural identity) and the type of communication involved (conventional, interpersonal, communal, and announcements). These categories are not mutually exclusive. I also analyzed message content for references to and demonstration of democratic values. Appendix I provides more detail on the methodology. I retain the original syntax in all quotations from webpages and Internet discussion forums.

Introduction to the Cases and Home Countries

Each of the selected organizations emphasizes a particular characteristic and/or type of contribution. For example, the Afghan case includes organizations that are primarily focused on community building on the one hand (AfghanistanOnline), and reconstruction and development on the other (Rebuild-Afghanistan, Afghans4Tomorrow). The Egyptian Copt case encompasses three organizations, each with a different emphasis: hybrid identity (MyCopticChurch.org), human rights policy (U.S. Copts Association), and improvements in quality of life (Coptic

Orphans). The case of the Somali diaspora (Somalinet), a cybercommunity, highlights how diasporas use the Internet to consider prospects for peace in their home country and generate understandings across clan divides within the diaspora. The Tibetan diaspora organization (TibetBoard) offers opportunities to explore how diasporas can use the Internet to sustain a homeland identity when repatriation is unlikely, and to question, shape, and promote political perspectives on the fate of the homeland. And the Nepali case, Thamel.com, demonstrates how the Internet can be used to sustain diaspora links to the homeland and channel remittances (particularly from migrant workers) to contribute to the local homeland economy as a whole, rather than to individual families alone.

What follows is a brief description of each of the home countries.

Afghanistan

Afghanistan has a volatile history, replete with external powers vying for its control. This began with the "Great Game" between the British and the Russians, followed by contestation between the United States (and Pakistan) and Russia. Only in 1880 was the country unified for the first time, under a despot, Abdur Rahman. This period saw the establishment of an Islamic state, governed by *sharia* law, and the establishment of the *loya jirga* or national council. Central governance remained weak, however, and the country continued to be ruled, de facto, by local warlords. Power continued to be contested. Afghanistan's first constitution was created in 1921.

The period 1963–1970, was known as the "New Democracy," with continued movement toward modernization and secularism. Further struggles for power ensued, which culminated in the overthrow of King Zahir Shah in 1978, and the Soviet invasion in 1979. Ethnic and tribal rivalries led to a full-scale civil war in the 1990s, followed by the Taliban seizing Kabul in 1996 and establishing its regime. In 2002, the United States invaded Afghanistan, ending the Taliban regime and establishing the Karzai interim government. A new constitution is now in effect and the process of rebuilding the war-torn society and infrastructure is ongoing.

Not surprisingly, this history yielded several waves of migration. While some immigrants trickled into the United States as early as the 1950s, the exponential growth and establishment of Afghan diaspora communities in the United States began to take shape in the 1980s. The U.S. census recorded 45,195 Afghans (defined as people born in Afghanistan) in 2000 (U.S. Census Bureau 2001), while Afghans in the United States consistently estimate their total number to be in the 100,000 range (Hanifi 2006). The first wave of Afghan immigration to the United States, from 1980–1996, consisted of relatively educated migrants from the merchant and professional classes, political elite, and "a heterogeneous collection of jihadist or mujahideen militants sponsored by the Central Intelligence Agency (CIA), informants working for the Drug Enforcement Agency (DEA), and translators for the Voice of America (VOA), as well as employees of other US Government agencies" (Hanifi 2006, 74). The second wave, 1996-2001, represented those who fled Afghanistan during the Taliban regime, and consists of relatively less educated and fewer wealthy individuals, with far greater numbers of women, children, and refugees.

The post-Taliban rebuilding of Afghanistan requires an effective and credible central state. Not surprisingly, this challenge has been referred to as more of a political than a technical one (Cramer and Goodhand 2002). Yet the technical challenges remain. Starting in 2002, reconstruction actors entered a country devastated not only by war, but also by drought. Beyond the well-known repression of women, general education levels were exceedingly low; health and social services largely nonexistent; and infrastructure had been destroyed (see Montgomery and Rondinelli 2004). It was this devastation and suffering, widely publicized in the popular press following the U.S. invasion, that inspired many Afghan diaspora members to commiserate and explore possibilities for contributing to their suffering homeland.

Egyptian Copts

Egypt is considered a semiauthoritarian regime. The 2005 presidential elections, while forwarding multiple candidates for the first time, secured President Hosni Mubarak a fifth six-year term with 88% of the vote. Subsequent parliamentary elections resulted in some opposition gains, but yielded some violence as well. Both elections saw low turnout, fraud, and vote rigging (U.S. State Department 2006b). The documented human rights abuses are many – including torture, political prisoners, arbitrary detention, absence of due process, and general restrictions on civil liberties. Some human rights abuses are specifically targeted to or have implications for the Copt community. Egypt's constitution specifies Islam as the official state religion.

Copts comprise a majority of the 8% to 10% of Christians in Egypt. According to the U.S. Department of State (2002b, 2006b), "for the most part, members of the non-Muslim minority worship without harassment." In its 2002 *International Religious Freedom Report*, the U.S. State Department (2002a) reported a continued trend toward "improvement in the Government's respect for and protection of religious freedom." Nevertheless, the report also detailed specific exceptions to this trend, which continue (U.S. State Department 2006b). In addition to ongoing challenges to church construction, the U.S. State Department reports continued government discriminatory practices against Copts, including discrimination in hiring and political representation, and a lack of cooperation with Christian families seeking to regain custody of their daughters who are forced to convert to Islam by Muslim men (U.S. State Deparment 2006b).

Perhaps most disturbing, 2005-2006 saw an upsurge in interreligious societal violence, mostly directed against Copts. In October 2005, the performance of an inflammatory play in a Coptic Church in Alexandria resulted in the murder of two Copts and sparked subsequent rioting. While such incidents have occurred periodically in recent years, many fear that the frequency and intensity of interreligious violence is increasing. In April 2006, an Islamist extremist attacked churchgoers at three Coptic Orthodox churches in Alexandria, Egypt. In an editorial responding to these attacks in *Al-Arahm Weekly*, the Editor-in-Chief, Ibrahim Nafie (2006) observes, "Never before have such wide scale sectarian skirmishes broken out in this country . . . there has been a fundamental shift in the dynamics governing Muslim-Copt relations in Egypt. A long history of trust is under threat."

Quality of life in Egypt ranges from adequate to very poor. Over the last decade, Egypt made sufficient progress on the Human Development Index to be reclassified from low to medium on human development, though regional and gender gaps are still prevalent (UNDP

2005). In 2004, there were approximately 2.15 million people unemployed, and 20.16% of the population lived below the poverty line. Upper Egypt, where the majority of Copts reside, remains the lowest performer on all indicators, with the highest rates of illiteracy, poverty, unemployment, and poor health (UNDP 2005).

It is impossible to gauge with any certainty the number of Egyptian Copts residing in the United States, as statistics on religious orientation of immigrants are not collected. Recent estimates of Arab immigrants range from 2 to 3 million, of whom 1.4 to 2.1 million may be Christians from the Middle East region (Coffman 2004). Legal permanent residence was granted to 51,698 immigrants from Egypt from 1996-2005, but the number of Copts within that figure is unknown (U.S. Office of Immigration Statistics 2006). During this period, 2,977 Egyptians were affirmatively granted asylum, and 1,782 were defensively granted asylum (U.S. Office of Immigrtion Statistics 2006). These asylum cases could reflect Egyptian government repression of political opposition, inclusive of Islamic movements, or societal tensions and persecution of the Copts. Repetitive confrontations between Christians and Muslims in Egypt began in 1979; the first waves of emigration can be dated to that time, though much of the subsequent migration is likely due to family ties and elective migration for economic reasons (see Fargues 2001).

Tibet

The People's Republic of China (PRC) has long considered Tibet a province of China. In the 1950s it acted on this belief, incorporating Tibet into its national territory and beginning a heavy influence over its politics, culture, and society. Some have even accused the PRC of genocide (for example, Sautman 2003). With the increasing severity of imposed reforms, a rebellion movement was born, first in the region of Kham (where people are known as Khampas), and later as a unified resistance army with other groups based in central Tibet. With Central Intelligence Agency support from the United States and a launching platform in Nepal, the Chushi Gangdrug resistance army fought against Chinese troops until 1974. It was no match for the Chinese army. Perhaps its most significant achievement was the successful escort of the Dalai Lama to India in 1959. The vestiges of the resistance army have since operated as a political and social welfare organization in the exile community (McGranahan 2005).

The Dalai Lama established a Tibetan Government in exile in Dharamsala, India, with a surrounding exiled community. Shortly after his establishment there, Tibetan refugees began arriving in the tens of thousands each year. As of March 2004, approximately 125,000 refugees were living in India, Nepal, and Bhutan, with an estimated 2,500 new arrivals each year; 10,000 Tibetan refugees are believed to be living in the West (Central Tibetan Administration of His Holiness the Dalai Lama; qtd. in International Campaign for Tibet 2005). In 2002, the U.S. Committee for Refugees reported that the number of refugees in Dharamsala fluctuates with approximately 1,000 new arrivals each year and an unknown number of returning Tibetans. An estimated one in five Tibetan refugees in Dharamsala suffer from posttraumatic stress, with various methods of torture reported (Crescenzi et al. 2002).

Nepal also hosts Tibetan refugees, estimated at 20,000 in 2002. Since the early 1990s, the government of Nepal has prevented newcomers from remaining in Nepal, though until recently they could legally transit through en route to India and other destinations (U.S. Department of State 2006c). Repression of Tibetans in Nepal continues to worsen. In 2005, the US Department of State (2006c) reported that local officials in Kathmandu prevented the Tibetan community from holding public celebrations, violating freedoms of assembly and religion.

Refugees continue to arrive in both India and Nepal, sometimes seeking assistance from the UN High Commissioner for Refugees. The UNHCR reported almost 3,500 new arrivals in each country in 2005 (U.S. Department of State 2006a). Thousands of Tibetans also transit to India for temporary stays, many of them in search of religious and cultural training (U.S. Department of State 2006a).

With time in exile, the Dalai Lama's political stance has evolved. It began with an absolute refusal to concede that Tibet is part of China and that, as peoples, the Chinese and Tibetans have any common bonds. It is now a less politically oriented power position, with a priority to maintain cultural and religious power in Tibet (Baogang and Sautman 2005/2006). Both China and exiled Tibetans worry that the so-called "Tibetan Question" would be better addressed during the

Dalai Lama's lifetime (Baogang and Sautman 2005/2006); as of 2007 he is 72. Tibetan independence supporters, among others, have sharply criticized the Dalai Lama and the Government in exile for distancing themselves from the perspective of China as the enemy and accommodating a need to negotiate (see Zupp 2004).

The Tibetan cause garnered significant support in the West from both politicians and Buddhist aficionados. In 1991, the U.S. Congress passed a nonbinding resolution declaring Tibet an "occupied country" and urging the U.S. government to recognize the Tibetan Government-in-Exile as Tibet's sovereign power. The "Free Tibet" movement became popular on college campuses, was endorsed by celebrities, and was further buttressed by the promotion and sale of Tibetan cultural goods in shops across the country. However, the United States continues to recognize the Tibetan Autonomous Region as part of the People's Republic of China and, in the aftermath of September 11, 2001, and with the long and continuing duration of China's control of the territory, interest in the movement has waned (Baogang and Sautman 2005/2006). A Tibetan expert (Goldstein 1995, xi) identified three options forward for the Government-in-Exile:

1) maintain the status quo by continuing the campaign of enhancing international support; 2) escalate the conflict by encouraging and even organizing violence in Tibet; and 3) compromise by sending Beijing a message that the Dalai Lama is ready to scale down his political demands in order to preserve a more homogeneous Tibetan homeland (Baogang and Sautman 2005/2006, 608).

While the options are not mutually exclusive, it seems that the Dalai Lama has adopted the third option and has already made significant concessions (Baogang and Sautman 2005/2006).

Following the March 2008 unrest in Tibet and concerned that international criticism would compromise its objectives for hosting the 2008 Summer Olympics, the PRC opened channels of communication, with Chinese President and Party Secretary Hu Jintao stating: "our attitude towards contacts and consultation with the Dalai Lama is serious" (Xinhua News 2008). The Dalai Lama's envoys have held a series of meetings with Chinese officials, wherein, according to his special envoy, divergent views were "expressed in a frank and candid manner" (Gyari 2008).

Perceptions of quality of life in Tibet are contentious. While there is a growing middle class, and the Chinese point to increased literacy and improved infrastructure, health conditions remain dismal (Singh 2004), with hospitals lacking infrastructure and equipment and suffering from minimal health worker training. In the 1990s child and maternal mortality rates were three times those of the rest of China. Child nutrition is a serious concern and almost two thirds of children suffer from rickets. The PRC has been accused of prioritizing infrastructure over health concerns (Watts 2003). Indeed, while Tibetans may be relatively better off economically than in the past, the Tibetan Autonomous Region remains the poorest administrative unit in China, despite disproportionate resource injections from the PRC. Equity between the Han Chinese and ethnic Tibetans remains a concern (Teufel Dreyer 2003). Access to information inside of Tibet is tightly controlled by the PRC, making assessments of human rights problematic (U.S. Department of State 2006a). Despite these challenges, the U.S. Department of State finds significant repression of religious freedom, and continued serious human rights abuses, including torture (U.S. Department of State 2006a).

Somalia

Somalia is a failed state. Historically, nomadic life and its constant challenge of resource scarcity created "institutionalized violence in the Somali culture of confrontation" (McFerson 1996, 21). Following decades of colonial competition, resulting in a division of the Somali historical territory, General Siad Barre established his military government in 1969. His model of "scientific socialism" repressed rights, discouraged private initiative, and outlawed any civic activity not explicitly sanctioned by the state. By extension, formal and informal institutions previously used for interethnic negotiation and conflict management were systematically undermined (McFerson 1996). Religious leaders were publicly executed and Western-trained intellectuals imprisoned. The Cold War was also fought in this territory: When the former Soviet Union backed Ethiopia in its war with Somalia, Barre switched his allegiance to the United States. During this time Barre also began to privilege or punish selected clans over others. This, in turn, led to clan warfare, notably with the Isaak clan in northern Somalia (1988), and the eventual collapse of the Barre regime in 1991.

Externally, repression and these wars led to massive accumulations of refugees in Ethiopia and emigration throughout the world; internally, the collapse of the Barre regime unleashed a "culture of vengeance" and fierce battles over scarce resources, fought with the abundance of weapons made available through the legacy of Cold War politics. As a result of this conflict, approximately 650,000 Somalis were uprooted (U.S. Committee for Refugees 2003),[16] with 31,889 Somali refugees arriving in the United States from 1996-2003, and an additional 23,736 arriving in 2004 and 2005 (U.S. Office of Immigration Statistics 2006).

While Somalia remains a stateless society, despite numerous attempts at international negotiation, de facto governance has reemerged in the North, with economic development spawned by diaspora investments. Until recently, conflict had significantly lessened, with some violence occurring in southern areas. A peace process, concluded in October 2004, resulted in the election of Abdullahi Yusuf Ahmed as Transitional Federal President of Somalia. The Transitional Federal Institutions were divided between Mogadishu and Jowhar. However, in 2006, Mogadishu was again seized, this time by Islamic militants, and Ethiopia dispatched troops to protect the Transitional Federation Government, challenging the legitimacy and efficacy of the negotiated government. As a result of the government's powerlessness in the face of these developments, twenty members of Parliament resigned in July 2006 (Olad Hassan 2006). Efforts to transfer security responsibility from the Ethiopians to an African peacekeeping force were unsuccessful. Amid concerns of an escalating and, possibly, regional war, in November 2007, Nur Hassan Hussein, a long-time humanitarian with the Red Crescent Society, was named prime minister.

Nepal

Nepal has a weak government and is plagued by a Maoist rebellion. Launched in 1996 with the intention of abolishing the monarchy and establishing a communist regime, within eight years the rebellion

---

[16] This number does not include voluntary migration.

spread from two districts to encompass almost two-thirds of the country (Manchanda 2004). Peace talks broke down in 2003, and as of 2004, over 10,000 deaths were attributed to violent clashes stemming from the rebellion (Machanda 2004). Both independently and in response to the insurgency, the monarchy has faced significant challenges, yielding many changes in government. This began in 2001 when the crown prince massacred members of the royal family and then committed suicide. In October 2002, the new king dismissed the prime minister and his cabinet. In June 2004 the king reinstated the most recently elected prime minister, but in February 2005 he dissolved the government and assumed power under a declared state of emergency (CIA 2006). After months of mass protest, organized by a seven-party opposition as well as the Maoists, the king allowed Parliament to reconvene on April 28, 2006 (CIA 2006).

In 2004, Nepal graduated from lower to middle status on the Human Development Index (UNDP 2004). However, it was still the poorest performer in terms of human development in all of South Asia, excepting Pakistan. Nepal remains one of the least developed countries in the world, with the majority of the population residing in rural areas, where human development performance lags behind. Indeed, huge disparities define the delivery of health and education services in urban and rural areas. This disparity corresponds with human poverty rates: 25.2% in urban areas and 42% in rural areas. Not surprisingly, the roots of the insurgency can be found in those regions with the poorest relative human development performance (UNDP 2005). The UNDP cautions that low levels of economic empowerment in Nepal are not sufficient even to sustain current social empowerment without expanded economic opportunities. Its findings suggest that the mismatch between levels of socioeconomic and political empowerment is likely to yield continuing conflict (UNDP 2004).

International migration is considered an important livelihood strategy in Nepal (Thieme et al. 2005); labor migration has long been a source of subsistence for rural families. Formally recognized remittances to Nepal are approximately $1 billion, or an estimated one-quarter of Nepal's gross national product, much of it transferred informally (see Seddon, Adhikari, and Gurung 2002). According to the Nepal Living Standards Survey conducted in 1996, remittances accounted for 25% of total household income for almost one-quarter of rural households (Seddon et al. 2002). Approximately 760,000 of Nepal's estimated 23 million population is "absent," 10.9% of whom are women (Thieme et al. 2005). Most of these emigrants can be found in India (roughly 77%). Increasingly since the 1990s, Nepalese find their way to the Gulf States, where they can earn more money with manual labor than in Nepal applying any technical skills they may have (see Seddon 2005); migration to the Gulf States accounted for 14.5% of emigrants as of 2005 (Thieme et al. 2005). Most emigrants are poorly educated and migrate temporarily, typically holding low-skilled jobs. About two-thirds of the migrants destined for countries outside of Asia come from urban areas (Seddon et al. 2002).

In 2005, Nepal was listed as one of the principal sources of refugees worldwide, with 201,800 (U.S. Committee for Refugees 2006). One hundred thousand new refugees sought support in India in 2005 alone. Approximately 12,636 Nepalis were granted legal residence in the United States from 1996-2005 (U.S. Office of Immigration Statistics 2006).

Outline of the Book

Chapter 2 explores the relationship between diaspora, identity, and the contributions of IT. I analyze how a diasporan moves from the challenge of migration – sometimes traumatic – to the creation of hybrid identity, inclusive of democratic values, and supportive of integration, peace, and security; and how this evolution can lead to contributions to the homeland. I consider identity, why it is important and how it emerges. I then introduce the factors that influence diasporans' ability to mobilize identity, and analyze what motivates this mobilization and its direction. Next, I examine how IT contributes to facilitating diaspora identity construction, building diaspora communities, and supporting identity mobilization. I end the chapter with a summary model that links diaspora identity, community formation, and outcomes, identifying the Internet's contributions to each of these.

In the following five chapters I present empirical data and analyze the case studies. These chapters develop and follow my analytic framework for better understanding and analyzing digital diasporas' functions and potential contributions. I analyze the Internet as a tool for sustaining homeland identity at the same time as fostering hybrid identities (Chapter 3), leading to the creation of cyber-communities (Chapter 4); who may prevent manifest conflict in the diaspora (Chapter 5); and who seek to influence policy (and human rights) regarding their homelands (Chapter 6) and improve quality of life for their homeland compatriots (Chapter 7).

In the final chapter I comparatively analyze the case studies, documenting the processes by which migrant communities may move toward diaspora identities, inclusive of liberal values, supportive of peaceful integration, and potentially mobilizeable for the purposes of preventing conflict and influencing policy and quality of life for the homeland. I analyze the interdependence of these processes, the relevance and efficacy of digital diasporas and physical diaspora organizations, and the likely evolution of this organizational sector. I close the book with a discussion of policy and practice implications.

2

Diasporas, Identity, and Information Technology

How does one move from the challenge of migration – sometimes traumatic – to the creation of hybrid identities, inclusive of democratic values, and supportive of integration, peace, and security? How might these identities lead to contributions of peace and prosperity in the homeland? How does the Internet support these processes? This chapter examines the relationship between diaspora, identity, mobilization, and the contributions of IT. Following a discussion of diaspora, I consider identity, why it is important and how it emerges. I then introduce the factors that influence diasporans' ability to mobilize identity, and analyze what motivates this mobilization and its direction. Next, I examine how IT contributes to facilitating diaspora identity construction, building diaspora communities, and supporting identity mobilization. I end the chapter with a summary model that links diaspora identity, community formation, and outcomes, identifying the Internet's contributions to each of these.

WHAT IS A DIASPORA?

Simply put, "Modern diasporas are ethnic minority groups of migrant origins residing and acting in host countries but maintaining strong sentimental and material links with their countries of origin – their homelands" (Sheffer 1986a, 3). Several features common to diasporas bind their members and suggest a potential for collective action. Cohen (1997, 515) identifies a range of these, including:

• A collective memory and myth about the homeland.

- An idealization of the putative ancestral home and a collective commitment to its maintenance, restoration, safety and prosperity, even to its creation.
- The development of a return movement that gains collective approbation.
- A strong ethnic group consciousness sustained over a long time and based on a sense of distinctiveness, a common history, and the belief in a common fate [and]
- A sense of empathy and solidarity with coethnic members in other countries of settlement.

Most scholars agree that diaspora members share a self-awareness or diasporic consciousness: They identify with each other as members of a dispersed identity group with continuing common ties to the homeland. This often leads to "institutionalizing networks of exchange and communication that transcend territorial states," linking diaspora groups between host countries (Vertovec 1997, 278). Chaliand and Rageau (1997) add "the will to survive as a minority by transmitting a heritage" (xvi). These features are but a few that are strewn throughout the literature, and are not without debate.[1]

As the attention to diasporas increases, we are actually losing conceptual clarity. Scholars have adapted and transmigrant groups of all kinds have appropriated the term. The inconsistent application of the term diaspora reflects, on the one hand, the neophyte enthusiasm of discovery, which leads some to apply the vocabulary of diaspora indiscriminately; and, on the other hand, a symptom of political agendas, where minority groups and their advocates seek inclusion in this conceptual territory in order to attract renewed interest and to support particular activist agendas. "Diaspora" is applied to groups as disparate

---

[1] Though not universally accepted, some scholars insist that a diaspora must result from dispersion to more than two countries, and require at least two generations to form (Butler 2001). For others, influential efficacy is a prerequisite. Linkages to the homeland must be "tangible and influential, not merely symbolic" (Orozco 2005, 1), or diasporas must have at least an "*ability* to mobilize international support and influence in both the homeland and hostland" [emphasis mine] (Clifford 1994, 311). Perspectives on "return" vary (see Safran 1999). Some scholars insist that to be a diaspora, members must share a committed interest in returning to the homeland; others hold that this commitment to return can become mythological or symbolic, with individuals never realistically intending to return, but maintaining linkages and discussing the possibility (Butler 2001).

as "expatriates, expellees, political refugees, alien residents, immigrants and ethnic and racial minorities *tout court*" (Safran 1991, 83), and recently to the 2005 New Orleans victims of Hurricane Katrina. The expanding application of the term prompted one scholar to title his review essay "Diasporama" (Tölölyan 1994). The term diaspora has been applied to those in the third, fourth, and fifth generations of assimilation. Gunderson (2000) calls these "the lost ones whose first cultures like unsettled spirits haunt their angst-filled reveries ... they are the shadow diasporas, consensually self-validated as groups, but only vaguely" (693). Members of the same migrant group may consider themselves diaspora and others may not.

Adapting from Cohen's (1997) short list, I define diasporas as those migrant groups who share the following features:

1. dispersion, whether voluntary or involuntary, across sociocultural boundaries and at least one political (i.e., nation state) border;
2. a collective memory and myth about the homeland, created and recreated across distances and generations;
3. a commitment to keeping the homeland – imagined or otherwise – alive through symbolic and purposive expression in the hostland and/or in the homeland;
4. the presence of the issue of return, though not necessarily a commitment to do so. The idea of return may be explored, discussed, and debated with or without specific intention of physical return; and
5. a diasporic consciousness and associated identity hybridity, expressed, in part, through the creation of diaspora associations or organizations.[2]

WHAT'S IDENTITY GOT TO DO WITH IT?

Identity is at the very core of diaspora and its influence in home- and hostland. Identity "transforms [migrants] from the physical reality of

---

[2] Contrary to Vertovec (1997, 297), I do not define as diaspora only those groups who are "unable or unwilling to be fully accepted by the 'host society' – thereby fostering feelings of alienation, or exclusion, or superiority, or other kind of 'difference'" (see also Cohen 1997).

dispersal into the psychosocial reality of diaspora" (Butler 2001, 207). Identity under any circumstance is a complex construct. It is even more complicated by the diaspora experience and the many influences that experience yields. Following is a discussion of the general notion of hybrid identity, the factors that contribute to it, the relevance of social capital to its formation, and the process by which it emerges.

Hybrid Identity

Diaspora identity encompasses important distinctions: between those who have migrated and those who remain in the home country; between those who assimilate whole-heartedly and those who retain an identification with the homeland; among generations of settlement; and among those who identify with a subset of the homeland culture versus the homeland as a whole (e.g., clans, ethnicities, religious communities). None of these distinctions is permanent. Four major components of diaspora combine to influence diaspora identity: "a distinct language, historical memory, a national religion, and the habitual status of a minority in larger societies" (Safran 1999, 280-281). Both the homeland and the host society influence diaspora identity.

The literature on cultural identity in the context of globalization calls for and confirms cultural hybridization (Friedman 1994; Lavie and Swedenburg 1996). Immigrants neither wholly accept their host country culture, nor do they automatically embrace their traditional ethnic culture to the exclusion of other influences. And it is not a question of zero-sum conflict among features of one identity versus the other. Shain (1995, 1999) argues that the United States' tolerance for hyphenization – that is, African-American, Asian-American, and Arab-American – affords diasporans a greater opportunity to pursue their cultural identity, within the context of their American selves. Even after several generations, research shows strong correlations between civic values of various ethnic groups in the United States and the prevailing values of their countries of origin (Inglehart 2000).

Diaspora identity "lives with and through, not despite, difference; by hybridity" (Hall 1990, 235). Hybrid identity can be viewed as synthesized or blended. At the same time, diasporans may develop competency to fully navigate one set of cultural norms and then the other, as required by the situation at hand. This "milieu moving" (Vertovec

1997, 294) is a relative capacity, reflective of the composite hybrid identity. For example, such competency may not hold when a diasporan seeks full (re)immersion in the home country. Acculturation is more than learning codes; it is fundamentally "a process of change in identity" (Friedman 1994, 28). According to the cultural-pluralist school, even for those who assimilate and begin to lose their language and customs, "their ethnicity continues to be recreated as a new form of identity that is not a simple repetition of what existed in their communities of origin" (Grosfoguel and Cordero-Guzmán 1998, 351).

The resulting hybrid identity is not a fixed end. Diaspora identities are constantly produced and reproduced. They emerge from trial and error experience, as well as give and take among perceived peer groups from the host society, one's diaspora, and the homeland. They are "a negotiated result rather than a reflection of an objective or described reality" (Friedman 1994, 71). Cultural beliefs and practices, the fodder for identity, are tools for adaptation. They help individuals make sense of their reality; they provide psychosocial comfort; and they yield "interactional experiences that have emotional meaning" (Weisner 2000, 142).

Factors Influencing Hybrid Identity

Diaspora hybrid identity results from a mix of characteristics from the homeland, the hostland, and lived experience. In the host society, the processes of socialization and integration are significant factors. Many diasporans may come to share civic and other values of the host country, learned through exposure and/or social pressure, or consciously sought (sometimes through elective migration). U.S.-based diasporas are believed to embrace American values of pluralism, democracy, and human rights.[3] This assumption builds upon the integrationist pluralist model, which "emphasizes the *protection of cultural practices that are compatible with liberalism*" (Spinner 1994; qtd. in Shain 1999, 26). Liberalism is both an assumption and a prescription. On the one hand, it assumes that "diverse cultures will ... prefer, express, and adhere to the same democratic values when allowed to flourish and attain the best

---

[3] Of course, this assumption does not universally hold, as the Hindu nationalist movement in the diaspora demonstrates (see Lal 1999).

that is in them" (Shain 1999, 26). On the other hand, it expects that citizens "will extend to others the same rights they themselves claim" (Shain 1999, 26). Even where traditional cultures are less tolerant, they will likely face pressure within the American multicultural society to conform to more liberalist tendencies (Raz 1994).

The manifestation of a particular diaspora identity can evolve from a defensive perspective or, as discussed previously, a hopeful and progressive one. Diaspora consciousness is "constituted negatively by experiences of discrimination and exclusion, and positively by identification with a historical heritage . . . or with contemporary world cultural or political forces" (Vertovec 1997, 281). Some circumstances may lead a diasporan to maintain some allegiance to the homeland for "emotional support and identity resources" (Kastoryano 1999, 198). Other circumstances might lead one to further embrace the hostland identity, for example, when thoughts of the homeland create psychic pain (Friedman 1994), as when the homeland is cast as a failed state and/or repatriation is impossible.

Several demographic features combine with experience in the host society to inform hybrid identity. Relevant characteristics include diaspora origins, generational composition, and religious identity.

Types of diaspora can be distinguished based on origin – e.g., captivity, conquest, forced exile, elective emigration (Butler 2001); and purpose – e.g., victim, labor, trade, imperial (Cohen 1997). The different types have implications for diaspora identity and potential mobilization (see also Armstrong 1976). These origins are "akin to the traumas of childhood; they mark the diasporan group and inform the direction of its development" (Butler 2001, 203). Origin yields a particular myth, which forms the basis of the diasporan's identity as distinct from the homeland and as a partial determinant of the diasporan's motivation to embrace the hostland or certain among its cultural characteristics. For some, it is a myth of return and/or reterritorialization; for others, it is the myth of economic prosperity in the hostland, and perhaps freedom and democracy.

Origins also determine demographic composition and illuminate religious, ethnic, and political differences both within the diaspora and between the diaspora and its compatriots remaining in the homeland. Diasporas may define themselves according to particular refugee waves, as in the Afghan diasporas of the Russian invasion or the

Taliban era; or pre- or post- some major event, such as the killing of American marines in Mogadishu in 1993. Within the diaspora, members may distinguish themselves according to clan, tribe, or social class. Religious diasporas define themselves primarily according to their religion, distinguishing themselves from the majority religion in their homeland (e.g., the Coptic Christian diaspora). Other diasporas may be relatively homogeneous in their religious faith but define themselves by another dominant criterion, such as the loss of an autonomous homeland, as in Tibet. Still other diasporas may create a meta-diaspora identity, moving beyond their individual or country diaspora origination, to encompass broader diasporic identities, whether based on faith, such as the Muslim diaspora in Europe (see Kastoryano 1999), or geographic region, such as Africans in North America (see Gilroy 1993, 1987).

Within the diaspora, generational differences inform motivations with respect to identity and its relative emphasis on homeland or hostland culture.[4] Some scholars still support a linear model of integration, hypothesizing that newer diasporas are likely to base their collective identity on a shared association with the homeland, whereas later generations may sense a stronger bond to the host country (Butler 2001). In his classic work, Hansen (1952) posits that the third generation is most likely to emerge as champion for the home country culture, as the first generation is likely to be focused on acculturation and survival in the hostland, and the second on rejection of difference in a full embrace of the host country. This linear model assumes there are incentives for subsequent generations to integrate.

Today, there is much stronger evidence to support segmented assimilation. Assimilation of successive generations depends on the opportunities, and social and cultural capital put in place by the previous generation(s) (Portes and Zhou 1993). Subsequent generations will lean toward the cultural identity that affords the greatest opportunities in terms of identity resources and quality of life.[5] "Downward

---

[4] Drawing on the case of Palestine, Mason (2007) argues that the number of generations diasporans have been exile is more important than their migration generation.

[5] For an application to West Indian immigrants, see Waters (1999). Suarez-Orozco (1987) provides an example of how some Central Americans used their homeland identity as a means to support their school performance. Sánchez Gibau (2005) analyzes how Cape Verdeans in Boston sustain a homeland identity to their advantage.

assimilation" is also possible, where subsequent generations lack the educational and economic opportunities of their forbearers, leading some to associate with marginalized subcultures in the hostland (e.g., ghetto culture) (Rumbaut and Portes 2001; Waldinger and Feliciano 2004).

Generational politics also come into play. Hybridity and "new ethnicities" are more common among youth (Hall 1991), who tend to be more exposed to "the cross-currents of differing cultural fields" (Vertovec 1997, 290). The young are more likely to select self-consciously and assimilate cultural identity artifacts (Vertovec 1997). This selectively extends to religious identity and practice. For example, research on the cultural production and reproduction of religious belief and practice among South Asian youth, finds that "young people adapt their own interpretations of belief, consciously decide the nature of their religious values, and specify for themselves modes of participation in 'religious community' activities" (Vertovec 1997, 291).[6]

Even beyond younger generations, the diaspora experience and the encounter with religious pluralism result in self-questioning, which may yield adaptations in religious belief and practice (Vertovec 1997). As early as 1968, Geertz summarized this change in diaspora consciousness as a shift of the primary religious question from "'What shall I believe' to 'How shall I believe it'" (Geertz 1968, 61; qtd. in Vertovec 1997, 283). Religion may flourish as a cultural defense, when individuals are confronted with alien cultures or religions, in part as a means for asserting a group's sense of worth (Wallis and Bruce 1992).

Identity and Social Capital

Being part of a collective identity is a primary psychological need. Therefore, individuals and communities need to cultivate various kinds of social capital. Social capital denotes resources (such as information and norms), generated by social relationships, which are useful for people's development, promote cooperation, and facilitate action (Bourdieu 1986). Cognitive social capital is the force behind more visible forms of social capital, and includes values, norms, civic responsibility, expected reciprocity, charity, altruism, and interpersonal trust

---

[6] See, for example, Baumann (1995); Vertovec and Rogers (1998).

(Uphoff 2000). Social capital is rooted in identity and shared identity negotiation processes.

Diasporans, in particular, need to cultivate bonding social capital (social bonds based on similar backgrounds), bridging social capital (relationships that develop among people with dissimilar backgrounds) (see Putnam 1993), and bridging-to-bond social capital (overcoming physical constraints, such as time, geographic location, and disabilities, to enable bonding to occur) (Brainard and Brinkerhoff 2004). Social capital is developed and manifested in association (Anheier and Kendall 2002; Putnam 1993). For diasporas, social capital is represented in the development of a diaspora community, complete with various types of diaspora associations or more formal organizations.

Diaspora communities are more or less self-governing (Ostrom 1990). Like all communities, they develop rules or norms of behavior that determine prescriptions for what is required, prohibited, or permitted (Ostrom, Gardner, and Walker 1994). By debating norms, values, and ideas, people create and enact organizations (Weick 1995). Rules need not be formally articulated; rather, they emerge through trial and error and are continuously negotiated (Brainard and Brinkerhoff 2004). These rules-in-use reflect shared meaning whose dynamic varies from community to community. Explicitly articulated rules are more common in formalized diaspora organizations, though even these operate according to rules-in-use, which may or may not be specified.

Diaspora communities provide one or more of the following benefits (Wilson 1995): purposive, material, and solidary. In the first instance, members engage in pursuing goals directed beyond the boundaries of the community or organization. These might include the provision of services to nonmembers or advocating for a particular cause. Material benefits may include information, referrals, and the tangible outcomes of service delivery. Solidary benefits refer to associational advantages that flow from feeling connected to others and belonging to a community. Diaspora-specific communities and organizations generate a fourth category of benefit. Cultural identity benefit relates to the opportunities for members to engage with others to explore and negotiate their individual, as well as community cultural identities. Diaspora organizations may be focused on influencing or contributing to the homeland, or geared toward meeting the needs of the diaspora, with respect to material and solidary needs and/or identity support.

Bonding social capital provides both a collective identity (solidary and identity benefits) and practical resources (purposive and material benefits) for advancing socioeconomically. Bonding social capital manifests as dense social networks that engender trust (Coleman 1998, 1990). Individual and collective identity, including a sense of meaning and purpose, are fundamental psychological needs. Collective identity, in particular, generates a sense of belonging that is necessary to ward off identity crisis (see Erikson 1975). By providing a collective identity, bonding social capital potentially raises the stakes for diasporans to foster instability, diminishing individuals' incentives to direct hostility toward an "other." Bonding social capital can counter the destabilizing forces of marginalization and provide a social safety net for group members (Gittel and Vidal 1998).

Bonding social capital also provides access to the kinds of social networks that more proactively support social and economic integration. New theories of immigrant adaptation highlight the importance of social capital, arguing that successful economic achievement may have more to do with social capital than assimilation per se. According to segmented assimilation, different opportunities and social capital may emerge for different diaspora groups, potentially creating ethnic jobs, networks, and values (Portes and Zhou 1993). Individuals' marginalization within the host society may have more to do with the social capital available than embrace (or not) of the host culture. By extension, maintaining a strong identification with the homeland culture does not preclude success in the host society.

Bonding social capital within diasporas has important security implications (see Brinkerhoff 2008a). Friedman (1994) maps how economic decline and increasing poverty can lead to "slummification," social disorder and then personal disorder. The latter, he argues, leads to criminal activity and/or psychic crisis. Psychic crisis, in turn, leads to the creation of identities alternative to modernity, including relatively extremist ethnic, fourth world (social isolationism), or religious identities. Bonding social capital provides the collective identity and instrumental networks that can ward off personal disorder and psychic crisis.

Diaspora community and associated organizations also may represent bridging social capital within the diaspora, and between diaspora members and the host society. Through repeat interaction and the discovery of shared needs and interests, bridging social capital prevents the dehumanization of "other" (see Northrup 1989; Rubin et al. 1994). Diaspora organizations can promote cross-categorization of identity as a means to promote common identities and understanding, where one unifying identity dimension can be privileged over conflicting ones, potentially fostering new perceived identities (Brewer 2000; Hewstone, Rubin, and Willis 2002). In this sense, diaspora organizations can bridge ethnic differences within the diaspora in order to promote bonding around the shared identification with the homeland. Similarly, these organizations may choose to promote cultural exchange with the host society in order to highlight common interests and identity.

The Emergence/Evolution of Identity

An important benefit of diaspora organizations is the opportunity to negotiate cultural identity and enact it through communication and collective action. Diaspora organizations can be "a shelter, sometimes a sanctuary, where culture, religion, ethnicity, and nation are interpreted, redefined, and internalized" (Kastoryano 1999, 193). But what occurs in these organizations that leads to identity negotiation and construction?

Life stories play a significant role in the formation of identity (Giddens 1991). Thus, storytelling and sharing is one approach to crafting identity (and cross-categorical identities). Stories "create recognition of common experiences that shape identity and link people's futures," leading to shared understandings (Navarro 2003, 138). Storytelling is a process of sensemaking, where individuals independently and collectively link and construct a meaningful logic among seemingly random, sometimes disparate occurrences and experiences (see Griffin 1993). Identity construction through storytelling is also a trial and error process. Building on Gergen's (1990) work, Navarro (2003, 129) puts it this way:

When people tell life stories, they do so according to models of intelligibility specific to the culture. Stories or 'accounts' are always produced and told under particular social conditions and constraints. ... These models are consonant with the conventions that stabilize the given organization of society. ... By contrast, stories that fail to conform to the models leave themselves open to questions, challenges, or resistance from any given society.

In this sense, diasporas do not construct a fixed identity. Rather, they continuously negotiate their identity, both in interaction with the host society, and among themselves, perhaps through multiple diaspora organizations each with a different perspective and/or purpose.

WHY DOES DIASPORA IDENTITY BECOME MOBILIZED AND WHY?

Homeland culture, host society, and experience influence the composition of diaspora hybrid identities, and these identities inform individuals' behavior. What causes diaspora individuals and communities to mobilize for collective action? A range of factors influence mobilization, generally and with respect to diaspora identities. Diasporans face various motivations for why they would mobilize around a diaspora hybrid identity and direct that mobilization toward the homeland, the host society, or both.

Mobilization Factors

Generally, successful mobilization is dependent on a number of factors, including a shared social identity (Pratkanis and Turner 1996), an organizational or networking base (Klandermans and Oegema 1987), opportunity structures (Esman 1986), and process factors. Shared identity is necessary for collective action (Ostrom 1990) and can contribute to developing a sense of efficacy, psychological empowerment, and a felt need to express identity. Heterogeneous networks allow for information diffusion, where individual actors act as bridges between diffuse sources of information (Burt 2000), and they can connect diasporans to power structures. Opportunity structures influence diasporans' access to power resources, e.g., economic, social, political, and physical (Uphoff 2005). They may include supportive regulation for diasporans' particular agenda in both the host country and the homeland, and other forms of legitimation of the diaspora's efforts and potential contributions.

Process factors influence diasporans' incentives to mobilize. Issues need to be framed in order to focus individuals' attention and energy and enable effective coordination of efforts (Snow and Benford 2000). Framing supports consensus on the direction of collective energy, including what is acceptable and what is not. To sustain motivation, organizers must generate a sense of efficacy and subsequent impact (see, for example, Klandermans 1997). Effective issue framing inspires confidence in an ability to enact change, in part, by referring to past as well as future success. These latter elements relate to psychological empowerment.

Psychological empowerment refers to "people's belief that they have the resources, energy, and competence to accomplish important goals" (Diener and Biswas-Diener 2005, 125). People are unlikely to pursue their goals without optimistic expectancy that they will achieve them (see Bandura 1997). Self-efficacy combines with motivation to determine the likelihood of mobilization. Groups are more likely to rapidly and aggressively mobilize defensively to a clear and present threat than offensively for uncertain future benefits (Esman 1994). Group norms may influence individuals' perceptions of and responses to initial conditions, including beliefs of self-efficacy vis-à-vis an individual's context. Diaspora origin may inform diasporans' motivation and sense of potential efficacy, that is, their perceived ability to integrate in the host country and/or influence the home country.

Motivation

The motivation for diasporans to mobilize is likely to be for the expression of their identity, for maintaining or acquiring power or other resources, or both. For some, the expression of homeland identity is based solely on a sense of belonging, in response to feelings of marginalization in their adopted societies. Cultural obligations and expected behavior vis-à-vis both the homeland and the hostland also influence motivation. These are first and foremost rooted in family relations and responsibilities, but also become shaped through the identity negotiation process and the context in which that occurs. Mobilization may be for the expression of a hybrid identity, which may encompass liberal values. The felt need to actively express identity may derive from various forms of marginalization (social, economic, political, or psychic), confusion and a sense that the homeland identity will be lost without proactive expression (e.g., when overwhelmed by pluralism), or simply in response to social reinforcement and perhaps pride. In the case of hybrid identities, such pride often encompasses liberal values and experiences associated with the adopted society. Ideally pride in hybrid identity gives rise to an embrace of basic freedoms and rights and psychological empowerment, reflecting a belief that these diasporans can effectively work to advance, protect, and embody these rights for themselves and potentially for the homeland.

The bonding and bridging social capital created within diaspora communities is crucial to these processes, as they influence perceptions and realities of vulnerability and marginalization. They can inspire pride in collective identities and confidence in the ability to mobilize for constructive change. And they frame how identity mobilization will be directed.

Directing Mobilization to the Homeland, Host Society, or Both

Mobilization of diaspora identity entails an implicit or subconscious cost-benefit analysis with respect to the individual's and the diaspora community's quality of life. These assessments account for "interests and obligations" resulting from diasporans' simultaneous engagement in the homeland and host society (Nyberg-Sorensen, Van Hear, and Engberg-Pedersen 2002). The higher the cost of a particular agenda to status and security in their adopted country, the greater the likelihood that the diaspora community will split and/or fail to mobilize (Esman 1986).

Just as diasporans may choose the identity emphasis that most supports their quality of life in the hostland (Portes and Zhou 1993), they may direct their mobilized identity toward improved quality of life for compatriots in the homeland, for diaspora communities in the hostland, or for both. The linear model of assimilation suggests that over time diaspora communities increasingly direct their mobilization toward quality of life in the hostland and potentially mobilize less and less as identity rooted in the ancestral homeland may dissipate. Recent evidence suggests otherwise. In the case of Salvadoran, Dominican, and Columbian immigrants to the United States, contrary to what one might expect, the longer a diasporan has been in the host country, the more likely s/he is to be politically engaged vis-à-vis the homeland (Guarnizo, Portes, and Haller 2003), perhaps due to socioeconomic power and psychological empowerment. Homeland crisis may also inspire renewed interest among later diaspora generations, as seen, for example, in Afghanistan (see Kerlin 2008). When the diaspora identity is not fully awakened until the homeland is in crisis, I call these latent diasporas. They may include younger generations who have never seen the homeland and may not speak its language (see Brinkerhoff 2004).

Specific purposive agendas vis-à-vis the homeland are shaped by the diaspora itself – its origins, generation, and religious orientation; its experience in the host society; its motivation (identity expression and/ or accessing power resources) and sense of efficacy (including available skills and other resources); and accordingly, the particular homeland challenges the diaspora perceives as most relevant. For some, these factors will combine to create an advocacy agenda, which may be targeted to the host country government, the international community, the homeland government, or all of the above. Others will seek to mitigate the potential for conflict within the diaspora and among its corresponding factions in the homeland. Still others will seek to contribute to socioeconomic development in the homeland, for example, through private investment, philanthropy, and skills transfer. This latter agenda and associated contributions may be especially prevalent among diasporas from countries in or emerging from conflict. In these cases, diasporans may evolve elaborate plans for postconflict reconstruction of the homeland.

Mobilizing on behalf of the homeland may also support integration in the host society, both in terms of relieving identity stress and in generating psychological empowerment. For example, Malugetah Asmallash, and others from the Ethiopian diaspora organization, Dir Foundation, organized a coffee project linking Dutch coffee companies to marginalized social groups in Ethiopia to generate sustainable livelihoods. In describing his experience Asmallash declared, "Sometimes I feel schizophrenic. I don't know who I am.... Through this project I know who I am." Implying that the experience of mobilizing to support the homeland was liberating, he added: "It has helped me to be myself; to be who I am. It's very healthy. I don't have to choose [between my Dutch and Ethiopian identities]" (Asmallash 2007). Similarly, Stéphanie Mbanzendore (2007), chairperson of the Netherlands-based Burundian Women for Peace and Development, shared:

Doing the work that I'm doing with the organization, I've become more integrated into the society here. Because I came here as a refugee, and it's an unhappy situation when you are here the first time to try to do all, alone, as an individual. Here it is a closed society. So to get a small door, you have really to fight. So, doing what I'm doing, I'm getting more integrated. ... I don't have time to think of my situation as a refugee, because now I can go back home and contribute to the situation there. ... So for me, I'm feeling very well in the world, because I am living again.

WHAT'S THE RELEVANCE OF INFORMATION TECHNOLOGY?

Information technology offers a host of advantages for diasporans: for forming communities – virtual and otherwise, providing solidary and material benefits, negotiating hybrid identity, and facilitating purposive objectives. Following is a review of the types of communities and organizations IT can facilitate, as well as a general discussion of the Internet's benefits and operations. Next, I discuss how diasporans create digital diasporas that capitalize on these benefits and operations.

IT: Organizations, Advantages, and Operations

The Internet promotes new connections and fosters new sets of cultural attributes (Greig 2002). It can generate a variety of communities. Aoki (1994) distinguishes three types: 1) virtual communities that are congruent with physical communities; 2) virtual communities that overlap with physical communities; and 3) virtual communities that are thoroughly distinct from physical communities (qtd. in Foster 1996). The first type of organization – a virtual community that is congruent with a physical community – may be a grassroots organization or even a formally registered nonprofit or business that maintains modes of interaction in cyberspace such that participants develop a sense of shared membership and shared community. The organization may provide services in the physical world and also include discussion forums for community building beyond these purposive objectives. For diasporas, such organizations are likely to support integration into the host society in the particular communities in which these diasporans reside. Virtual communities that overlap with physical communities but are not congruent with them may include those that connect dispersed populations and use the Internet to discuss and plan for purposive engagement in the physical world that they later execute, for example in the homeland. Another type of organization is the completely virtual type of diaspora CGO, where the organization is cocreated by members and exists only online. Diasporans may individually "connect" offline to mobilize for purposive objectives in the physical world but these activities take place outside of the cybercommunity. The inclusion of e-mail addresses in communications "provides the basis for more multiplex relationships to develop between participants" (Wellman and Gulia 1999, 182).

Beyond these cyber-community types are more traditional organizations that exist primarily in the physical world, but utilize the Internet to access its identity and mobilization advantages. They may provide all types of member benefits – material, solidarity, purposive, and cultural identity, but any solidary benefits are generated in the physical world, not in cyberspace.[7] The overlay of virtual communities can enhance the physical communities. Research shows that virtual interaction can intensify support and relationships in physical communities (Hampton and Wellman 2002).

IT provides a dialogical space where tradition and modernity converge to produce new self-understandings (Bhatia and Ram 2001). In his seminal work on virtual community, Rheingold (1993) stressed that communication technologies are not politically neutral, given that they influence human beliefs and perceptions. A general argument and perception of the Internet's promotion of liberal values persists. IT may promote cosmopolitanism, or "a universal moral code transcending state boundaries and state interests" (Jacobsen and Lawsen 1999, 205). Such moral codes increasingly encompass respect for human rights and democratic practices. Others argue that IT also facilitates increasing parochialism (see Barber 1995). Using IT, individuals can more easily selectively pursue information and interaction opportunities (Elkins 1997). However, this thesis only holds for limited increases in the range of communication; larger increases in communication tend toward homogeneity (Greig 2002).

---

[7] Sökefeld (2002) argues that diaspora communities are sometimes "*represented* in cyberspace... [and] not – or are only to a very limited degree – *sustained by interaction* within that space" (emphasis in the original, 108).

Intra-community organization and communication reflect the characteristics of the Internet as a tool: to at least a limited extent, it will be relatively more democratic and representative of freedom of speech. The Internet facilitates the expression of liberal values such as individualism and freedom of speech, either through anonymity or access opportunity. In this sense, CGOs can become a test bed for experimenting with liberal values. In fact, many CGOs are expressly democratic in their functioning. Cyberspace provides a platform for the member-construction of organizations (Brainard 2003) that are democratically based and participatory as opposed to hierarchical and control oriented (Brainard and Siplon 2004).

Internet technology facilitates issue framing, both through established social norms, and through the structuring of interactive components and the rules regulating participation. Virtual components of communities ease the formation of voluntary communities. A voluntary community, a conception combining social ties with autonomy, has three defining conditions: low barriers to entry, low barriers to exit, and "interpersonal relations shaped by mutual adjustment rather than hierarchical authority or coercion" (Galston 2002, 43). Like their physical space counterparts, cybercommunities operate according to member-created norms. Norms in cyberspace emerge in response to three kinds of imperatives: promoting shared purposes, safeguarding the quality of group discussion, and managing scarce resources in the virtual commons (Galston 2002). Through communication, members evolve organizational norms, such as, for example, the extent to which they tolerate diversity of opinion, personal attacks, and political entrenchment. In this regard, cybercommunities are self-regulating.

Beyond these organic efforts, listserv managers and founders/managers of websites more proactively regulate community behavior. Through member registration, discussion moderation, and participation rules, they establish what may or may not be legitimate to debate. Members can be banned (temporarily or permanently) for breaking rules, such as spamming or including forbidden content. Filtering and message delay can be used to frame discussion. For example, the Burundi Youth Council implements a highly structured filtering process, postponing messages, when deemed appropriate, to enable discussants to "cool down," and disallowing messages altogether when they are not deemed constructive by board members (Kadende-Kaiser 2003).

Through content regulation (community norms, formal rules, and filtering), participation rules, and delay, the Internet becomes a tool for moderating potentially inflammatory sentiments.

Community members and/or external antagonists may also occasionally use "violence" to prevent participation, including flaming sites (i.e., inundating them with hostile or offensive mail), hacking and infecting sites with viruses, and using "kill files," indicating addresses from which a user will not receive messages (Graham and Khosravi 2002, 221).

The Internet is a mobilizing tool for the various types of organizations it supports. It facilitates the formation of shared identity necessary for collective action; it is an organizational/networking resource for assembling and communicating among individuals and groups, providing information and referrals to other actors; and it facilitates issue framing and confidence building. Results of mobilization agendas can be posted and disseminated to inspire continued commitment and subsequent mobilization.

The Creation and Benefits of Digital Diasporas

The defining conditions of voluntary communities – low barriers to entry and exit, and nonhierarchical and noncoercive – are particularly salient to diasporans. Migration stress may create fear and distrust of formalized activities. The nonhierarchical nature of these communities may be especially welcome for those who migrate as a result of authoritarian rule and/or conflict. Research on CGOs (Brainard and Brinkerhoff 2004) demonstrates their ability to provide solidary member benefits, as well as material ones.

Through the Internet, geographically dispersed diasporans can connect and bond, providing to each other a quality of benefit – a sense of shared understanding – no one else could possibly provide. Given their dispersion within and across host countries, without the Internet such bridging-to-bond social capital would not be possible. For some, the Internet is crucial to maintaining religious practice and belonging to a congregation. Encountering religious pluralism in the host society may inspire cultural defense among diasporans. This may encourage the migration of religious discourse and practice from the physical world into cyberspace, inclusive of "long distance ritual practice, cyberpilgrimage, and other religiously-motivated undertakings" (Helland 2007, 956; see also Rao 2004).

Digital diaspora communities provide members material benefits, solidary benefits based on a shared homeland identity, and opportunities to explore and express alternative hybrid identities – cultural identity benefits. Regarding material benefits, a common feature of diaspora websites is news and information on the homeland. News coverage may include mainstream media stories, links to homeland media sources, and members' own op-eds and analyses. These sites also provide a wealth of information about the homeland culture, history, and religious practices – some of which may be translated in order to reach subsequent generations of the diaspora who may not speak the homeland language, and to reach broader publics. Other types of information may address how to do business in the homeland as well as patronize diaspora businesses. The sites often provide opportunities to link dispersed diasporans beyond the ad hoc connections made through discussion forums. For example, dating and matchmaking services may be available. Through online discussions members may provide referrals to other members for their own socioeconomic opportunities and advancement, and they may discuss and share information and referrals pertinent to helping the homeland.

Websites supporting the Russian immigrant community illustrate each of these benefits (Sapienza 2001). Material benefits support immigrants' participation in cultural events, as well as integration in the host society, such as with referrals to public services; the websites also supply business guides and dating services. Personal narratives, as members seek and provide advice, confirm solidary benefits. And cultural identity benefits ensue from members expressing nostalgia and, together, easing their anxiety from crosscultural encounters.

The solidary and identity benefits cybercommunities provide are especially salient to diasporans, providing comfort and identity support as they cope with the sometimes traumatic experience of dispersion. The anonymity the Internet provides may ease diasporans' participation, especially when sharing painful memories or discussing potentially conflictive topics. For example, individual Bosnian refugees used the Internet to create mausoleums to their history and culture through personal webpages, or "cyberhomes":

In the imagination and representation of the home on the Web, the trauma is being erased. Bosnians use the Internet as a new symbolic order that grants them a possibility to patch their fractured identities, to construct coherent stories about their obviously incoherent lives and to obfuscate the shock of uprootedness and alienation (Hozic 2001, 5).

These refugees thus "articulate their loneliness," process their trauma, make sense of their current realities, and recreate and sustain their homeland identity.

IT may reinforce the self-conscious selection and assimilation of cultural identity artifacts, especially among youth. New media, such as text messaging and Internet discussions, emphasize the development of self-positions among youth (Cortini, Mininni, and Manuti 2004). Furthermore, while first generation diasporans may use the Internet to extend their offline social networks, younger diasporans are more likely to connect exclusively online in support of hyphenated identities (Ven den Bos and Nell 2006).

Studies of digital diasporas confirm diasporans' use of the Internet to experiment with and express hybrid identities. An examination of Russian immigrant websites reveals "varying degrees of juxtaposition and mixing of local and global" as opposed to cultural polarization (Sapienza 2001, 435). In one of the earliest studies of diasporas' use of IT, Rai (1995) found that members of the Hindu diaspora could at once support affirmative action in the United States and be against reservations in India, expressing tolerant pluralism for the West and narrow sectarianism for the East.

This experimentation with hybrid identity can include homeland representatives themselves, where these communities cocreate a collective metaphor that bridges the homeland and its diaspora (Tsaliki 2003). The bridging between homeland and diaspora can be a cultural project, as with the Greek diaspora (Tsaliki 2003), or a political one, as with the Eritrean Peoples Liberation Front during the Eritrean War of Independence from Ethiopia (Redeker Hepner 2008). Bridging may also occur online between the diaspora and members of the host society, finding common ground and advocating to each other for an agreed cause vis-à-vis the homeland. The Tibetan case is a telling example (see Santianni 2003). Studies of the Eritrean diaspora confirm that cyberspace can be used at once to "produce and debate" identity narratives and to purposively influence the homeland (Bernal 2006, 161). The Internet thus becomes "an emotion-laden and creative space" (Bernal 2006, 161).

Still other studies focus primarily on how diasporans use the Internet to sustain their traditional homeland identities, or reinterpretations of these, leading one scholar to emphasize "virtual nation" and declaring, "nationality: cyber-Russian" (Saunders 2004). Some cultural identities are relatively obscure (see, for example, Sökefeld 2002), or dramatically dispersed suggesting that their survival may largely depend on the efforts of dispersed diasporans using the Internet to sustain and support them with strong bonding social capital. Among the dramatically dispersed are white Rhodesians, who either voluntarily or forceably exiled, use the Internet to maintain their sense of a Rhodesian identity as distinct from a Zimbabwean one (King 2003); and the Polynesian diaspora (Franklin 2003).

The Internet can also be used to create hybrid identities that, in the view of their creators, offer the best that home and host society may have to offer. Cyberspace provides a safe haven to discuss taboo subjects or simply those that are emotionally laden or potentially conflictive; and it provides a repository for emerging consensus. This is often seen, for example, with regard to women's rights, such as efforts to create "cyber-feminist e-spaces" for the South Asian diaspora (Gajjala 2003).

Diasporas from failing states may similarly incorporate values and ideas from their host societies as they challenge homeland values and practices that they perceive are the roots of conflict and make plans for a more peaceful future in the homeland. The Internet enables these discussions and shared meanings to continue and be sustained until which time it may be possible to enact them in the homeland. For example, the new understandings so generated by the Sierra Leonean digital diaspora were "held in conceptual escrow, waiting for the institutional structure to return" (Tynes 2007). Similarly, the Palestinian disapora formed PALESTA (Palestinian Scientists and Technologists Abroad) to create and maintain networks of skilled diasporans waiting for when they might return to contribute their skills to a new Palestine (Hanafi 2005).

Interactive components of IT are an efficient, easy-access tool for diaspora storytelling and sharing, enabling members to make sense of their experiences and feelings in the encounter between cultures and identities. Diasporans use these tools to experiment with hybridity. Digital diaspora communities, like formal physical world diaspora organizations, self-regulate and negotiate acceptable norms of behavior. They can provide validation or correction in the experimentation with hybrid identity and they can frame issues in order to ensure continued shared social norms for group solidarity. In other words, escape into cyberspace does not mean discussions are unregulated. Rather they are regulated differently, by the communities themselves, in addition to organization founders and moderators, and in ways that may be more or less exclusive and agenda focused than what members might find in some physical world groupings (Graham and Khosravi 2002). Some evidence suggests that digital diasporas organized for cultural purposes may be more inclusive than those that are focused on political ends (Van den Bos 2006).

The Internet provides a place for diasporans to consider the plight of their homeland, contemplate its future, and explore ideas for purposive activities. The Internet's tools for issue framing can assist diasporans to build consensus and direction for purposive ideas, which may originate from a sense of dismay and helplessness if the homeland and/or compatriots are suffering. Through material benefits of information sharing and referrals, diasporans can further develop purposive proposals. Through the networking IT provides, they can identify and potentially access necessary resources to enact these proposals. And once a project is underway, diasporans can use the Internet to report on progress and successes, inspiring further commitment as diasporans build their confidence in their ability to contribute to the homeland.

DIGITAL DIASPORAS: IDENTITY AND TRANSNATIONAL ENGAGEMENT

Diasporans face distinctive challenges owing to the experience of dispersion and acculturation. This leads individuals and groups within diasporas to transform their identity, selectively embracing elements of both the home and host culture. Rather than following a linear path, with subsequent generations following a predictable pattern, diasporans are likely to assume a hybrid identity leaning in one or the other direction based on the opportunities that identity may afford to them. Younger diasporans, in particular, are likely to be consciously selective in their identity components and this may lead to religious beliefs that differ from their forefathers and foremothers.

Collective identity is supported and represented by a diaspora community, replete with a variety of diaspora organizations and associations serving different purposes. These diaspora organizations and associations are self-governing, evolving norms that set the parameters for what is expected, acceptable, and permitted (or not). They generate a range of benefits to their members and beyond, including material, solidary, cultural identity, and purposive benefits. These organizations may focus on influencing or contributing to the homeland, supporting the diaspora and its integration into the host society, or both.

This diaspora community and its composite organizations provide bonding and bridging social capital. Bonding social capital provides support for socioeconomic success, raises the stakes for participating in or promoting instability, provides identity support, and ultimately prevents psychic crisis. Diaspora organizations and associations may also cultivate bridging social capital within the diaspora as well as between the diaspora and the host society. In shaping crosscategorical identity, this bridging social capital can prevent dehumization of other groups, potentially deflecting conflict.

Within diaspora communities, members continuously negotiate their hybrid identities through storytelling, promoting consensus on shared understandings, and sense making. With respect to their identity and associated behaviors, they test the boundaries of shared identity, providing affirmation and correction as needed to sustain a collective bond.

Choosing to mobilize based on one's diaspora identity depends upon ability, as determined by access to collective identity, organizational resources, and opportunity structures; and perceptions of what may be gained, and whether or not one might be effective. Benefits and costs of mobilization include social rewards and sanctions related to complying with cultural expectations and obligations. The likelihood of identity mobilization can be summed up in the following equation (Brinkerhoff 2008a):

$$\text{Mobilization} = \text{Perceived Value (Benefits } - \text{ Costs)}$$
$$\text{Perceived Efficacy}$$

Each of these components is subject to social influence and is a product of individuals' perceptions. Perceived efficacy results from opportunity structures as well as issue framing and psychological empowerment.

Issue framing and opportunity structures also influence selected agendas. The direction of that mobilization may be toward purposive activities in the homeland, the host society, or both. Liberal values may shape these agendas. Mobilization on behalf of the homeland may also support integration into the host society.

The Internet can facilitate the creation of horizontally structured voluntary communities that present opportunities for identity negotiation and the spread of and experimentation with liberal values, such as respect for human rights and democratic practices. IT's interactive components support storytelling and hence identity negotiation. IT enables homeland identity maintenance, reinterpretation, and hybridity. Particularly among youth, the Internet may support the self-conscious selection of cultural artifacts. These may include experimentation with and adoption of liberal values. Digital diaspora communities may replicate aspects of their homeland culture that are inconsistent with liberal values, and they may use cyberspace to promote and potentially mobilize for nonliberal purposive agendas, but these outcomes are decreasingly likely the larger and more diverse the digital diaspora becomes.

Digital diaspora communities demonstrate self-governance with social norms and rules, a host of benefits, and advantages for issue framing. The Internet enables the creation of bonding, bridging, and especially bridging-to-bond social capital. As a resource for cultivating solidary benefits, it is particularly important for diasporas. Diasporas also use the Internet as a mobilization tool, capitalizing on the collective identity it may support and its functionality for networking and material benefits, such as information sharing and referral. The Internet affords particular opportunities to frame issues through the structuring of interactive components and rules regulating participation.

Figure 2-1 summarizes this model of digital diaspora identity and engagement as supported by the Internet. It illustrates how hybrid identity negotiation creates communities that generate various forms of social capital and member benefits. These may then be mobilized for purposive activities directed to the host society, the homeland or both. Purposive activities may include policy influence, conflict mitigation, and/or support for socioeconomic development in the homeland and integration in the host society. The Internet facilitates each of these components. Its functionality for the mobilization of identity and social capital for purposive benefits is quite broad and may build upon the

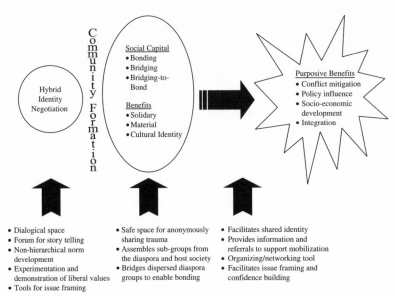

Internet Contributions

FIGURE 2-1. Model for Digital Diaspora Identity and Engagement

contributions of earlier stages, perhaps as achieved by different organizations. A range of organization types may be implicated in these processes and may complement each other. For example, CGOs may be most targeted to the earlier stages of the model, while overlapping the virtual/physical world and exclusively physical world organizations may be most focused on mobilization for purposive action. The following chapters illustrate various components of this model through specific organization case studies.

3

Keeping the Dream Alive

This chapter describes two diaspora CGOs and a transnational business founded by a diasporan and targeted to other diasporans. The three cases demonstrate how diasporans may retain ties to and cultivate a homeland-oriented identity at the same time that they negotiate a hybrid identity, inclusive of host country values, with religious (MyCopticChurch.org), political (TibetBoard), and business (Thamel. com) implications. Following a brief discussion of diaspora hybrid identity, I introduce each of the three cases. The chapter closes with an examination of their religious, political, and business implications.

DIASPORAS AND HYBRID IDENTITY

One defining feature of diasporas is an allegiance to and even romanticizing of the ancestral homeland (see, for example, Cohen 1997). That allegiance may be focused on geographic territory, culture, religion, family ancestry, and, sometimes particular political regimes or governments. For some, the idea of returning to the ancestral homeland is the primary focus. However, the notion of a return movement, or the issue of return, does not require an actual intention to return; it may only represent an idealized dream. Safran (1999, 280) differentiates three meanings of return: "(1) instrumental: that is, an active attempt to return as soon as possible; (2) millennial: a return 'at the end of days'; and (3) intermediate: that is, living in exile, but constantly thinking of the homeland." Diasporas may romanticize and sustain a homeland identity through different ideologies of return – physical repatriation and cultural return in the case of Africa, and symbolic projections, including membership in a great civilization on the part of Indians (Singh 2001). For religious diasporas, the geographic homeland may be less salient than a community of faith and keeping ties with one's brethren in the faith. In all these ways, the issue of return assists diasporans to keep the ancestral homeland alive in their hearts and minds.

Diasporas may proactively promote and recreate homeland identities, and these efforts may be more acute in the absence of a physical homeland. For example, in the 1990s, Kurds in London broadcasted Kurdish language television throughout Europe and into Turkey at a time when Turkey did not permit Kurdish language television. The program featured folk dances and children's programming (Marcus 1995; qtd. in Koslowski 2005), and alternative news reporting, including issues of Kurdish human rights (Verrier 1997).[1] Commonly, diasporas visit the homeland in search of their roots. Sometimes, perhaps surprisingly, these visits yield a better understanding not of their homeland identity, but of those features of their experience and values that make their identity somehow different (see, for example, Louie 2001); that is, these diasporans confirm elements of their identity that are associated with the host society. Several governments proactively cultivate connections among diaspora youth, and earlier generations of diaspora are eager to see their children participate. The governments of Israel, Mexico, South Korea, and Taiwan all offer intensive summer programs targeting diaspora teenagers and college-age youth for learning culture and language.

Diasporas represent those permeable boundaries between cultures where individuals and communities mutually adapt, producing cultural hybridization. This does not mean that some shared identity core is not sustained:

Groups negotiating their identity in contexts of domination and exchange persist, patch themselves together in ways different from a living organism. *A community, unlike a body, can lose a central 'organ' and not die.* All the

---

[1] MED-TV's broadcast license was revoked by the UK Independent Television Commission in 1999. Turkey lifted the ban on Kurdish radio and television programming, though retained heavy regulation, and several private companies began legally broadcasting in 2006 (*Turkish Daily News* 2006).

critical elements of identity are in specific conditions replaceable: language, land, blood, leadership, religion (Clifford 1988, 338; qtd. with italics in Hermans and Kempen 1998, 1116).

Adding to and transforming their homeland identities (though not wholesale replacing them), many diasporans come to share civic and other values of the host country, learned through exposure and/or social pressure, or consciously sought (sometimes through elective migration). U.S.-based diasporas are believed to embrace American values of pluralism, democracy, and human rights. Commonly, individuals who self-identify as members of a diaspora maintain dual allegiances to ancestral and adopted homelands.

The Internet may be an essential repository of information about the homeland, providing opportunities to continuously educate subsequent diaspora generations, as well as more general publics. Beyond the one-way transmission of information, it also provides an opportunity for diasporans to engage and ask each other questions, clarifying historical points and issues surrounding religious practice, and/or seeking advice for how to reconcile perceived clashes between the homeland culture and the host society. Even further, through the Internet, diasporans can put their identities into practice, for example, engaging in online religious ceremonies (Helland 2007).

At the same time, identity negotiation in cyberspace may reinforce hybridity. Beyond explicit advice seeking, diasporans may more subtly solicit feedback and correction as they assert their identity through storytelling. In the exchange, communities may frame issues and sustain a particular shared identity and associated solidary benefits. The very nature of CGOs represents liberal values such as democracy and freedom of speech, and in a way that may be alien to diasporans' previous cultural experiences. Diasporans use cyberspace to experiment with the relevance of these and other cultural artifacts they encounter in the host society. Prior to joining a cybercommunity, some diasporans have never before allowed themselves to consider the implications of basic freedoms for their homeland.

Similarly, CGOs may represent the first time diasporans are able to self-consciously consider aspects of their identity, question traditional interpretations of religion and culture, and choose for themselves what their identity "truth" is. In the homeland, cultural identities may have been sustained and institutionalized through social or religious hierarchies, which represent, instruct, and promulgate one identity interpretation. By moving beyond these physical communities and structures and into cyberspace, diasporans can more freely propose, debate, and self-correct (whether their identity interpretations are historically "correct" or not). And in cyberspace, through cybercommunities, these individual processes can be mutually reinforced, with communities forming around similarly selected constructs, without the need for or constraint of more formal or "official" endorsement of traditional identity arbiters. Thus, cyberspace reinforces the identity dynamics among diaspora youth, where youth are more likely to self-consciously select cultural and religious identity artifacts. Without cyberspace, these diaspora youth "would be consumers of knowledge and representation, not producers and distributors" (Sökefeld 2002, 109).

There are limits to the extent to which negotiated identity becomes rooted in accurate descriptions of the ancestral identity, and resulting identities may not always represent liberal values. To illustrate, focusing specifically on the Alevi diaspora,[2] Sökefeld (2002) argues that the websites (or CGOs) he describes at once represent "a *kind of democratization or empowerment of Alevi self-representation*" (emphasis in the original), and "the possibility that elements of Alevism and their meaning may be simplified or even distorted, out of ignorance or even intentionally, to make a case" (105). Similarly, Lal (1999) describes the historical revisionism present on Hindu diaspora webpages based in North America, where even the Taj Mahal is recast as a Hindu monument. Posted articles are presented as pseudoacademic, complete with questionable references and invitations to check them. In these cybercommunities, the operative objective of identity construction trumps historical and cultural accuracy. Sato (2005) recounts how Urfalli Syrian Orthodox Christians practice selective amnesia in their reconstruction of identity in diaspora in order to better situate themselves in Syrian society and changing political contexts.

---

[2] The Alevi are a religious subgroup, found primarily in Turkey (with pockets in Albania and Bulgaria). Alevism is related to Shia Islam and also encompasses elements of pre-Islamic religions of Anatolia and ancient Turkic Shamanism.

As self-governed communities based on a shared identification with the homeland, cybercommunities can also recreate social hierarchies, replicating discriminatory aspects of the homeland culture and/or recasting them in the context of diaspora community and its hybrid identity. The tone of hybrid identity is likely to vary from CGO to CGO and generalizations are problematic.[3] Thus we can only confirm the *potential* for cybercommunities to *selectively* promote liberal values.

Diaspora members are likely to experience a motley identity, not exclusively of ancestral homeland, not exclusively of the adopted society, and not exactly a dual identity. Immigrants neither wholly accept their host country or adopted homeland culture, nor do they automatically embrace their traditional ethnic culture to the exclusion of other influences. Emerging identities may represent significant distortions of homeland history and culture, and/or may reinforce illiberal elements of these. Nevertheless, the Internet is a powerful tool in keeping a homeland identity – however constructed – alive. This is illustrated by the communities of MyCopticChurch.org and TibetBoard, as well as in the consumer base and activities of Thamel.com.

MY COPTIC CHURCH[4]

George Andraws has been disseminating Coptic religious information to the diaspora for some time. At only age 17, wanting to learn more about the Coptic Church, Andraws started an Internet service called "Verse of the Day." He discovered that the Coptic Church had a wealth of knowledge and spiritual information that was largely overlooked. It was overwhelming in size and lacking in organization, which would facilitate its dissemination. Andraws saw a need, and particularly for English speakers in the diaspora, like himself:

I thought people should have access to liturgical readings everyday.... A lot of sites had very poorly written articles or fluff, with no value. So I wanted to put up good quality content.

---

[3] For examples of less liberal manifestations, e.g., regarding gender relations and the application of human rights, see Rai (1995).

[4] Unless otherwise indicated, information on My Coptic Church derives from my personal interview of George Andraws on May 27, 2003. In this and all other discussion forums cited, I maintain the original syntax of thread titles and posts.

He was also driven by the common angst of youth, exacerbated by his diasporic identity:

When I started Verse of the Day I was still in high school. I faced the problem of living between two cultures and I was often frustrated. Pretty much everyone at that age is. But I was frustrated that not a lot of services were tailored to people like me who didn't know Arabic very well. . . . In churches [leaders] wanted everything to be in Arabic. There was not enough in English. We all want it to be in the language we understand the best, but there is a middle ground.

Building on this daily email, Andraws created MyCopticChurch. com in late 2001. His website includes an archive of his Verse of the Day and a link to its continuing content. Having established his Internet presence, he began receiving email requests and learned what other members of the diaspora Copt community wanted. He developed MyCopticChurch with the intention of creating "a universal site for Coptic resources. I wanted it to be very practical and I wanted it to be a site for the Internet community and so I included things like daily readings, stories from the saints, articles. . . ." After he added the Copts Forum, a discussion space, the site began to grow in popularity. When it first began, the number of unique hits grew an average of 50–100 each month. By 2003, the site was receiving an average of 575 unique hits per day.

Andraws' dedication to MyCopticChurch is a reflection of his identity. He came to the United States when he was five years old and continued to visit Egypt fairly regularly. While in junior high school, he spent at least two months in Egypt during the summers. These experiences reminded him of his heritage and also compelled him to reflect on his identity:

The culture had a huge impact on me. I came back very intrigued. I visited lots of Egyptian churches and monasteries. From a Coptic tradition point of view and from a cultural point of view. I liked watching daily life. Things you'd never find in America. . . . I know I'm going to live here the rest of my life . . . but I don't consider myself 100% American. I am an American citizen. I'm a patriot. But I see myself not as 100% Egyptian. I see myself more Coptic than anything. . . . I feel most comfortable around other people who are just like me: other Egyptian Copt families who have immigrated.

TABLE 3-1. *MyCopticChurch Reply Rates*

Reply Range	Number of Threads
50–100	4
26–50	10
20–25	6
11–20	24
6–10	51
1–5	216

As a result, Andraws founded MyCopticChurch with pride in and commitment to his Coptic identity, as he confirms on his webpage:

The Coptic Church is truly unique in respect to its culture, language, liturgy and overall feel. There is a certain feeling you get when you look at a Coptic icon, attend a Coptic service, read Coptic writing, or even talk with a Copt. This is the Coptic experience and that's what I try to harvest and share with Copts and non-Copts alike.

Especially through its discussion forum, MyCopticChurch is a vehicle through which Andraws and others in the diaspora create their own community of Copt émigrés who share the experience of living in the United States and interpreting what being Copt means to them in this environment. Discussion topics address identity issues, either as titled, such as "Coptic Language," "Coptic Church," "Orthodoxy," "Relationships & Marriage," or "Moral/Contemporary Issues"; or as the members define their interests under general labels, such as "Other & Miscellaneous" and "Asking for info."

I observed and analyzed discussion threads from February – April, 2003. I selected 311 threads, which received approximately seven replies on average. More specific reply rates are reported in Table 3-1. The most popular topical areas are reported in Table 3-2.

The reply rates suggest that many of the posts are announcements and/or members may respond directly by email to specific questions, because email addresses are publicly visible. By far, the most popular topical area was "Other & Miscellaneous," with 157 threads. While "Moral/Contemporary Issues" had only four threads, two of these received replies in the 50–100 range (100 and 80 specifically). These

TABLE 3-2. *MyCopticChurch Popular Topical Areas*

Topical Area	Number of Threads
Other & Miscellaneous	157
Asking for info	34
Coptic Church	29
Relationships & Marriage	29
Orthodoxy	11

results suggest that the "Other & Miscellaneous" topic is the one members use by default, and members are very interested in "Moral/ Contemporary Issues" – of those "Other & Miscellaneous" threads, 91 concerned religion and 29 were about culture. Andraws initiates provocative posts to try to explore religious and other controversial issues, such as *why can't I cover my head or do kitchen service?*, about the role of women, and *Does God Love His Enemies?*

Within these topics, many threads address particulars about the Coptic religion. Members receive spiritual support from each other, for example, in confronting fears about confession (*I'm Scared To Have Confession*), committing adultery in one's heart (*Forbidden Love -*), and spiritual crisis (*Seeking Advice- very long post, please be patient*). They also pose and answer religious questions, including: how certain practices are done (e.g., whether one bows down and/or does the sign of the cross when taking communion (*Communion*) and what traditional Coptic marriages are like (*Coptic Marriages – Urgent!*)); why certain practices exist (e.g., why priests wear hats while serving at the altar during certain ceremonies and other church leaders do not (*Asking for info*); and how the Church is organized (e.g., asking if anyone could list the order of the Coptic Hierarchy from the Pope downward (*Coptic Hierarchy*)). Some of these posts highlight or explain differences in practice between Coptic and other churches/traditions, such as: why Coptic Orthodox churches do not celebrate the liturgy of the Presanctified Gifts on the days that other orthodox churches do (*Liturgy of the Presanctified Gifts*), why Eastern Orthodox followers use more icons than Coptic Orthodox followers (*Icons*), whether Catholics sing their masses and use incense as Copts do (*Pre-VaticanII and VaticanII??*), and what the difference is between Copts' "expression of Christ" and the Chalcedonians' (*Chalcedon: What is the difference?*). Many of these discussions included reference to other sources and websites.[5]

These threads contribute to keeping the Copt identity alive. They transmit and sustain knowledge and information about Copt tradition, history, and religious practice. One thread even asked, "what is being done to create 'neologisms' or new words in the Coptic language?" (*New Words for Coptic*). This member argued that if the Coptic language was going to come "back to life ... there is a big need to create new words to use in our world." Several suggestions of new words and phrases were posted, some of which draw from Greek.

Members also seek clarification about Coptic traditions as they confront lifestyles in the West. There are many threads about marriage and the role of women, as well as debates about religious tolerance (*'my religion is the right religion'*) and secularism (*Diaspora, relations before marriage*). Members post questions about their own love lives, including falling in love with people of other faith (*Coptic marrying a Catholic, conversion, marry an American, interracial marriage*), and/or who are divorced (*Marrying a Divorced Person??, copt/can he marry a divorced person*) or younger (*marry a man younger than me*). They also ask about appropriate pre-marital physical contact (*kissing, relations before marriage*) and post-marital sexual practices (*Anal sex between legitimate married couples*). They discuss the pros and cons of marriage versus singlehood, especially for older women, and the challenges of meeting potential mates (*Most Wonderful Love*), raising children in diaspora with a different religion who want to learn about their heritage (*Re: Coptic marrying a Catholic*), and how to meet the right person to marry (*websites on preparation for marriage, Husband Hunting, attraction and marriage*).

Several discussions concern the role of women in the church. For example, in *Women keep silent in the churches*, a member quotes I Corinthians 14:34-35, where St. Paul asserts that it is shameful for women to speak in church and they should be submissive. After posting a series of questions about this, the member writes: "These questions

---

[5] People of other religious faith seeking information about the Coptic religion initiated some of the threads. For example, a Lutheran pastor asked about a Coptic Easter rite he had heard about (*Question on Easter Liturgy – Help!*), and an Eastern Orthodox Russian asked specific questions about Coptic religious traditions (*your beautiful coptic religion*).

might seem ignorant, but I always thought the men and women had equality (while being given separate roles) in the Coptic Church and this seems to contradict that idea." Several members respond indicating an intended interpretation that women should not be priests. In one response a member writes:

If I walked into Church and the priest decided that along with allowing the readers to give sermons, a few women would be picked to give the sermon, I'd walk out and go to another parish, write the bishop, and I'd say that the shame would be firstly on the priest, secondly on the women, next on the husbands, and finally on the members of the congregation who condone it. It's not that the women are inferior, it's just that God chose to ordain men, not women, and so they simply can't have the same graces to allow them to speak with authority in Church. ... It's not a superiority any more than a servant is superiors to the person they serve, it's just a different God given role.

Following additional comments about what makes men and women different, the poster adds:

I'm sure a lot of women reading this will be upset, and probably men too, and probably I haven't quite gotten it right; but I don't think I'm completely off, St. Paul did say that women are the weaker vessels, and this does seem to be how things work in many families. It doesn't mean that the man is better than the women, or vice versa, just that we are different, and better strengthening each other.

Members write of the role of deaconesses in the early church, and other women members seek further clarification. One member questions the source of interpretation regarding men having the responsibility to raise children: "somehow, the part about the man being the source of information on how to raise the children seems wrong to me. I always thought the mother would be the leader in this aspect of family life." Regarding being "source of information on the faith for the family," another member retorts: "Yeah he [the husband] may have that responsibility, but how many times do I see the mother participating in church only??? How many mothers do I see with their chidlren alone in church without their husbands on sunday morning?" One core member who often writes about Church history and religious practice writes: "[I] belive let ur women be silent in churches, was meant to refer to the 'side talks' this is the same as we would say now, to men, women, and kids as well, to keep scilent in churches." Interestingly, this thread was initiated by a man.

In another thread, the founder, Andraws, questions, *why can't I cover my head or do kitchen service?* He writes:

Why is it that when a women wants to take on the roles traditionally done by men in the Church, and required by the laws to be done by men in Church, we think yeah, it's not fair, how come they can't. But when you turn it around the other way, it just seems rediculous. I'm sure that the North American ideology that men and women are the same and not different other than reproductively is seeping in to us and contributing to our feelings that there shouldn't be these different services, but why is it that it seems right and just to us in one direction, and silly in the other?

In response, a member recounts how her Coptic community worshipped with a Lebanese orthodox church until they were able to build their own church. She reported on the mixed-gender choir and the lead role the priest's wife took with the congregation. She questions: "That is a church that's both ORTHODOX and arabic, and they have surpassed us culturally. What's holding us back?"

Even when instances of progress and change in women's roles in Coptic churches in Egypt are pointed out, some members resist new ideas for the sake of preserving Coptic identity in diaspora:

we can try to be open minded like that priest, but Egypt is different from the Land of Imigration. Here (Canada) we can easily lose our traditions if not properly preserved. If girls are allowed to play the cymbals in the church, then the new generation will grow up in this country thinking that they can do that. Then little by little, they'll askk why they can't serve in the alter and we will lose our tradition (*Holy Week: female readers?*).

Another thread asks the question, "Better to be a Copt in an Islamic dominated Egypt or a Copt in the Diaspora?" (*Diaspora*). Noting one of the advantages of diaspora, a member responds:

our natural tendency is to keep our faith hidden, having been a minority in an Islamic state. So, this [being surrounded by other Christians] is encouraging us and teaching us to glorify God more publicly, in the open square, and not only in the inner closets, and teaching us more about evangelism.

On the other hand, this same member laments an erosion of culture and tradition:

However, I have seen the influence of the more liberal and secular American mindset. Whether we like it or not, while the former (Christian) influence is present in America, with all its positive attitudes ..., the latter (secular) influence is actually dominant, and penetrates every moment of our daily lives, whether in school, at work, on television, or in the newspaper. So, sadly, this has definitely had an influence on us, and it's so hard for a lot of us to see that this has happened (and therefore many will deny it), because it has occured so universally that almost everyone has been poisoned with the same venom and our mindset is so engrained and deepled rooted that it seems to us that these are the correct and natural perspectives and conclusions. It takes one coming fresh from Egypt to notice this change of mindset occuring in our youth.

In a similar vein, though in a different thread, another member expresses unresolved angst rooted in the diaspora reality:

White and Black American culture are corrupt. I will marry my fiancee in 5 months. If the Lord blesses us with a child, I would like to spare him/her from the culture I was raised in. The prospects for accomplishing that goal are grim. Filth and degradation drip from the t.v. and radio, and I simply cannot reconcile my Regenerated nature with the media culture, or even the society I live in every single day of my life. The media culture influences young people in ways that older generations simply cannot understand (*relations before marriage*).

TIBETBOARD[6]

Dorjee Nudup was born in Darjeeling, India, after his parents fled Tibet. While Nudup's father returned to Tibet, having found the adjustment too difficult, Nudup and his mother eventually came to the United States, where at the time of our interview, he had almost completed his university studies in computer systems. Nudup founded TibetBoard in 2000, just two years after his arrival in New York. He describes it as "more of a personal website," noting the interpersonal interactions and contrasting it with purely information dissemination sites, such as Tibet House, a physical 501(c)3 in New York, whose mission it is to preserve Tibetan culture. TibetBoard is an interactive and comparatively informal destination for those who may want to learn about or negotiate the Tibetan identity in diaspora.[7]

---

[6] Unless otherwise specified, information on TibetBoard derives from my personal interview with the founder, Dorjee Nudup, October 12, 2003.

[7] Commercial advertising supports the expenses for TibetBoard's maintenance.

Nudup created TibetBoard, in part, to serve instrumental functions:

I based it on my interest and also for people who want to get more information about America, who want to come to America. And also for the main parties, like people in New York City, because we don't have any media which we can use to advertise for a conference or meetings. I advertise for them so people know where we gather and where the festivals are happening.

In addition to posting information and web links for immigration, including how to apply for a visa to the United States, discussion forums enable individuals to ask specific questions and provide to each other more personalized advice regarding immigration processes. The website also includes a lively chatroom, with as many as eighty to ninety people chatting at one time.

Nudup posts links to all the Tibetan-related organizations in which he is active, as well as others he is aware of or upon request. He sees his advertising of events and activities as particularly important for mobilizing people to take action, again emphasizing, "We don't have big media, like a TV station or newspaper. So a lot of people are depending on my website nowadays. ... People will contact me to promote their activity, like through a banner." While many of these activities concern rallies or fundraising in support of Tibetan human rights and political rights, and improved quality of life for Tibetans in Dharamsala, many events also concern cultural celebrations and festivals.

Beyond the material benefits of providing such information, Nudup emphasizes the importance of the discussion boards for exploring Tibetan identity in diaspora:

Tibetan people, because of the traditional system, we don't speak openly all the time because of the situation, so that's my purpose. I want people to talk about anything, like politics, without boundary and also have fun.

According to Nudup, this free discussion is particularly important to Tibetans because:

In our culture, traditional system, our Tibetan government, if we have a different opinion usually they don't – in the mentality – accept that you should, well – whatever the government says then you should do it. Our main conflict is, well, with the Dalai Lama, whatever he says, you have to follow. But people have different opinions .... You can feel whatever you want online. People are afraid to voice their opinions, but you can post without anyone knowing. You can comment on anything.

Participation requires registration, though Nudup acknowledges that, as with other sites, one can easily hide one's identity, choosing whichever username one likes. Among the broader number of registrants, Nudup confirmed a smaller, more active core membership. Guests can also post, though they are sometimes prevented from participating in certain discussions, at the discretion of the initiator. As on other sites, members may masquerade as guests to post different ideas without divulging their identity. In fact, members accuse one another of doing so, taking guesses or asserting the identity of "guests" in particular discussions.

TibetBoard appears to bring together Tibetans from all over the world, and Nudup seems to take for granted that these participants are first and foremost Tibetan. Nudup shared the results of a survey he conducted, confirming membership from Switzerland, India, and Nepal, as well as North America. When asked why he decided to survey his membership to learn of their location of residence, the reasoning had nothing to do with potential differences in interests or preferences; Nudup surveyed his membership in order to ensure that he was using the appropriate technical interface so that his members could most easily access and view his website. Like many Tibetans in diaspora, Nudup has several friends in Dharamsala. These friends often provide feedback to him on the occasional real-world outcomes of TibetBoard's discussions, reporting resulting marriages, for example.

The discussion forums include topics related to Buddhism, poetry, education, and human rights.[8] I observed and analyzed discussion threads from May – July, 2003. I selected 241 threads, which received approximately seven replies on average. More specific reply rates are reported in Table 3-3. The most popular threads are reported in Table 3-4.

---

[8] While not formally analyzed, the poetry area affords members the opportunity to experiment and post their own poetry. Members respond, often with praise and/or encouragement related to both the writing/composition and the subject matter, which frequently concerns cultural and religious expression, as well as more secular love.

TABLE 3-3. *TibetBoard Reply Rates (by number of threads)*

Reply Range	Politics of the People	Buddhism	Education	Human Rights	Totals	%
51–101	4	1	0	0	5	2%
21–50	13	1	1	0	15	6%
11–20	35	2	1	1	39	16%
6–10	35	2	1	1	39	16%
1–5	80	9	4	3	96	40%
0	35	6	3	3	47	20%
TOTALS	202	21	10	8	241	

TABLE 3-4. *TibetBoard Most Popular Threads*

Thread Name	Replies/Views	Topical Area
Tibetan violence	101/2059	Politics of the people
Why do Tibetans hate the khampas?	96/1724	Politics of the people
U.S. Visa, why why	82/1879	Politics of the people
Marriage divorce tantrism sex	63/1145	Buddhism
Ok guys, I'm leaving this board, good luck.	55/402	Politics of the people
SARS … from China	27/861	Education
Education is NOTHING	17/1216	Education

"Politics of the People" is clearly the most popular topical area, and may be the posting place of default. The reply rates suggest a high percentage of announcements.

The basis for thread popularity is difficult to determine. In some instances, it seems clear that the thread name inspires interest, but perhaps the discussion itself is less interesting. This may explain the large differences between numbers of replies and views. On the other hand, interest (demonstrated by a large number of views), but few responses may also be a function of the subject matter being uncomfortable. For example, issues surrounding violence and ethnic tension may be of great interest, though as Nudup suggests, it may be difficult for some to express their opinion on these subjects, perhaps even online. In still other instances, the thread name may be misleading. This is the case, for example, for *SARS . . . from China*. It is possible that some members viewed the thread out of concern about the spread of SARS, especially in Tibet. However, the discussion begins and continues somewhat as a commentary on Chinese karma (though that term is not explicitly mentioned).

Threads may be popular because of their initiators. *Ok Guys, I'm leaving this board, good luck.* was initiated by a member who calls himself ChineseGuy. ChineseGuy provocatively engages other members throughout the forums by advocating for the Chinese. Whether or not he does this in order to provoke and seek attention or because he is expressing his true beliefs is impossible to determine. However, his controversial presence and contributions keep many of the discussions lively, often contentious, and sometimes inclusive of angry name calling and profanity. Similarly, the most popular thread, *Why do Tibetans hate the khampas?*, was initiated by Chris, a non-Tibetan core member, who sometimes writes in support of the Chinese. The discussion oscillates between responding seriously to the question and accusing Chris of asking it in order to foment disagreement. Finally, number of replies cannot, alone, indicate popularity. Upon investigation, *Marriage divorce tantrism sex* was discovered to be primarily spamming by the same author using different, though related usernames, sometimes in conversation with himself.

While it's impossible to know the true identity and demographics of participants, many posts allude to study and midterms and some members make their age and identity explicit when it is other than a Tibetan teenager. During the period analyzed, one member tried to learn more about the identity of others. In *A Genuine Suggestion, introducing ourselves*, WakeUp_Tibet asks members to introduce themselves and initiates by listing his nationality, current location, age range, occupation, and gender. The thread received only fourteen responses, and only three were serious responses. These responses, if they are to be believed, indicate that one of the most active members, ChineseGuy is sixteen to seventeen. Other indicated years or age ranges were: thirties, twenty-six, and twenty.

Posts indicate that members are self-conscious about diaspora identity issues and explicitly seek to preserve their Tibetan identity by participating in TibetBoard. For example, in response to a criticism that the discussions are sometimes more about gossip than issues relevant to Tibetans worldwide, one member writes:

For me Tibet chat has acted as a platform where i can meet Tibetan people and preserve the Tibetaness in me. I live in white area, my social ciricles have been blonde girls all the time who I get along very well. I am thankful to Tibetchat for making me more Tibetan than I was before (*Time to Move on.*).

Other members lament the influence of Western culture on Tibetans in diaspora. For example,

the stuff that I read are not very intelligent too and that is the education standard of our society. i know it's not very impressive with regards to sensibility and emphasis on the values of real genuine Tibetans we once used to be .... this is the affects of the chain reaction caused by the western influence on us. And what i have seen is that we tend to leave our good virtues and pick up the petty characters from the West which are called COOL (*Time to Move on.*).

Elsewhere, a member named "Preserve the Tibetan Culture" explains to member "Ghetto Child" what ghetto means and implores Tibetans not to adopt the ghetto culture, even though they think it's cool (*Hello Ghetto Child*).

The thread, *What's there in Future for Tibetans?* also takes on this issue. It opens with the observation that "Lot of Tibetan teenagers are losing touch with our culture. Parents are working and their sons/daughters don't get the proper guidance that they need and we are all turning into the All American Theory of Consumerism." In response, a member questions the relevance of Tibetan culture to the modern world and suggests that at least the language should be kept alive:

One thing you have to forget, the old culture, which is not fit for the modern wolrd then you have to forget, but our tibetan language is not this kind of matter, but on the other side we have to improve it and have to rewrite the grammtic rule, in order to learn it easier way and easier way to speak, then may many teenager tibetan learn the language, eventhough it takes little place for their every day life (*What's there in Future for Tibetans?*).

The focus on language is reminiscent of MyCopticChurch. Another member responds offering some comfort in the fact that the discussion is about teenagers:

unfortunately tibetan teenagers will be influenced by many things that are not in line with our culture but from experience i believe that with age comes understanding and realisation one's own identity. In other word, majority of tibetans will develop their own unique character but will not loss their sense that they are a Tibetan (*What's there in Future for Tibetans?*).

One of the defining features of the Tibetan diaspora is the perceived inability or impossibility of return. In response to these laments about Western influence, some members encourage others to remain authentic despite these influences:

the Tibet should learn how to be the authentic independent Tibetan without any foreign compulsive influence!! We cannot avoid the foreign influence, but we can think independently and select the best things for us (*Should the Tibetan object to the USA?*)

In other threads, members discussed which destinations would be better for the sustenance of Tibetan culture. In *AMERICA...!!! IT'S NOT WHAT YOU THINK* ... the initiator warns Tibetans in India that life can be very difficult in America, and that America is different from what they may have seen from "bollywood movies." He argues that the quality of life in India, while not as luxurious, is otherwise better, contrasting "From the moment you land the JFK international airport, your life of slavery begans," with "people in India are living a richer life considering the luxury of time to sleep, to hang with friends, to have emotional people all around you and time for yourself." Later in the thread, this same member asks the community to consider, what would happen if all Tibetans came to the US, leaving only the Government in exile in India? He argues that this will lead to the end of Tibet's political struggle and that the Tibetans themselves will become extinct.

In another thread, members express similar concerns about the loss of Tibetan identity:

we could preserve our identity and culture better in India and Nepal-(East). I have been in America for seven years and i have seen the worst of cultural destruction.... WE can't even shape our kids character coz over here it's called abuse and control. This is another planet here and you either forget about tibet or love where you are (*US Visa, why why*).

In response, another member defends Tibetans in America reminding the poster that people come to America not just for money or consumption, but also for a better education and more opportunities for their children than might be found in Nepal. Another member adds, passionately, that TibetBoard members should recognize that many Tibetans come to America (United States and Canada) to escape from poverty.

In the same thread, members begin to identify positive attributes of American society. Invoking the famous John F. Kennedy line, a member defends the Dalai Lama and reminds others that most Tibetans in diaspora have probably not contributed much, if anything, to helping their government to re-secure the homeland or at least improve the plight of Tibetans worldwide. She urges others to pursue scholarships in the United States and become educated without relying on the Tibetan Government in exile (*US Visa, why why*). More explicitly, a member writes:

There are good things to learn too in America. Just look around and watch how a kid from decent middle class American family talk or behave. They don't just go around cursing everyone or using those slangs from the streets. This is surely a land of opportunity, but it doesn't mean you forget your origin, identity and culture (*US Visa, why why*).

These posts turn the discussion in a much more optimistic direction. For example:

going to America or any European countries is a good thing for all of us.... we should think of going to America legally, come on we should atleast trust ourself this much. its is not just about going there, but becoming a better human being and being on a better stand to support our cause. ... be a good human being anywhere you go, and be a good tibetan (*US Visa, why why*).

In seeking to sustain their Tibetan identity in diaspora, members ask questions about traditions and at the same time seem to look for ways to connect their Tibetan identity to their adopted host culture. Like MyCopticChurch, members may ask questions specific to Buddhist religious practice, such as whether or not the Eight Auspicious Symbols should be learned in any particular order (*The Eight Auspicious Symbols, and particular order?*). This thread begins with an exchange between the questioner and a knowledgeable respondent but then prompts requests for clarification from other members. The original poster then asks additional questions, this time about the four sects, adding with appreciation "There are no substitutes for learning from people who are born into and live this culture" (Ibid.).[9]

Looking for Tibetan identity in the West, one member asks, "do you people notice there seem to be a lot of movies made in Hollywood with rich buddhist themes?" (*O)*)). The discussion leads to a somewhat detailed analysis of the film *The Matrix* (1999) from a Buddhist perspective. Elsewhere, invoking democracy, a member initiates a thread with:

Tibetans have to learn to express their individuality. That is the essence of a healthy democratic society and we should not be swayed by all the "negative" influences that come with it. Instead when people are allowed to express themselves this allows for –strangely a better platform for dialogue and understanding. Sadly the Tibetan community has a huge gap within – intellectually. A part remains in the medieval mindset and a part western educated and aware. Then there are the in betweens who are torn between these seemingly opposing groups choosing to take sides when convenient (*wasted opportunity, ignorance*).

The author uses this statement as the basis for arguing that encouraging all Tibetans to stay in India or Nepal to better preserve Tibetan culture is misguided. A Tibetan living in India responds defensively.

Even a seemingly superficial thread about a popular Tibetan singer evokes issues of "true" Tibetan identity. It also reinforces the merit of admiring those who serve the Tibetan people. After a few posts about the singer Yangchan Lhamo, a member with the username "Real Tibetan" asserts that Jetsum Pema is a better woman to revere. Yangchan Lhamo, some members argue, is more concerned about her popularity and marketability in the West, championing Buddhism, but not the freedom of Tibet (*Who is the most Eligible Women?, Tibetan*

---

[9] It is impossible to know whether or not this member is of the Tibetan diaspora or is of another culture/nationality with an interest in Buddhism (in which case the thread would demonstrate bridging social capital). In any event, the initiator prompted other members – presumably Tibetans among them – to contribute and to seek further clarification.

Entertainment). "Instead", writes a member, "why don't you call Jetsum Pema lak as the most eligible tibetan woman. Lokk how she is staying and what she has been doing since so many years. Looking after thousands and thousands of tibetan students" (*Who is the most Eligible Women?, Tibetan Entertainment*). At the Dalai Lama's request, Jetsun Pema has been running the Tibetan Children's Village in Dharamsala since 1964. She was officially awarded the title "Mother of Tibet" by the Tibetan National Assembly-in-Exile in 1995 (The Tibetan Cultural Center 2006).

Perhaps in a similar effort to maintain "true" Tibetan-ness, the Dalai Lama as a religious figure is often defended and supported; this can occur at the same time that some members question the effectiveness of the Dalai Lama's nonviolent approach and criticize the Tibetan Government in exile. For example, one member takes on the username "Dali Llama" and often argues on behalf of the Chinese. At one point, he defends the Chinese colonization of Tibet "in order to civilize an otherwise backward province" (*FINAL SOLUTION TO THE CHINESE QUESTION!*). Another member entreats Dali Llama to change his username:

could u please kindly change the name becouse I do not like someone playing with His Holiness name.I myself respect him so much and he means so much to me (*Are Tibetans Terroists?*).

Elsewhere, a member pleads, "Please do not say anything bad about His Holiness the Dalai Lama. He is the only hope we have. H.H. is not just himself, but he is a symbol of Tibet" (*Ban Chris! Ban all opposition to the HH Dalai Lama*). In fact, feelings about the Dalai Lama run high. In the thread *What do you think about Dalai Lama?, Let's see how modern your thinkings are*, a member initiates a poll with four voting options: "1) He is a holy man, the reincarnation of all past Dalai Lamas; 2) He is an ordinary good human; 3) He is a disgraceful beggar; and 4) He is a disgraceful beggar, who shall be reincaranted as a dog." Guests were not allowed to vote, and only three votes were cast. It may be telling, though, that one vote was cast for each of the options except that the Dalai Lama is an ordinary man.

The Tibetan diaspora is both a political/territorial diaspora and a religious one. And these identities are not always compatible. For example, one member writes, "Getting political independence has nothing to

do with Buddha Dharma as long as we interpret it as something car-
ried out by the mind" (*How can we get Freedom, do you have any
opinions about Tibet*). An unregistered guest initiates another thread
with a Buddhist perspective on the Tibetans' diaspora:

I do not think that it is in our innate nature to be part of a perticular region
where ones ancestors have inherited. its natural to gradually get assimilated
into or with other societies and this simple process has produced all the different people. in buddhism too we are all equal. so why do we, the tibtean have to
fight for something that is inevitable? what is the reason for our struggle when
every thing is deemed 'empty'? why??? (*why Tibet*).

The thread only received three posts – none of which were substantively
responsive, and 36 views. In the context of a more popular discussion
thread, representing bridging social capital, one member defends Chris,
a non-Tibetan pro-Chinese and contentious contributor, arguing that:

My concept is totally different from Chris (I want Chinese out from Tibet and Let
Tibetan have their own country. I will even use violence to get my country back in
the future) but that doesn't mean I have to avoid him or hate him. Instead I love
him so much (*Ban Chris! Ban all opposition to the HH Dalai Lama*).

Later this member invokes Buddhism and argues that "there is no
ultimate truth" (Ibid.).
    This post inspires an exchange about how Tibetan Buddhism differs
from other forms of Buddhism, and just what the essence of Buddhism
is. This further leads to a discussion of how religion is a form of social
control and that, even in Tibet, historically it was a political tool. The
poster of this historical perspective, tibetan warrior, goes on to outline
the incompatibilities of Tibetan Buddhism and democracy:

anyone who supports violence is looked down upon the rest of the people and the
government in exile treats that person with contempt.well if that is not a dictator
in action than what.think about it. tibetans need a new political system where
monks and lamas are banned then only true democracy and development will be
possible (*Ban Chris! Ban all opposition to the HH Dalai Lama*).

These tensions further underscore the importance of the Dalai Lama,
whether as a symbol, a religious leader, or a political leader of the
Tibetans in diaspora. As one member puts it bluntly:

We still believe in non-violence because of H.H. Dalai Lama. The fact is I am afraid to tell you that in the future without Dalai Lama, all Tibetan will use violence against China (*tibetan violence*).

The fact that Tibetan diasporans use TibetBoard to negotiate their identity, questioning their traditional home culture as they embrace values, experience, and culture from their hostlands, is confirmed succinctly by the contentious non-Tibetan, Chris, in explaining why he chooses to participate in the TibetBoard community:

the reason i am on this board as when i was on the free-tibet boards they say stero typical things about the tibetans, i.e. you were a peacefull nonviolent country, all tibetans worship the dalai lama. they glorify serf/slavery tibet. etc etc i thought they were racist towards you (*tibetan violence*).

THAMEL.COM[10]

Following his undergraduate business studies in Portland, Oregon, Bal Joshi returned to Nepal and, after initially selling beverages out of a pushcart on the streets of Katmandu, successfully designed and implemented Nepal's first national lottery. Unfortunately, the lottery's success attracted the attention of a new government administration, and individuals' demands for kickbacks led Joshi and his investors to close up shop. Based on the success of U.S. dot coms, several of Joshi's former employees suggested an information portal on Nepali businesses. The original idea was to market a guide to local businesses to entice tourists both to come to Nepal and spend money with local businesses. They named the company after the Katmandu street that hosts the business core: Thamel.

Joshi and his associates soon discovered that most of the interest in Thamel.com was coming from diasporans, not the tourists they had anticipated. At the same time, Thamel.com's staff was energized by the

---

[10] The following case description draws on my personal interview and correspondence with the founder and his associates, a review of empirical data, observation of the Thamel.com webpage (www.thamel.com), and organization reports and media coverage. Unless otherwise noted, the source of information is my personal interview with Bal K. Joshi, Cofounder and Managing Director of Thamel.com, Codirector of Thamel International, September 17, 2004a.

prospect of fully exploring and introducing Nepalis to the latest technology available at the time. For example, they launched Nepal's first web-based audio learning tool and mapping system. This was 1998, before Yahoo and Microsoft had popularized their sophisticated chatroom and discussion forum platforms. Thamel.com, with very basic technology, had become an important vehicle for diasporans to communicate inexpensively with their family members in Nepal. From his own experience in Portland, Joshi could well appreciate the value of this communication link for diaspora communities.

On the other hand, this alone would not make Thamel.com profitable. Joshi had agreed to fund the operation for the first year with the understanding that after that it would need to be at least self-sustaining. As an experiment, Joshi and his associates decided to post a few items for sale and explore whether or not diasporans would want to purchase gifts for their families. They had already developed a network of over 500 local businesses with the intention of attracting customers, so why not market their products to the diaspora via the web?

Thamel.com got off to a slow start and encountered many expected challenges. Because of its novelty as well as Nepal's history with business scams, their biggest initial hurdle was trust. Thinking ahead to their own family plans, they stumbled on a new idea related to the upcoming Dashain Festival, the most important cultural and spiritual celebration in Nepal. A major component of the celebration is the sacrifice of a ceremonial goat to ensure prosperity in the year to come. This is such an essential component of the festival and its related blessings that families sometimes secure loans to pay for it – the cost ($80–100) can be as high as 40–50% of average yearly income. For Nepali diasporans, the cost might not be as prohibitive. However, the means of ensuring the money transfer and its application to the intended use were complicated at best. And how would customers know the goat had been delivered? How would Thamel.com develop trust with their customer base? Joshi's staff suggested taking a digital picture of the recipient and the gifted goat and e-mailing it to the customer.

A further challenge remained: how to deliver the goats? What happens if they died or lost weight in transit? They soon realized that to be culturally relevant, the families would also need to select their own goat; this is a very important ritual in preparation for the festival. In fact, this became the easy solution to delivery. Thamel.com had only to inform the family of the gift, delivering a gift certificate that could be redeemed at a particular goat market. In the first few days, business was slow at best, but then Thamel.com was quickly overwhelmed. They caught the attention of the BBC, which did a story on them, further expanding the demand.

With an estimated customer base of 18,000–20,000, by 2004 Thamel.com offered a range of products for diaspora gifting to their families (e.g., flowers, cakes, jewelry, musical CDs – even limousine service for weddings).[11] Thamel.com continues to focus on culturally relevant products and services using the digital photo as their signature touch, having evolved the motto: "We are the messenger of your sentiments" (Katauskas 2004). For example, Nepal's equivalent to Father's Day is roughly translated as "looking upon father's face." Joshi received a long distance phone call from one of his Father's Day customers:

She was crying. She had sent her father in Nepal a Father's Day gift through our website. He had received the gift and his picture had been forwarded to her in acknowledgement of the delivery. She was overwhelmed with joy. This was the first time she had seen her father's face in 13 years (Joshi and Granger 2003).

Father's Day photograph delivery is coordinated to ensure early morning delivery. Gift delivery has become an event with a ritual all its own. Family members assemble in formal clothes to enjoy the gift together.

Thamel.com's evolution follows a course of trial and error. Despite their success with the diaspora gift market, they continued to promote selectively exports, marketed on a subsidiary webpage called "Freak Street" after the tourist shopping street in Katmandu. Joshi and his staff soon discovered that the demand for Nepali exports was much more segmented than they originally anticipated. They decided to specialize by launching individual platforms for specific products (e.g., pashminas) in partnership with local (Nepali) producers. The diaspora community became their greatest advertiser. For example, during the world wars, Nepali warriors were famous for their Khukuri knives. Some

---

[11] Approximately 66% of sales originated in the United States, with another 15% from the UK, Canada, and Australia. Access to information technology has hampered marketing in some areas, such as the Middle East.

diasporans already possess them, or, desiring a symbol of Nepal, acquire them through Thamel.com. When their adopted/host country friends see them and express interest, diasporans direct their friends to the webpage. Of Thamel.com's export business, the diaspora is estimated to represent only 10%.

AS of 2003, Thamel.com employed 50 full time staff in Nepal, maintained over 500 business affiliates (ranging from the largest businesses in Nepal to street vendors with annual revenues under $1,000), serves 18,000–20,000 people in 25 countries, contributed over one million U.S. dollars a year in revenue to the local economy (Joshi and Granger 2003), and generated $1.3 million revenue in 2003 (Katauskas 2004; Joshi 2004b). Thamel.com represents a multifaceted business model, encompassing three kinds of services: home market, remittance, and business development (to be discussed in Chapter 7). The home market services are largely described above and concern the acquisition of goods and services from Nepal for either the local gift or export markets. In tandem with the evolution of these services, Joshi and his associates also recognized a strategic business opportunity, as well as a social interest, in developing remittance services and business development services for its business affiliates. Table 3-5 illustrates how each of these service areas draws on different actors for financing, employment, and consumption.

Formally recognized remittances to Nepal are approximately $1 billion. Joshi estimated that another $2 billion was being sent through the Hundi system, with a risk of loss or leakage. Alternatives, such as Western Union, can charge as much as 10%. Thamel.com offers

TABLE 3-5. *Diasporas and the Poor in Thamel's Three Service Areas*

Home Market Services	Diaspora as customers, poor as employees and consumers
Business Development Services	Poor as business partners, diaspora and poor as customers
Remittance Services	Diaspora as customers, poor as consumers

these services for 2.4–3%. Because the home market services were well-established and trust in Thamel.com was strong, it was relatively easy for Joshi and his associates to launch remittance services. No advertising was necessary, and on occasion, money is transferred without initial identification and instructions. According to Joshi, "There is no question about credibility. There is no question that we would not deliver the money."

Thamel.com leverages money transfer into products and services. Customers have the option of transferring money in the conventional sense – for use at the discretion of recipients; or, they can transfer money to invest in specified outcomes. Because these services are provided in partnership with producers and banks (with some profit sharing), Thamel.com does not charge additional transfer service fees. As Joshi puts it, "We want to help you manage your funds. We want to help you obtain loans. We also want to make sure that if your wife or your husband runs away with someone else, your money that you invested is yours."

Thamel.com enables diasporans to set up bank accounts in Nepal for specific purposes, or with restricted access (to make sure the money gets to the intended beneficiary). For example, for those who can afford it, private schooling in Nepal is considered to be good quality, at a cost of $200–300 per month. Previously when this money was transferred to a family member, the sender could not know for certain that the money was used for that purpose. Thamel.com organized private schools to set up specific accounts with a banking partner, where the funds can be transferred directly. Now, Thamel.com, with its banking partner, establishes a bank account for the sender and the bank automatically makes the school payments on a schedule. The bank account is solely for that purpose.

HYBRID IDENTITY AND ITS RELIGIOUS, POLITICAL, AND BUSINESS IMPLICATIONS

All three organizations link diasporans to homeland identity – and in the case of Thamel.com, to the homeland itself – in both materially and psychologically instrumental ways. Simple information exchange enables: Copts and Tibetans to better understand how their religions are traditionally practiced; Tibetans to learn about how to migrate to

North America; Tibetans and other interested parties to politically mobilize in support of a free Tibet, or simply to participate in Tibetan cultural events; and Nepalese to learn how to acquire Nepali products and refer their friends.

These organizations also provide identity benefits. They provide opportunities for members to: negotiate hybrid identities and suggest their own interpretations of religion and culture (MyCopticChurch and TibetBoard), receive support in understanding and expressing the homeland culture and religion (all three), and, in so doing, potentially strengthen and extend that identity and its practice, with religious, political, and business implications.

Regarding religion, both CGOs provide opportunities for diasporans to seek clarification and become more educated about the religious practice, while at once providing a forum for questioning and potentially modifying or encouraging modification of religious practice and traditions. Even a private business, Thamel.com, enables diasporans to connect with and in some way participate in cultural/religious festivals, such as Dashain and Father's Day. CGOs, in particular, may help to keep religious practice alive and make it relevant in diaspora. The two cybercommunities reveal members' defensiveness of their religion resulting from the diaspora experience. For example, some members of MyCopticChurch explicitly argue that the practice of the Coptic religion in diaspora cannot afford to reform its gender practices as Coptic churches in Egypt can, else "little by little ... we will lose our tradition" (*Holy Week: female readers?*). One member of TibetBoard asserts that it is better to learn religion from those who have directly experienced and grown up within its culture.

In encountering religious pluralism and alternative lifestyles, members pose questions, assert their own interpretations – sometimes with inherent contradictions, and promote tolerance, provide correction, or simply ignore remarks that might jeopardize the continuing community. Both communities clarify their religious identity by exploring its difference with other forms of religious practice. Some of the questions and discussions on MyCopticChurch are quite personal and the efforts to resolve lifestyle issues in accordance with the religion appear quite sincere, even if the answers are not what one might have hoped for (e.g., regarding marrying outside of the faith, or women as church leaders). Criticizing and defending the Dalai Lama are a favorite pastime of TibetBoard members, though no members seem to question that he is a religious leader and not an ordinary man. Religious discussions sometimes lead to implicit cost-benefit analyses, such as women Copts in diaspora wondering if the traditional practices are reflective of reality as they have experienced it or are in their interest (*Women keep silent in the churches*), or Tibetans in diaspora questioning if their religious identity inclusive of nonviolence has served them well and whether religion is an undemocratic form of social control (*Ban Chris! Ban all opposition to the HH Dalai Lama*). On Tibet-Board, one member promotes tolerance for Chris, invoking peace and love for him even as s/he asserts support for violence against the Chinese.

TibetBoard is the most politically oriented of the three organizations. I will further explore this characteristic in Chapter 7. Already, the description provided here suggests a number of political implications of hybrid identity. Certainly, digital diasporas can be politically mobilized and Dorjee Nudup sees that mobilization as a major service to his community. By providing a means by which cultural and political events can be advertised, he enables the Tibetan diaspora to assemble as a physical community and share and develop a common political platform. Beyond this physical mobilization, the process of negotiating a hybrid identity may influence the direction of this potential mobilization. Some diasporas originating from a more traditional dispersal – whether through forced migration or voluntary exile – may be inclined to embrace individualism and find empowerment potentially for violence from embracing selected Western values (such as basic freedoms and human rights). The Tibetan diaspora is likely tempered in its physical world violent engagement by its religious identity of nonviolence. TibetBoard includes many calls for embracing violence as a potentially more effective approach to preserving a Tibetan homeland, however, it is unlikely that these would become real-world intentions and these calls are often met with reminders of Tibetan religious values. As will be argued in Chapter 5 (examining AfghanistanOnline and Somalinet), cybercommunities afford diasporans the opportunity to potentially deflect their frustration and animosity through verbal as opposed to physical confrontation.

Thamel.com demonstrates how transnational businesses can promote the retention of links between diasporas and their homelands, and in creative ways. Thamel.com provides these links through: 1) simple online communication; 2) support for cultural festivals, allowing diasporans to participate from a distance; 3) visual connection to family and community through a digital photograph; 4) diaspora consumption of cultural products, which also provides opportunities to discuss the homeland with friends who may themselves purchase these items; and 5) facilitating and encouraging remittances by providing services at lower costs, higher trust, and with opportunities to make long-term investments. This latter service may arguably sustain as well as make remittances more productive. By providing opportunities to open bank accounts to make regular payments for schooling and large purchase items, Thamel.com secures a longer term financial investment with market accountability built in. Thamel.com may be a particularly creative and sophisticated model for sustaining homeland identity in diaspora, but alongside it many businesses have long provided linkages to the homeland, including telecommunications, travel/tourism, and more traditional cultural exports.

Identity hybridity may be a natural, even automatic outgrowth of diaspora experience. However, diaspora organizations that foster its negotiation and enable the sustenance of a diaspora identity inclusive of at least some homeland values and traditions, may arguably sustain hybridity and homeland identity across generations of diaspora. And this sustenance may be more likely with the advent of the Internet. This process may yield new identities that become ever distant from identity practiced in the homeland – whether considered more traditional or more modern. These cases suggest that either one of these hybrid options will have implications for how religion is practiced, how and why diasporans mobilize politically, and how they consume and maintain economic links to the homeland.

4

Digital Diasporas as Cybercommunities

Chapter 3 illustrated how the Internet's interactive components become an efficient, easy-access tool for diaspora storytelling and sharing, enabling members to make sense of their experiences and feelings in the encounter between cultures and identities. Over time, these interactive processes create on-line communities and organizations. This chapter examines how these cyberspaces become communities. I present two cyber-grassroots organizations (CGOs), AfghanistanOnline and Somalinet. Each organization retains few, if any, offline resources. They are truly *cyber*-grassroots organizations in which the bulk of organization activities take place only online. The websites associated with each have substantial interactive components, such as online discussion boards, which facilitate communication between and among members. The use of these interactive components make these cases living communities and organizations (as characterized by Weick 1979, 1995), complete with interpersonal communication, a range of member benefits – most especially solidary benefits, and rule making.What follows is a brief discussion of community formation and outcomes.

INFORMATION TECHNOLOGY AND CYBERCOMMUNITIES

The contribution of IT to diaspora identity and potential mobilization begins with the Internet's enabling features for the formation of voluntary communities. A voluntary community has three defining conditions: low barriers to entry, low barriers to exit, and nonhierarchical and noncoercive (Galston 2002). These characteristics are highly relevant to dispersed diasporans who may be experiencing identity stress. Communities – and especially *virtual* communities – are developed based on the expression or eliciting of feeling/emotion and communication/discussion (see Rheingold 1993).

CGOs may create voluntary communities. They have no physical presence. Their only "infrastructure" is the webpage and its associated Internet-based technologies, such as email listservs, online chatrooms, and electronic bulletin boards. By debating norms, values, and ideas, people create and enact the organization (see Brainard 2003; Brainard and Brinkerhoff 2004). The interactive components of the Internet provide for the exchange of ideas, debate, and the mobilization of opinion, potentially culminating in strong social bonds and relationships (Rheingold 1993; see also Walther 1995; Wellman and Gulia 1999).

These communities generate bonding, bridging, and bridging-to-bond social capital. As members provide validation and correction in the process of identity negotiation, they ensure continued shared social norms for group solidarity. This solidarity and the anonymity the Internet affords provide a safe space for members to share painful memories, even trauma, both personal and collective, and experiment with new ideas, as they relate to the diaspora experience and the fate of the homeland. In doing so, members collectively generate bonding social capital. The Internet also fosters bridging social capital. The communities assemble diasporans from dispersed countries and locations of settlement and a range of generations, often representing multiple social and ethnic factions of the homeland. Furthermore, they may include nondiasporans, who may be connected to the idea of the diaspora and its homeland through family relationships, personal experience, or shared religious faith. Beyond the online community, the inclusion of e-mail addresses in communications enables members to selectively communicate and engage beyond the cybercommunity, possibly in the physical world as well (Wellman and Gulia 1999). By connecting members across locations and time and between cyberspace and potentially the physical world, cybercommunities also create bridging-to-bond social capital.

Like their physical space counterparts, cybercommunities operate according to member-created norms. Through repeat interaction, members discover shared needs and interests and evolve social norms to address them. Norms in cyberspace emerge in response to three kinds of imperatives: promoting shared purposes, safeguarding the quality of group discussion, and managing scarce resources in the virtual commons (Galston 2002). Rules need not be formally articulated; rather, they emerge through trial and error and so are continuously negotiated (Brainard and Brinkerhoff 2004). These rules-in-use reflect shared understandings.

Listserv managers and founders/managers of websites may more proactively regulate community behavior. Through member registration, discussion moderation, and participation rules, they establish what may or may not be legitimate to debate. Members can be banned (temporarily or permanently) for breaking rules, such as spamming or including forbidden content. Filtering and message delay also can be used to frame discussion. Through content regulation (community norms, formal rules, and filtering), participation rules, and delay, the Internet becomes a tool for moderating potentially inflammatory sentiments.

Through these self-generating norms as well as the intentions of the site founder(s), communities can frame the discussions, establishing parameters for the content, tone, and openness of participation. Interactive components may be moderated minimally (e.g., removing posts upon request) or more extensively (such as through filtering), solely by the founder/staff or in collaboration with volunteer moderators from the community. Occasionally, outsiders may attempt to prevent participation, including flaming sites (i.e., inundating them with hostile or offensive mail), hacking and infecting sites with viruses, and using "kill files," indicating addresses from which a user will not receive messages (Graham and Khosravi 2002). At such times, the community may assert itself in a common defense, confirming individuals' shared identity as members of the particular community.

Diaspora CGOs offer all of the benefits of brick and mortar grassroots organizations (see Brainard and Brinkerhoff 2004), and the Internet facilitates several of these. Cybercommunities at once provide to members solidary benefits based on a shared homeland identity and opportunities to explore and express alternative identities (cultural identity benefits). CGOs and other diaspora organizations with an Internet presence also provide material benefits to their members, enhanced through IT. In cybercommunities, material benefits come primarily in the way of information dissemination. The Internet reduces transaction costs for acquiring and disseminating information. Diaspora organizations on the Internet provide material benefits focused on information and referral related to homeland identity (e.g., historical, cultural, and current event information), as well as in support of adjustment in the homeland (e.g., where to find a lawyer, how to get a driver's license). In CGOs, members provide both kinds of material benefits to each other through discussion forums and chatrooms, creating sometimes close-knit communities. Material benefits may also include dating/marriage service, and business promotion.

AfghanistanOnline and Somalinet demonstrate these communal and organizational attributes.

AFGHANISTANONLINE[1]

Abdullah Qazi initiated what would later become AfghanistanOnline (www.afghan-web.com) in 1996 as a way to learn about the country he left as a child. Beginning with his own research, he started his site with just a few pages, posting materials he deemed interesting as he researched his home country. He made no effort to solicit visits to his site; he simply posted a webpage. Initially he received only one to two hits per day; eventually he began to receive significant positive feedback so he continued to develop the webpage. Visitors to his site soon began to contribute content, such as pictures and stories from visits to Afghanistan. Some of this material was rare – old pictures, for example – and Qazi and his visitors believed others within the Afghan diaspora would also be interested. The more Qazi posted these, the more positive feedback he received. Approximately eighteen months after AfghanistanOnline's launch, readers suggested he add a discussion page to enable them to interact. The following is based on monitoring and analysis of AfghanistanOnline from August 1–November 1, 2002.

AfghanistanOnline (AO), with over 5,000 hits each day, is a place where Afghans from all over the world can interact and learn more about Afghanistan. Qazi ensures that his site is the first listed for web

---

[1] This description builds largely from Brainard and Brinkerhoff (2004). Unless otherwise noted, case information derives from Qazi (2002).

searches for Afghanistan from major search engines (e.g., google.com). The site has won numerous awards, including honors for web design, technical excellence, general excellence, outstanding multicultural website, and the Global Choice Cuisine Award for its page on Afghan cooking. The site aims to provide "the most current and reliable information on Afghanistan." Page topics range from news to culture, politics, history, biographies, and even plants and animals. AO also provides a variety of online discussion forums. Abdullah Qazi describes AO as "a hobby" that he shares with his wife. With her support, he alone manages the site and its content. Commercial activities on the website include advertisement and the sale of Afghanistan-related products. Qazi reinvests associated revenues in technology for the site.

Discussion forums range from the general (e.g., "General Discussion Forum on Afghanistan") to the specific (such as a German language forum created by request from Afghans living in Germany). Within these categories, individuals can create and add their own threads. Thus, within the five discussion forums, there were 737 topics with a total of 8,065 postings (as of November 1, 2002). The most active forum was the "General Discussion Forum on Afghanistan." Topics addressed here included continuing developments in Afghanistan, the prospects and progress for the future of Afghanistan, current events and their implications for Afghanistan, and history, culture, and personal memories of Afghanistan.

Membership

The website (including its forums) is publicly available and requires no registration. Yet in order to actively contribute to the forums (i.e., create and add discussion threads and participate in the ongoing conversations), one must register. Those who register are considered "members." As of November 1, 2002, AfghanistanOnline counted 244 registered members. Individuals may achieve a certain level of membership. Membership levels range from "newbie" (0–10 postings to the discussion boards) to junior (10–50), full (50–100), and senior members (100+). As with any organization, a subgroup of people is particularly active and constitutes the core group of members. These core members typically initiate discussion topics/threads and are among the most active responders.

During the registration process, one sets up a personal profile thus creating and sharing one's personal identity (Brainard and Brinkerhoff 2004). A member can identify his or her name, age, and instant messenger information. One can also create a personal avatar, which is often embodied in a picture or a quote, or both. For example, one core member adopts a picture of the popular Star Wars character, Yoda (a reflective Jedi warrior from the movie *Star Wars*) holding what appears to be a cigarette and a cocktail. Another is represented by a picture of a cartoon tiger with the quote, "I am in love with the land of flying eagles/ tigers," a reference to his homeland, Afghanistan. In addition to simply using them as identifiers, members enact their avatars. For example, one member uses an animated graphic of a dolphin leaping in and out of an ocean and goes by the name Peace. Peace, in fact, does play the role of a peacemaker and tries to keep the dialogue relatively light-hearted.

Members are encouraged to honestly identify themselves and join the community. For example, in a conflictive thread, a member divulges personal information about her identity and family life – a white woman who has had a child with a Pashtun man. Two other members encourage her to identify her username rather than posting as a "Newbie." In another instance, a member admitted to falsely representing herself. In the thread *AOP Forum and the Afghan American Community*, this member confesses to having initially posted under a masculine name, for fear of how the other participants would react and relate to her and her posts. She referenced another woman member who "was always wading through the occasional insults or crude jokes of some of the members." She continues:

There seemed to be strict sense of how an Afghan woman should write, or what topics to which she should contribute. This sense was shared by both male and female participants.

When, once in a while, a lady did contribute, either her words were ignored or they were treated with a gentle but heavy arrogance. That the comments of women were largely ignored, I think, had less to do with prejudice than in being unfamiliar with discussing political and social issues with a woman of the same Afghan origin.

The post sparked some exchange between the two women and sixty additional views. That the initiating woman eventually became comfortable enough to share her true identity implies her increasing affinity with the AO community. It may also represent a general positive feeling among members about the opportunities the forum presents to explore hybrid identities, inclusive of gender roles, and improve relations through open and honest dialogue.

Interpersonal Communication

Table 4-1 reports data on AO's forums for the period August 1 – November 1, 2002. The quantity of threads and posts demonstrates high participation among the membership as a whole. The ratio of threads to replies demonstrates interaction among members. The most active forum, the General Discussion Forum on Afghanistan, included 6 threads with more than 100 posts.

These data, and the content of these threads and forums, suggest continuing and/or lengthy conversations. However, almost one third (32.8%) of the General Discussion Forum threads received 0-1 response. This is consistent with one member's analysis of the first 100 threads (*100th post of the forum! Some stats so far*). He showed that 42% of these threads were initiated by two members, whom he called spammers, and that these threads received only 24% of the total replies. In other words, a few individuals can skew the findings suggesting less interaction than what actually occurs overall.

Members also take advantage of the chatroom.[2] At least one random check revealed between sixty-eight and the seventy-five maximum participants in the chatroom. When the chatroom came back after an outage, a member used the General Forum to express his disappointment that others had not yet discovered it was back up. Another member responded by making an appointment to join this member in the chatroom.

Community Rules/Norms

Membership comes with very few obligations (Brainard and Brinkerhoff 2004). There is no requirement to participate in conversations once

---

[2] I did not systematically analyze the chatroom as it occurs in real time and does not yield a lasting record.

TABLE 4-1. AO Discussion Forum Statistics (*August 1–November 1, 2002*)

Topic	Most recent post	# of threads	# of replies	Avg replies	Highest reply rates (Thread title, # of replies)
General Discussion Forum	11-01-02	663	7532	11 (129 avg views)	• Israel/Palestine Thread (193)
Islam (Religious Discussion)	10-25-02	11	59	5	• Afghan Cuisine: Recipes (178) • Hasanhh (13)
Deutsch-sprachiges Diskussionsforum	11-01-02	34	273	8	• Open your eyes (13) • Lasst uns anfangen: Diskussionsthema Nr.1 (54) • Zanburaks "poetically" Gefühl (26)
Issues Concerning The Forums	10-28-02	18	124	7	• To:Mr. Sardar (27) • Questions about New Forum (14)
Social/Cultural Issues	11-01-02	11	77	7	• Just for laughs (24) • Embroidered Afghan Pakols (16)

Adapted from Brainard and Brinkerhoff (2004)

a member is registered. Upon registration, a member need only agree not to post vulgar or defamatory messages. Anyone who feels that a posting is objectionable may contact the Administrator (Qazi), who reserves the right to remove such content. However, as the removal process is manual, removal of content and ejection of a member is extremely rare. Rather than relying on "rules" of membership, the members continuously develop their own community and organizational norms through a continuous and ongoing discussion of appropriate behavior, as illustrated below. In some threads, name calling and personal attacks seem to be accepted without question. In others, members request respect and tolerance for different views.

Members appear to be very interested in their community as a whole. As referenced previously, this interest led one member to compile his own data on the General Discussion Forum on Afghanistan in a thread titled 100th *post of the forum! Some stats Stats so far.* Statistics provided on the first 99 threads and 870 posts, included the top three posters, average posts per member (8.6), average topics started per member (0.9), and average replies per topic (7.7). Not counting the two identified "spammers," he calculated an average reply per topic of 11.6. This member's initiative to examine the forum's statistics and report on the spammers confirms his sense of belonging to the community and represents an effort to regulate behavior in order to preserve community solidarity.

This thread prompted a lively discussion about the nature of communication, communication norms, and the role of the two alleged spamming members in particular. For example, in defense of his labeling another member a spammer, a member writes to one of the alleged spammers:

I enjoy your posts 'from the heart,' the ones you write yourself. And *some* of your articles are interesting. All I am asking is that you try to edit a bit – only post the 2 most interesting articles of the day, not 5 or 6 OK? But it's a free country – you can do what you want anyway.

Another member responds invoking the authority of the nonparticipating, unobtrusive Administrator (Qazi):

Sadar said, if the post is popular it will stay afloat if its not popular it will sink like the titanic, that's the nature of the forum.

These discussions illustrate the continuous process of negotiating and collectively determining what the appropriate norms are.

They also confirm members' embrace of liberal values as the implicit basis for these norms. For example, there appears to be a let-the-market-rule approach to spamming, as illustrated above. The initiator of the Forum's statistical analysis also concludes with a recommendation regarding the two identified spammers: "Ignore anything posted by these guys until it gets at least 10 replies. I know I do!" In addition to the reference to freedom of speech noted above, when the forums were temporarily down and seemed to have disappeared from cyberspace, one member wrote to the Administrator:

Here today, gone tomorrow. Is it just technical, or is there somebody out there who doesn't like this wonderful forum? This is the closest to a true free-speech dialog opportunity that I have ever encountered. Hope it's fixed again soon. Thanks for all your hard work Sadar & Co.

Freedom of speech is also explicitly discussed in a thread about Jerry Falwell, where, in response to a strong opinion, a member responds, "Dearest Grace . . . I believe in freedom of speech." Grace then confirms that she did not intend that freedom of speech should not exist.

Beyond community norms regarding communication processes, the AfghanistanOnline community also checks content related to identity. For example, in a thread titled *Afghan Dance* a native American inquires about Afghan dance and laments the loss of her own Cherokee dance traditions. While some members responded with websites and pictures, one member replied "There is no 'Afghan Dance,'" comparing dance in his native Herat to that practiced throughout the Middle East. He also indicated his preference for Arabic music and dance. To this, several members angrily replied. One argued that his perspective implied, "I hate Afghans and Afghanistan." He continued:

. . . so **why are you posting in Afghan Message Board?** I mean there are plenty of other message boards, like Arab message boards and Iranian message boards for you to strengthen your ethnocentrism.

Another member requested that he not refer to "we" but instead to his own family and preferences when responding to questions about Afghanistan.

These members seem very concerned with maintaining the AO community as one that is proud of Afghan identity. This general orientation is confirmed by a post from the community's most active member:

Hope one day I end my very long exile and return to the land of sunshine-mountain and beauty my mothers land Great Afghanistan that I missed dearly and see fundamentalists, traitors and foreign stooges free Afghanistan. Regards

Members also check the veracity of posters' identity. For example, a member claiming to have been a soldier in Afghanistan is grilled by other members who highlight inconsistencies in his service description. This member also admits to having posted anonymously in the chatroom. Another member investigates other websites and pastes a somewhat vulgar post by the username, asking him if he is the same individual. He posts:

Curious though . . . his postings on Monster.com started 3/8/02 a mere four days after the start of the ground offensive at Gardez. . . . I wonder . . . is it common for combat infantrymen to be searching Monster.com for a job as they "fight" the taliban?

Member Benefits

Of the threads analyzed, approximately 89% provided some material benefit, 20% provided solidary benefits, and 67% provided identity benefits. Very few threads provided purposive benefits, though members appear to share an interest in helping the homeland. One thread, *The Children of Afghanistan*, prompted several ideas to help Afghan children (Brainard and Brinkerhoff 2004). For example, one member suggested that members donate to a charity called Help the Afghan Children. The member noted that he had done research on this particular charity, via an online charity watchdog organization, and provided some background information on the charity, the URL, and the link to provide donations. Another member suggested that the members of the forum join together to give directly to Afghan families; he solicited information on how money could be transferred to Afghanistan and how the banking system was operating. In another thread, a member encourages members of the skilled diaspora to return and help rebuild Afghanistan. In response, a member proposes:

If you folks ever get the AFGHAN FESTIVAL going in California or wherever, you could have a booth there set up to recruit educated Afghan-Americans, etc., to actually go to Afghanistan and help rebuild it

There is no way of knowing the results of these efforts since communication between forum members takes place through instant messaging and private email to which the research team did not have access.

With regard to striving for individual purposive goals, members are often a resource to each other (Brainard and Brinkerhoff 2004). For example, a member created a topic thread, *Let's talk about Old memories*, where with great emotion he related the nature of his formative years in Afghanistan (discussing family members and neighborhoods). Through the course of the thread, it became apparent that another member intends to make a documentary film about Afghans living in Toronto. Members joined in to offer suggestions on the film, how he could go about making it. One member even offered to assist him.

Discussions of purposive issues also yield identity benefits. In *Are the afghans serious of going back?*, a member writes:

Wonder if our fellow afghans who live as immigrants, refugees or citizens in other countries seriously think of going back to afghanistan? Are you guys serious or is it only an emotional thinking? As far as I see many have settled either legally or illegally. . . . hence i find it a difficult task for afghans to move into afghanistan. . . . leaving behind the so called "Freedom" they enjoyed in the west

The thread's initiator at once promotes repatriation and sacrifice among diasporans and expresses concern about cultural influences they may bring:

Frankly speaking . . . what I see . . . is unfortunately westernised afghans . . . sometimes i tell myself . . . its better these guys don't go back to afghansitan . . . being afraid of the ideologies which they shall be taking back. Afghans in West have left the path of education and knowledge . . . and are just running after money . . . a character of a capitalist society

Another member replies in defense of the diaspora:

Please, stop giving patriotic lessons to the Afghans that are in the West. I don't know how much you know about Afghans in the West. But I can assure that there are dozens of thousands of educated men and women Afghans who dream one thing in their life - to go back to Afghanistan

Yet another member then provides an analysis of the Afghan diasporans who share an ambition to return. He categorizes them as those who see it as a business opportunity; those who are young and idealist, "who for the love of country and nation are joining any type of ventures in order to help the country"; and those whom he calls "the educated ones," who are the "opportunists" seeking government posts. (Other members join the discussion and it quickly devolves into personal attacks).

Threads like *Let's talk about Old memories* also illustrate identity benefits. Some members promote their tribal identities such as in *Why!*, where a member posts links to several websites promoting Tajik pride and unity. In some threads, members seek reinforcement of their homeland identity; in others, members debate this identity in the face of other value influences. In *Shari'a in Afghanistan* members explore the appropriate role of Shari'a law and whether Afghanistan should pursue a secular government. One member notes the relativity of secularism, pointing to the United States as an example of a secular society where there is a separation between religion and state in all practical affairs, but religion is still very much a part of civil society. In response to the suggestion of Turkey as a model to follow, he writes, "Turkey's system ... is totally inconsistent with the norms of freedom. ... We should model ourselves after the best model, the American system."

One active post, *Should the United States Go Home?* (45 replies, 681 views) raised a series of questions: "Do you see any positve changes since the U.S. has been in your country? How many innocent Afghans died in the bombings? I havent seen any numbers or statistics?" The discussion led to various comments about Americans and American culture, as well as a fierce debate about whether or not there was anything good about the United States. In this context, one member posted an article from the *Washington Times* called, "10 Great Reasons to Celebrate America" (Dinesh D'Souza, July 4, 2002). While some members responded in concurrence and thanking the poster, others attacked the ideas expressed as well as the member who posted the article. Through these interactions, members are negotiating their own identities as they find common ground with others, though not in all respects or with all of the members of the community they cocreate.

Some threads combine identity with material benefits. For example, in *pakhto brother in need of help to rediscover roots*, a member writes:

i am a pukhtun that was born in the area of chach also known as ghoghushti. my father speaks small amounts of pushtu my mother non, i can only speak some words
i request help from anyone who can teach me how to speak pushtu and its english meanings

All of the responses are encouraging, with several offering webpages and other sources of information. The thread ends with the initiator posting thanks to his "brothers." In another thread (*Buying things from Afghanistan*), a member asks if it is possible to find Afghan goods for under $150. One member suggests looking for less expensive goods in U.S. stores. Another writes in with a link to Afghans for Civil Society which, he says, sells "Afghan clothing and shawls, among other things, made by Afghan women working in their homes."

Material benefits derive from both the forums and the broader website (Brainard and Brinkerhoff 2004). As noted above, the site is a font of information about Afghanistan and its history for all those wanting to learn more. In fact, the site claims to be "a point of reference for many schools and organizations" regarding information about Afghanistan (Qazi 2002). The forums provide additional opportunities to share information about current events and opportunities. Some members have returned to Afghanistan and occasionally, members will ask for updates on what is happening on the ground there. Members often announce a planned trip to Afghanistan, whereupon others are quick to offer tips and good wishes. On a more mundane level, members swap Afghan recipes, and discuss locating wives for each other.

Members of AO excel at delivering solidary benefits to each other through the nature of their online interaction (Brainard and Brinkerhoff 2004). For example the above-noted thread, *Let's Talk About Old Memories*, serves as a verbal postcard of old Afghanistan prior to the

Soviet invasion. The initiating member discusses his old memories of neighborhoods and people and happy times. Others respond by asking him if he knew certain people when he lived in Afghanistan, to which he, in turn, responds by discussing his memories of those people, of playing soccer, and of his grandfather. Others join in to provide support for his apparent regret at not being able to pursue his university education as a result of the Soviet invasion. A personal discussion ensues where the member shares details of his family life and hopes for the future.

Other examples of solidary benefits include the mutual support and admiration expressed between the two women interacting in the thread *AOP Forum and the Afghan American Community*, and the "chat date" noted above, where one member set a time to meet another member in the chatroom who was lonely. In several instances, when a member was absent for a time, due to travel or illness, his absence was acknowledged and he was welcomed back.

SOMALINET[3]

Abdi Osman left Somalia as a teenager and moved with his family to Canada in 1987. He completed his schooling there and in recent years moved to the United States. He started Somalinet in 1998, as a simple links page to help Somalis connect to sites that would be of common interest. The site and its popularity quickly grew, resulting in e-mail requests to Osman for help in locating Somali friends and family members. Rather than facilitate each of these exchanges, Osman established discussion forums in 2000 so that individuals could post and respond to inquiries without his intervention. The site has now evolved into one of the largest digital diasporas, receiving approximately 3.7 million page views per month,[4] with an online directory of Somalia-based or Somali-owned businesses, a matrimonial service, an extensive links page, 126 discussion boards, and an estimated 20,000 members.

I systematically analyzed threads from the General Discussions, North America – USA, North American General Discussions, Women

---

[3] Unless otherwise noted, the source of data/information is my personal interview of Abdi Osman, October 2, 2003.

[4] Abdi Osman provided this figure, drawn from his Internet server statistics page.

General Discussions, and General Discussions – Members Only during
the three-month period, May - August 2003.[5]

Like AfghanistanOnline, the website (including its forums) is publicly
available and requires no registration. Here too, individuals may
achieve a certain level of membership. Membership levels range from
junior (0–50 postings to the discussion boards) to senior (50–100), to
"Somalinetizen" (100+). When they register, members choose a username. They do not have personal avatars as on AfghanistanOnline, but
their usernames are often reflective of their personality or political or
religious orientation. For example, Beards is an Islamist who frequently
promotes an Islamic state as the solution to Somalia's state failure, and
Concerned posts updates on the peace conferences underway in Kenya
during the research period.

Osman estimates membership to be about 20,000, with approximately 60% from the United Kingdom, Canada, and the United
States. Members outside of these countries often self-identify. In
*The Somali Diaspora Moral Decay threaten our very National Iden-
tity!* a member provides her/his own analysis of the diaspora communities in Europe, North America, Australia, and New Zealand. Here,
another member likens the diversity within Somalinet to the diaspora
as a whole:

If we take this forum as a model of a Somali community in Diaspora, we would
find the apostate who threw the religion, the values, and the traditions of his/
her forefathers behind, the atheist who discovered that leading a godless life is
the wise escape of the earthly riddles, the homosexual who took his desires as
his god and never looked back, and the lost soul who has caught between two
fires of two identities.

---

[5] Somalinet includes discussion forums for Somalis residing all over the world. Its
forums range from general discussions to geographically based forums, to more
specific subjects such as literature, health, and education. Some forums are inter-
spersed with comments in Somali or are solely in the Somali language. Given the
complexity of the website and the location and citizenship of the founder, I chose
to limit my analysis to the forums most relevant to Somalis residing in North
America, as determined by the forum name, topic, or affirmed identity of
participants.

Drawing upon this diverse membership, in *Somalis = the most beautifull and most beloved people on earth* a Norway-based member asks about racism in other host countries as he describes racism and discrimination against Somalis in Norway, posting a recent newspaper article to prove his point. Others respond sharing their own experience of being discriminated against. Some compare the experience of Somalis to discrimination against other minority groups. Others blame the Somalis for not rising to "really catch up to the standards of their hosting populus."

Given its diversity, the site provides interesting examples of bridging social capital among members. One of the most active members is Mad Mac, a self-identified Caucasian American citizen who served in Somalia with the U.S. Army in 1993. He actively engages others in debate, sometimes matching their profanity and personal attacks, and sometimes thoughtfully posing or contributing to questions concerning the future of Somalia. In one thread (*when will this "war" end?*) a member identifies two factions within the community and appeals to them to stop arguing based on clanism. In other threads, three factions are identified generally: Islamists, nationalists, and tribalists.

Members take great interest in their community. When a large influx of new members is noticed, one member initiates a thread, *A question to Somalinet newcomers*, asking them if they have come because other Somali internet forums are currently down. Another member hypothesizes that the expansion is due to a change of registration rules such that members can no longer post (as Cowards or Chickens) without registering (see below). A newly registered member confirms that he previously posted as a Coward. In *Somalinet Counterparts*, a member asks others if they visit other diaspora websites and, if so, how they compare to Somalinet. He even asks if there is a "Mad Mac" equivalent on these other sites.

Interpersonal Communication

Table 4-2 reports data on Somalinet's forums for the period May 1–August 1, 2003. The quantity of threads and posts demonstrates high participation among the membership as a whole. The ratio of threads to messages demonstrates interaction among members. The most active forum, the General Discussion Forum, includes seven threads with more than 100 posts.

TABLE 4-2. *Somalinet Discussion Forum Statistics (May 1–August 1, 2003)*

Topic	Most recent post	# of threads	# of replies	Avg Replies/Views	Highest reply (with view) rates (Thread title, # of replies, # of views)
General Discussion Forum	7-31-03	283	5432	19/255	• Entire City of GALCACIO...gets TAP water.....except BARXLEY (370, 3707) • U ARE FROM *KISMAYO* IF........? (152, 1809) • Do We Need the UN? (122, 1239) • The Psychology Of The Somali Hoz?? (117, 2008) • Stop The Somali FGM Insanity! (109, 1323) • WHATS SO GOOD ABOUT BEENG ARAB???????? (101, 1274) • the former somalia should be divided! (101, 1081)
General Discussion – Members Only	7-31-03	9	137	15/174	• Whats worse.....(106, 931)

North America General Discussions	7-28-03	11	79	7/274	• FOR THE ISSACK PRINCESS..... (27, 767)
North America – USA	7-28-03	27	561	21/522	• who's the best lookin boy/gurl in seattle schools (99, 2575) • PRE-MARITAL SEX (ESPECIALLY SOMALIS), IS IT A TABOO OR SOME KIND OF SCAPEGOATISM? (82, 2002)
Women – General Discussions	7-25-03	33	1994	60/1402	• Poems...... Love..... Hope..... Life..... (620, 9091) • WHO IS THE BEST BOY AND GIRL ON PATALK....THE SOMALI VOICE CHAT(330, 13523) • HAVE YOU EVER BEEN IN LOVE (209, 6883) • I HAVE A CRUSH ON AN ADOON!!!!!!!!!!! (178, 2247) • Why most of us are choosing to be with none-Somali man..?? (108, 3042)

These data imply lengthier conversations than those found on AO. Overall, threads received an average of 23 replies and 378 views. The most replies were to a thread on *Poems ... Love ... Hope ... Life ...* (620 replies, 9,091 views), followed by a thread concerning clannism and economic development (*Entire City of GALCACIO ... gets TAP water ... except BARXLEY {habr githir section}*, 370 replies, 3,707 views). Approximately 17% of the threads received 0–1 reply. No habitual spammers were identified.

Community Rules/Norms

Somalinet's discussion boards are open to anyone and exhibit an extreme penchant for freedom of speech bordering on the chaotic and, sometimes, the offensive. Osman attributes Somalinet's success, in part, to this openness and its nonpartisanship:

I think one of the successes of Somalinet is that it's not political or anything. It's not religious or exploitive. .... If people come there and want to sell their ideas, why not let them do it? I don't care. People fight over there all the time, you know, fighting in every thread. .... This is purely for Somalis and I don't care who they are, their religion or whatever they do.

Members are free to post any opinion on substantive issues. For example, in response to a complaint about a post stating "President Bush is a killer," Osman suggested the claimant "insult his president if you know where he is." Denigration, inclusive of profanity, of one clan by members of another is quite common.

Osman maintains a system of volunteer moderators who enforce some limits on what is acceptable to post. Osman and these moderators remove posts deemed inappropriate as identified in their own monitoring or in response to complaints from other members. Rules regulate personal content, length, and repetition of posts; the rules do not extend to use of profanity or personal attacks. In one instance a member wrote about a friend, indicating her legal name, who was dating a non-Somali, opining that this was not acceptable in the Somali culture and religion. The subject of the post wrote to Osman indicating that her personal life was on public view, whereupon he removed the thread. In response, a member from the Middle East accused Osman of being non-Muslim.

He removed that post as well. In order to combat spamming, Osman designed the discussion boards so they prevent posting of an article more than once in ten minutes. In one instance a member tried to repetitively post "Allah Akbhar." When s/he was unable to post a second time s/he complained that Somalinet was banning the praise of God.

In addition to this general monitoring and associated removal of messages, designated moderators (and other members) provide some structure to interaction by initiating substantive threads calling for debate and discussion around specific questions related to identity and the future of Somalia. Concerning identity, threads include: *What are we celebrating?* (referring to celebrations of Somalia's independence from Italy), *Who we are we Somalis?*, *Can religion and evolution coexist?*, *Arranged marriage for it or against?*, *LETS TALK ABOUT POLYGAMY*, *What is American Values?*, and *What would you miss?* (referring to what U.S.-based diasporans would miss if they returned to a rebuilt Somalia). Members discussed Somalia's future, for example, in: *Would non-violent protest work in Somalia?*, *Shall we forgive each other of what?*, *What is the Duty/ Agenda of Somali Wadaads? Discussion*, *What should Somalias future government look like?*, and *Do You Think Somalia Needs a Foreign Help?*.

In some cases, moderators not only introduce a topic for discussion and debate, they also provide ground rules specific to that thread. For example, in *Tribalism, Religion and Nationalism: The Future of Somalia*, the moderator posts the following rules:

1. Be specific with your claims, back up all your claims with credible evidence to be taken seriously.
2. Be brief as much as possible.
3. Be fair, treat others the way you like to be treated.
4. Be objective, remember that we need to get somewhere at the end.
5. Remember that Allah is a witness of all we do.

Similarly, another member posts rules for his proposed discussion in *A Dialogue Between A Nationalist DALMAR and Islamist Nur*. Interestingly, it is Nur who initiates this thread, intended primarily as a debate between himself and another member (DALMAR), but open to others who want to participate. He outlines the following "Rules of Engagement":

This thread is primarily for clarifying the Nationalists and Islamists point of view on the fate of our homeland, it is meant to be educational and intellectual, all are invited to participate but we kindly ask all to abide by the following rules:

1. No Insults of any kind to anyone, anyone who insults anyone on this thread should not be taken as a serious debator, and should be ignored, that pesron is worth the words he speaks.
2. Be specific with your claims, back up all your claims with credible evidence to be taken seriously.
3. Do not generalize, make sure not to take an incident and say that all people with Red shirts are bad because the killer wore a Red shirt.
4. Be brief as much as possible.
5. Be fair, treat others the way you like to be treated.
6. Be objective, remember that we need to get somewhere at the end, going in circles is not economical.
7. Rememver that Allah is a witness of all we do, so be careful.

The similarity of suggested rules across members and substantive threads suggest general agreement on the appropriate norms for serious discussion. There is also an implicit divide between those discussions and other threads where anything goes. Indeed, the same members behave very differently, depending on whether or not they are participating in a thread with specified rules.

Identification in the discussion forums is an important subject of debate and rule making. During the period of investigation a new system was put into place. Initially, individuals could post as "Coward," "Chicken," or "Hiding." In fact, this was a popular approach to posting. Osman attributed its use either to those who were "dropping in" to spam and leave, or, more commonly, to members who did not want to identify their usernames in the context of discussing sensitive subjects. In fact, members would sometimes identify others or themselves as "cowards," making the system the subject of community discussion and debate. Eventually, these debates led members to request the removal of these options. Osman complied and now everyone must register as a member in order to post to the discussion boards; usernames automatically appear with each post.

Initial reactions to the change varied among members. The outcome was debated in *YIPIIIIIIIIIII*, where the initiator thanked Allah that there would no longer be anonymous posters and made a plea that the forum be "clean." Much agreement was expressed, such as, "ALLHU AKBAR . . . after all this is what we been waiting for. . . No[w] no one can hide from anyone." Others felt that anonymous postings made the forum more interesting. For example, one contributor wrote, "With Anonymous you could post something, reply to it, reply to the reply and create controversy. This makes the forum more entertaining. So we need anonymous for the controversy and drama." Beyond this thread, forum discussions continued and members seemed to accept and adapt to the change.

Members also self-regulate with respect to identification by questioning the attribution of posts to particular individuals and investigating appearances of posts by the same individual under different names. For example, when a racist, provocative post is made by a proclaimed "redneck," suggesting that all Somalis should go home and get off U.S. welfare (*WHEN ARE YOU SOMALIANS GOING HOME?*), it is Mad Mac who replies, noting the poster's ignorance and suggesting that the poster could just be a Somali trying to "stir the pot."

Member Benefits

Somalinet provides all four types of organization benefits to its members. During the research period, over 47% of the threads provided identity benefits; 21% concerned solidary benefits; and 5-6% were purposive in orientation, though 16.4% of overall threads explicitly focused on rebuilding Somalia's state, society, and economy. Over 26% of the threads focused on material benefits, many of them providing information about current events and political developments related to Somalia.

Like AfghanistanOnline, members are keenly interested in the community they have created on Somalinet. They pose general questions about the community, seek to acknowledge members with desirable traits, and single out core members, confirming their importance to the community. Among the threads with a significant number of views were those concerning the community itself, such as *Who are the most poetic souls in Somalinet forums? Vote* (1,061 views), *Nur, Viking,*

where the [expletive] are you guys? (215), *Happy 21st BirthDay
Basra!!!!!!!!!!!!!!* (214), *im leaving* (433), *Viking - you still out there?*
(408), *why the excessive use of vulgarity and profanity in the forums
and chat rooms?* (36 replies, 486 views), and *The sweetest Guy or Girl
in the Somalinet Chatrooms* (247).

Members also seek solidary benefits. For example, a member
announces her return after a three-year absence (*Dear Somalinet: I'm
Back*):

Yes I'm back, and life has never been better. I have loved, I have triumphed and,
yes, I have cried. My life has been a whirlwind of activity these past years,
falling in love, overcoming old fears. . . . I cannot believe it has been so long.
And what have all my favorite characters been up to: Sirrus, Basra and all the
rest.

Basra is the first to respond and welcomes her back inviting details on
her news and admonishing her for not at least checking in on occasion.
She replies:

Oh my goodness, how could I have forgotten you ninxoon. Well I missed you
too, I haven't had a conversation with a psychotic in a long long time.

Unfortunately, the conversation quickly devolves into a sexual discourse among other members without much further comment from
the returning member.

Whether or not members always find the solidarity they are looking
for on Somalinet, there is no doubt they seek it. One of the more
popular threads was *On Friendship*, receiving 50 replies and 717 views.
*What makes SOMALI PEOPLE so hateful in Somalinet Formz any-
how?* received 270 views (though only 15 replies). Other threads included, *i never new there was a lot of Somalis* and *damn how come
there aint no somalian livin in LA, NYC, and them big states.*

Members sometimes receive unsolicited support from others. This
was the case in *attention guys!*, where a UK-based woman (uk_babe)
expresses discontent with Somali men in the UK and makes an appeal
to Somalis in North America. She indicates that if anyone is interested
in having "a relationship with with a nice/decent/religious girl PLZ
contact me and i promise u will like me." After some inappropriate
responses, members express concern, addressing her as "dear" and

"sis." One warns her that her post makes her look desperate and suggests she is just looking for men in the wrong places. Other advice includes trying to meet men at weddings instead of bars, and a recommendation that she "just relax" and giver herself time; "don't rush things."

In contrast, in *THIS BLACK GIRL TOLD ME THAT I WAS STUPID BECAUSE SOMALIS ARE BLACK*, the young girl who initiated the thread received no support whatsoever. Instead, she was personally attacked for being "stupid" and, once again, respondents resorted to sexualized accusations. The thread seemed to have struck a nerve in the community. It received 94 replies and 1,886 views. It wasn't long before the initiator was lost in the discussion and members simply attacked each other alternately claiming Somalis are not black (with many racist comments) and arguments to the contrary, encouraging black pride. Toward the end, out of embarrassment, a member requests that the thread be closed and another member (Clanfree) apologizes to any African Americans who might have read the posts and underscores the shame and embarrassment the posters should feel. This response represents an effort to correct and redirect members' behavior, and confirm desirable community values.

The thread *Does Aanyone of us miss Somalia or have homesick?* generated a different reception. Here, a member expresses identity stress:

I have to say that Im extremely homesick and it gets worser with the minute. Strange how alotta Somalis lived outsite Somali so long and still dont plan to go back and see their country ... Do we still have passion for our country?

  you cannt imagine how sad I feel when my friends talk about their country and I cannt call their country mine and cannot talk positive about Somalia ... do anyone of you have that feeling? ... the sad thing is that I have a feeling which is that I dont belong nowhere ...

In this case, members respond sharing their feelings upon returning to Somalia for a visit, their hope that the Somali culture and country will survive, and their love for their country. Indeed, this thread struck a different kind of chord, as one member replies: "Homer, for the first time you have a written about an issue that is important to every somali."

One wonders why so many members remain engaged in the discussions after personal attacks, profanity, and sexism. It would seem that Somalinet has created a culture that embraces or at least accepts this behavior. Members seem to take pride in outdoing each other in these tirades. This is confirmed in *A question to Somalinet newcomers*, where, in commenting on other Somali Diaspora sites, a member seems to be urging honesty/realism and denigrating those who go too far in adopting Western culture:

SomaliaOnLine is a place where a bunch of hypocrites complement one another, they not somalis they are blond and blue eye somalis who seem the West and the capitalist hype gone into their little cubic heads.

SomaliaOnline is prison for the ill informed it breeds a mentality called "lets all agree on everyhting just for the show."

Later in the thread, he confirms: "What I like about Somalinet although it banned me several times is the hard cold honest opinion good or bad take it or live it." In a similar thread, *Somalinet Counterparts*, Somalinet's freedom of speech is again praised, and the absence of freedom of speech is linked to the conflict that created Somalia's failed state:

Most of the somali websites I visited are under strict censorship. Differing views are not welcome. Remember, the problem of somalia started with silencing critics. I think somalinet has succeeded in allowing people to air their opinions.

The so called moderators . . . should be more active if a discussion results in personal attacks or if there is a religious blasphemy.

Still, I wouldn't trade somalinet with other sites that encourage the views of people from particular tribes.

As implied in this post, there remain those members who prefer more serious and less offensive discussion, for whom the structured debates are a welcome novelty. For example, in one such thread a member writes:

I have been off and on form somnet for past one year. i remember days when no descent topic could be discussed at all without muscle flexing, insult and women bashing. but it appears to me things are changing for the better. and it seems nawadays people have nerves to raise and discuss meaningful topics that have real effect on our daily lifes and national affairs. surely if somalis in general approach their problems in this manner surely a solusion could be found in our little world (*A Dialogue between a Nationalist DALMAR and Islamist Nur*).

As with solidary benefits, members who seek material benefits may or may not obtain what they are looking for. In *What is life like in Somalia?*, the initial reply is: "Don't u have relatives back home who can tell u more, or are u not a somali?" However, this poster and others do respond with more helpful (and sometimes flippant) responses and descriptions of life in Somalia. Much of the material benefit comes from posts related to current developments in peace talks occurring in Kenya during the research period, and to other developments in Somalia (e.g., *Somaliland's First University gives birth to 32 Undergraduates*). Beyond the discussion forums (and sometimes within them), Somalinet also facilitates the finding of potential spouses and dates.

Members receive identity benefits in the many debates on identity issues, ranging from dating and marriage to religious practices, to Somali culture and clan. Here, members demonstrate their embrace of hybrid identities inclusive of host country or liberal values. One member explicitly states his surprise that Somalis put down American values yet are so desperate to live in the United States (*What is American Values*). On several occasions members have stressed the importance of Somalis still residing in Somalia determining their future, indicating that "those living abroad do not have the knowledge and understanding to make that decision" (*the former Somalia should be divided!*). In response to the question, *What would you miss?*, one member clearly indicates her identification with American culture: "I would miss the simple freedom as a woman now I can sit a outdoor cafe & enjoy a glass of chianti without being look at as a slut." In *Ala . . . Somalis can't be deported :o*, two women debate Somali culture preservation. In response to an accusation that she is a "Western kid," Foxxy-Gal responds:

Am I a Western Kid? Probably seeing as I am living in the West. You don't expect me to go out wearing a dirac and a malkahabad do you? I think people need to stop obsessing about preserving an ever changing culture, and just live their live's according to their goals and aspirations. . . .

Quman_Girl responds: "Honestly there is nothing wrong in holding on to ur culture. For instant, a Chinese person will never lose their culture no matter where they are so why can't Somalis do the same...?"

Threads that address purposive discussions often yield identity benefits as well. In *WHO IS PLANING ON RETURING BACK TO SOMALIA*, LovelyFarhia announces that she plans to return to Somalia once she completes her nursing degree to contribute to her country. Two posters compliment her on her intentions. One supports her idea, linking it to identity:

well i hear that same thing all the time, "why would i go back to Somalia?", i dont really understand their way of thinking because first of all as much as ya'll love being in the state of DENIAL this aint ur home, and 2nd of all, getting too comfortable is a total waste of time seeing as there's a country waiting on us to rebuild . . . i think everybody has a responsability to their family and country to go back and apply your NEW and IMPROVED skills, NOTE: this doesnt mean u have to have a degree, we need blue color workers up in that spot just as much as we do somebody behind a desk, i think ya'll have taken a long enough nap and its time to wake up and serve your country, coz u aint canadian and u sure as hell aint american . . .

Even more explicitly, a member solicits commitments of return in *Reconstructing Somalia: Help Wanted* (49 replies, 749 views). He initiates the thread by asking, "When Somalia returns to peace and the reconstruction phase begins, what kind of skills would you be able to bring to the motherland?" He indicates that he will contribute as a volunteer teacher and in economic reconstruction, and he inquires about what other forum members will do. Numerous forum participants weighed in with their thoughts on how they could/would contribute to the rebuilding of Somali. Offers to help included offers to teach, establish a Somali stock exchange, work for National Security, be a builder, and assist with health care. One member posted a specific proposal and solicited participation from other Somalinet members: "If you are Genuine and sincere lets setup a Somali Youth Confederacy and help our people . . . hold me on this, there is no one out there who help Somalia if we dont." This suggestion was brought up repeatedly throughout the thread by this member and others who were concerned about the status of youth in Somalia. In another thread a member expresses a more instrumental perspective on why the Somali diaspora should help the reconstruction of Somalia, referring to family requests for remittances: *PEACE & Your POCKET: Good for your $$$$*.

One of the most popular posts takes on a cultural issue, which is confronted in Western media and, hence, confronts the diaspora's identity: female circumcision, or female genital mutilation (FGM) (*Stop The Somali FGM Insanity*, 109 replies, 1,377 views). Members debate whether the popularity of discussions on the issue within the forum is a result of Western media attention and "hype." Others consider its relation to Islam. Still others call for action and education to stop it. For example:

it's about time that FGM is put on the Agenda. It has been hidden in the closet long enough!! Bring it out in the light!! Enlighten people!! FGM is plain cultural and needs to be treated as such. Only information, information, information and lots of patience can change that cruel tradition

AFGHANISTANONLINE AND SOMALINET: CYBERCOMMUNITIES IN ACTION

AfghanistanOnline and Somalinet exhibit all of the characteristics of voluntary communities. They have low barriers to entry, low barriers to exit, and are nonhierarchical and noncoercive (Galston 2002). Yet rules are made, respected, and occasionally enforced. And members potentially receive a range of benefits: solidary, identity, material, and purposive.

Like all communities, the sites differ in their culture. Members of AfghanistanOnline are almost unequivocally proud of their homeland and culture. When several members criticize a member for denigrating Afghan identity, no one comes to his defense. Cultural defense and identity confirmation are subjects of the community's self-regulation. In contrast, Somalinet members are ambivalent about their identity and culture. Some express pride in contrasting their identity from African Americans, while relying on racist epithets; others are at times similarly racist in identifying with an African American ghetto culture; still others express pride based on pan-Africanism, Islamism, and Arabic heritage. The overall tenor of identity discussions suggests shame rather than pride. Members freely express these varied points of view. In fact, both sites embrace freedom of speech and engage in tribal or clan-based in-fighting, though there is less vicious in-fighting among members of

AfghanistanOnline and they tend to discourage posts that are critical of Afghaniyat, or the Afghan-ness that unifies members. "Somalinomo" (Somali-ness) is variously supported and questioned as a concept. In both communities members appear to be proud of their membership, self-consciously embracing it through ranking (sometimes competitive), reflection on the communities' evolution, and in contrast to other like communities.

The nature and structure of community rulemaking differs. Members of both communities check each other's identity and attempt to verify authenticity. Rules are minimal at both sites. At AfghanistanOnline explicit reference is made to market mechanisms, underscoring the value of freedom of speech. Here, members make requests with respect to spamming, and occasionally to personal insult. Some members may request more respect in the context of a discussion; other times, name calling and personal attacks are tolerated. Somalinet seems to have two operating cultures, one where anything goes, and – perhaps because of this dominant culture – one where more structured and explicit rules become necessary. Members adapt their behavior depending on which rules are in play. The rule making in both communities is demand-driven, relies on self-regulation, and demonstrates the cocreation of the community – members collectively define the community.

Both sites offer a range of member benefits, perhaps to varying degrees of effectiveness. In both communities, while purposive ideas are discussed, the emphasis appears to be focused on the diasporans themselves and the benefits they directly derive from participating in these communities. Both sites provide material benefits among members in the discussion forums, and by the founders outside of these forums (on the webpage). Identity benefits are the most apparent in both communities. AfghanistanOnline provides compelling examples of solidary benefits as well.

It appears that members seek these various benefits from Somalinet, though perhaps not all of them find what they are looking for. As illustrated above, some members explicitly ask for support due to identity stress and/or seek solidary benefits. Sometimes this yields heartfelt exchanges that seem to unify the community across ethnic and clan divisions (e.g., *Does anyone miss Somalia or have homesick?*). Sometimes these calls remain unanswered, or worse, are greeted with personal attacks and profanity. As a result of such responses the original poster may simply disappear from the scene while other members continue to attack each other (e.g., *THIS BLACK GIRL TOLD ME THAT I WAS STUPID BECAUSE SOMALIS ARE BLACK*). Some members report that they stop participating when this subculture takes hold. For others, this is the very outlet they seek. Members seem to compete with each other to generate the most profane personal attacks. At the same time, these members engage in more serious debate when threads are structured accordingly. This demonstrates respect for the moderators of those threads and, perhaps the issues salient to their identity and homeland.

While the two member-created communities differ and exist only in cyberspace, they are communities nonetheless. Together, they illustrate demand for membership benefits that are particularly salient to diasporas. Solidary benefits may be sought and provided to different degrees, but both sites excel in their provision of identity benefits and the opportunity to negotiate hybrid identities. They also confirm digital diasporas' contribution to keeping the homeland alive, the subject of Chapter 3.

Chapters 5–7 examine how these communities and the social capital and benefits they generate can be directed toward conflict mitigation, policy influence, and socioeconomic contributions to the homeland. Next, Chapter 5 returns to AfghanistanOnline and Somalinet to analyze how digital diasporas potentially mitigate conflict.

5

Digital Diasporas and Conflict Prevention

Diasporas potentially contribute to conflict; preventing their participation in conflict is the subject of this chapter. Chapter 4 analyzed how digital diasporas create cybercommunities and emphasized bonding social capital. Such communities can counter the marginalization conducive to violence. Here, we return to Somalinet and AfghanistanOnline to investigate how digital diasporas use cyberspace to potentially prevent conflict through opportunities to: express feelings of marginalization, explore cross-categorical identities and develop bridging social capital, negotiate hybrid identity inclusive of liberal values and shared norms of behavior, and frame issues to explicitly avert conflict/violence. I introduce the descriptions of each organization's approach to conflict prevention with additional information about the history and nature of the homeland conflict. First, I examine identity and conflict prevention generally.

RESTRUCTURING IDENTITY AND THE POTENTIAL FOR CONFLICT PREVENTION

Conflict prevention aims not necessarily to eliminate the sources of latent conflict, but to reduce the likelihood that conflict will become manifest through violent action. This occurs not only at the beginning of a conflict, but throughout various stages of conflict, resulting in three types of prevention (Leatherman et al. 1999): conflict prevention, that is, preventing the initiation of violent conflict; escalation prevention, that is, preventing the vertical and horizontal escalation of hostilities involving additional actors and more destructive means of violence; and postconflict prevention, that is, preventing the reemergence of disputes by reintegrating and rebuilding the society. Diasporans may participate in peace or conflict at any of these stages – beginning, escalation, and reemergence. The potential for manifest conflict is a function of the product of desire, or motivation to act, and the ability to act (Fuller et al. 2000), or perceived efficacy.

Mobilizing individuals to violent action entails a change in their power, resources, and/or psychological state (see Leatherman et al. 1999). By extension, manifest conflict can be prevented by targeting each of these components to reduce the likelihood of conflict engagement. Through their emphasis on identity, identity negotiation, and support for identity stress, digital diasporas excel in addressing psychological states that may prevent manifest conflict. Psychological states encompass four components or stages: perception of threat, distortion of information, rigid interpretations of the world, and dehumanization of other (Northrup 1989).

Beyond differences in interest, conflict occurs more fundamentally over meaning, that is, the social construction and management of meaning (Vayrynen 2001). This cultural perspective suggests that "conflicts are shaped by shared and opposed fears about human existence and identity, and their projections into the future" (Leatherman et al. 1999, 60; see also Ross 1993). Situated between purely subjective (e.g., individual perceptions, misunderstandings, and attitudes) and objective (e.g., objectively verifiable structural causes) perceptions of conflict, the culture model of conflict focuses on the interplay between the individual actor and the social group. Conflict is defined as the breakdown of shared reality (Vayrynen 2001).

Conflict is most likely when social identity is defined in mutually exclusive terms, leading each group to perceive the fulfillment of the other's identity as occurring at the expense of its own (Northrup 1989). Yet ethnic group boundaries and preferences are not necessarily fixed ends. A more nuanced understanding of ethnic identity can help us to see beyond presumed intractability of ethnic group demands to consider ways of structuring options and institutions to avoid inter-ethnic conflict (Chandra 2001). Privileging a single dimension of identity "might over time destroy the capacity to organize politics along other dimensions" (Chandra 2001, 350). Groups mobilizing around a general *diaspora* identity may overcome ethnic divisions and the possibility of mobilizing around these identities.

Crossed categorization of identity, where group membership is shared or overlaps, can reduce polarization among groups. Crossed categorization decreases the importance of any one in-group/out-group distinction, increases classification of others in terms of multiple dimensions, and increases the degree of interpersonal interaction and trust across category boundaries (Brewer 2000; Hewstone et al. 2002). Resulting multiple loyalties, mutual dependencies, and common interests between homeland and hostland, and among cleavages within the diaspora, may serve to discourage diaspora participation in violent conflict concerning the homeland.

Conflict prevention is most effective when the interests of the parties are still malleable and their internal unity has not yet crystallized (Zartman 1991). At this stage, several factors influence diasporans' motivation to engage in violent action. Mobilization is driven by identity concerns and is influenced by a perceived sense of potential efficacy. For example, "'defensive' mobilization in response to a clear and present threat to a group's established position will produce more rapid and aggressive collective action than 'offensive' mobilization to exploit opportunities for uncertain future benefits" (Esman 1994, 30). Diasporans often assess their interest and willingness to act with consideration to their interests in their adopted countries. The higher the cost to status and security in their adopted country, the greater the likelihood that the diaspora community will split and/or fail to support the home government (Esman 1986). As a potential alternative to mobilization, diasporans may also rely on their American identity when thoughts of their homeland create psychic pain (Friedman 1994).

Crosscategorization of identity relates to another perspective on conflict – social capital. Diminished social capital is both the cause and the result of conflict. Bonding social capital can counter the destabilizing forces of marginalization and provide a social safety net for group members (Gittel and Vidal 1998). In doing so, bonding social capital can potentially remove individuals' incentives to direct violence toward an "other" who is perceived as being of an exclusive in-group and having access to the social, economic, and political advantages that this membership might afford. Bonding social capital provides the basis for collective identity. Those who lack such identity have been described as "psychologically desperate" and easy prey for terrorist organizations – or perhaps conflict entrepreneurs – who seek to fill this psychological void (Taylor and Lewis 2004).

Conflict prevention may not result, however, without a minimal degree of bridging social capital. The absence of social networks across groups can lead to tension and distrust among ethnic groups (Fearon and Laitin 1996). When exogenous shocks, tensions, or rumors lead to intra-ethnic engagement, the common result is ethnic violence; but when these lead to inter-ethnic engagement the result may be ethnic peace (Varshney 2001). Bridging social capital emphasizes heterogeneous networks, where members have greater opportunities to access information and understanding beyond their current intra-group resources (see Burt 2000). Through repeat interaction and the discovery of shared needs and interests, bridging social capital prevents the dehumanization of "other" (see, for example, Northrup 1989; Rubin et al. 1994). Game theory also suggests that when individuals have experience of repeat interaction with representatives of the violator ethnic group, they may be disinclined to associate norm violations with the entire ethnic group (Fearon and Laitin 1996).

Cognitive social capital is the force behind more visible forms of social capital, and includes values, norms, civic responsibility, expected reciprocity, charity, altruism, and interpersonal trust (Uphoff 2000). Thus, social capital is rooted in identity and shared identity negotiation processes. It is also reflected in the rules or norms of behavior communities develop to prescribe what is required, prohibited, or permitted (Ostrom et al. 1994). Norms set the parameters for acceptable matters for discussion and debate and "sanctify the speech" of some parties over others (Benhabib 1992, 48). In this way, issues are framed to focus individuals' attention and energy and potentially enable effective coordination of their efforts (Snow et al. 1986), including consolidating agendas toward peace or conflict.

Internet technology facilitates this framing of issues, through established social norms, and through the structuring of interactive components and the rules regulating participation. It also may incline the particular frame toward discussions and agendas consistent with liberal values. As noted in earlier chapters, in negotiating and expressing hybrid identities, digital diaspora communities may include liberal values in both the content and process of their deliberations. And even in reinforcing nonliberal values, intra-community organization and communication will reflect the characteristics of the Internet as a tool: to at least a limited extent, it will be relatively more democratic and representative of freedom of speech. As Somalinet and AfghanistanOnline demonstrate, the Internet facilitates the expression of liberal values such as individualism and freedom of speech, either through anonymity or access opportunity, and, in this sense, CGOs can become a test bed for experimenting with liberal values. This experimentation may have implications for promoting or mobilizing in support of peace or conflict.

Somalinet

Historically and persistently, Somali society is nomadic and extremely individualistic. Somalis have been described as fiercely independent, with "each man his own sultan" (Lewis, 1961; qtd. in McFerson 1996, 20). Given the scarcity inherent in its pastoral society, conflict is frequent and intense: "Force and the threat of force are always present, and violence is an institutionalized and socially approved means of settling disputes" (McFerson 1996, 20). At the same time, traditional Somalia has been called "a nation of poets" (McFerson 1996, 23); oral poets had special status as mediators and conflict mitigators, often fulfilling a public relations function for the clan (see Samatar 1982). The territory's first experience with centralized authority came through colonization, which divided the territory among the Italian, British, and the French (what is now the Republic of Djbouti). In 1960, the former British and Italian colonies were united to form Somalia.

Under General Siad Barre, formal and informal institutions previously used for inter-ethnic negotiation and conflict management were systematically undermined. Somalia became opportunist in the Cold War – or a pawn, depending on one's perspective – leaving a legacy of widely distributed arms. And selected clans were privileged or punished over others, leading to clan warfare and the collapse of the Barre regime in 1991. After Barre's demise, former British Somaliland in the North declared its independence but has not received international recognition. United Nations intervention was ended following the killing of U.S marines in 1993. Recovery in various regions differs dramatically, with de facto government established in the North along with diaspora investment and economic development (see Battera 2004; Nenova and Harford 2004), while the Center (including Mogadishu), the South and West remain ungoverned, unstable, and persistently poor and undeveloped. Despite external support for negotiations and planning for a new government, Somalia remains a failed state, as witnessed by the renewed warfare and the Ethiopian intervention in 2006.

Marginalization

Upon first visit, Somalinet is striking for its members' apparent identification with marginalized communities in the United States, as demonstrated by rampant use of ghetto-talk, sexism, and profanity. In fact, members occasionally express shame at the categorization of Somalia as a "failed state" and are at times quite cynical with respect to future prospects for their home country. Members seem to at once denigrate and embrace their Somali identity. In the words of one member:

I have seen many young people of all tribes dismissing the Somali culture because of its obsessiveness with tribal hatred.... [P]lease, let them grow to love their own people and culture instead of the emulating and yearning to belong to an alien culture such as the black American one (*Who we are we Somalis?*).

Discrimination and welfare are frequent topics of conversation. A thread on comparative discrimination among hostlands, *Somalis = the most beautifull and most beloved people on earth*, is a case in point. The enormous interest in one thread is also telling with respect to feelings of marginalization. As noted in Chapter 4, *THIS BLACK GIRL TOLD ME THAT I WAS STUPID BECAUSE SOMALIS ARE BLACK* received 94 replies and 1,886 views, compared to an average of 23 replies and 378 views per thread. African identity is also discussed in *lost, blind, and stupid*, where Coward from Morocco initiates, telling Somalis that they need to remember their roots and realize that they are Africans. He asks, "why is that somali people still act like they are really apart of the muslim umahh when in fact that most muslim people look down on somali people and don't think of them as brothers." Coward (Mohamed) responded asking the poster not to generalize because all Somalis do not have drug problems and are not abusive.

Another member references "arab racism" and claims Arabs "introduced slavery to the white man." He adds, "and by the way we are sooo proud to be AFRICANS." In the final post, a member writes, "what do you expect from people who destroyed killed and raped their own people to be good muslims."

With respect to welfare, in *Biggest Welfare handout by City, or State/Province*, LazyBoy announced that he was looking to move from the UK to the United States and wondered where the best welfare benefits were available. Some members responded that he must be joking or that he was giving the UK a bad name. Other posters took the question seriously indicating, for example, that Chicago provided $490 a month for single people. To which another member posted that one could only get about $250 a month in Chicago, but in Toronto he had a friend who received $520.

Other threads focus on Somali youth, aspirations, and opportunities, for example, *how come there are no high dreams?*. The thread *Why are Somali youth on the bottom of the education league?* opened with an essay about Somali youth. The author listed the following needs for Somali youth: older role models, parents who set high expectations for them, to be taken to mosques and to their homeland to remember religion and their culture, and to think about implications of different cultures on marriage traditions. In a similar thread, *Why we don't acquire higher degrees?!!*, the initiator noted that even in the United States where there is free education available, people do not take advantage of it. A reply confirms, "most younger Somalis appear to follow and imitate the wrong kind of company; rap music, partying, uneducated local people and etc." Another member lamented:

Here is new Zealand we've a new fever immigration to Western Australia. As usual, the whole issue revolve around welfare (centerlink) and cheap housing. More Somali New Zealand families are moving to Perth for just simple short gaining without career planning. Wish to see a website dedicated to our career planning than this fragmented discussions.

In fact, a discussion of careers and career planning ensues with suggestions on what type of careers might be the most fruitful. One such post concluded, "our country needs any degree though, so everything will be important to the motherland."

Cross-Categorical Identity and Bridging Social Capital

As noted in Chapter 4, Somalinet brings together a host of identity groups from within the diaspora, including various clans, as well as,

... the apostate who threw the religion, the values, and the traditions of his/her forefathers behind, the atheist who discovered that leading a godless life is the wise escape of the earthly riddles, the homosexual who took his desires as his god and never looked back, and the lost soul who has caught between two fires of two identities (*The Somali Diaspora Moral Decay threaten our very National Identity!*).

Groups who identify around various approaches for a future Somali government also assemble here to debate, including those who self-identify as Islamists, nationalists, and tribalists.

Despite this diversity, members are willing to suspend their personal attacks to collectively debate issues related to identity, ending the conflict in Somalia, and rebuilding governance structures. A particularly telling thread, *The Decepting Nature of Many Somali Diaspora!*, illustrates clan loyalty while still embracing a common Somali identity:

the word nation first dont exist in somli dictionary. it is me and my clan first. so why dont we all start there ... "me and my clan first" ... cos it is the only common ground we all share ... and then see what we can do for our country. i beleive this is a practical solution for those who wanna a tangible solution

Another member, Mr. Somali, responds confirming his belief in "Somalinomo," or Somali-ness. Another thread begins with a focus on one clan and moves to a discussion of clannism generally. Here a Coward writes:

I still see every Somali as a brother. But never would I allow myself to be at the mercy of another Somali. I would extend the hand of friendship to every Somali but I would prefer to be wielding a weapon in the spare one. That is just a reality (*The Suffering Barawaani*).

The diaspora experience seems to have inspired an interest in Somalinomo that might not have emerged if these individuals had remained in Somalia. In *ORIGIN OF SOMALI PPL*, a member requests information about Somali origins – without reference to clan identity.

Some members seek to foster a shared and affirming Somali identity. One member initiated and moderated ten threads on topics concerning nonviolence. In one of these he writes:

A united Somalia, without distinction of your tribe is where I yearn that I want to live, and I know that many do have similar dreams How could we make a reality of our dream? A simplistic answer would be that we should approach nation building from the premise of shared customs, such as language, religion, and culture. It has never happened before (from independence to the last regime), and it is time that we should commence it (*Who we are we Somalis?*).

From a far more immediate instrumental perspective, another member underscores a common Somali identity: "In the end we are Somali. We will get pulled to the side at immigration counters, stopped by Kenyan, Habashi police, continue being passportles ... we look alike and will get the same kind of harsh treatment" (*WE HAVE DONE OUR HOMEWORK*).

While clan perspectives may be promoted, even with vicious personal attacks, members seem to share a desire for peace and prosperity in Somalia, a despair over the current suffering, and some shame at their own relative comforts. And some attempt to constructively, yet critically, consider prospects for the future while still encouraging hope within the diaspora. *Any Hope for Somalia?* is a good illustration:

Asking hard questions is not being negative. Of course there is hope for Somalia, but what hope? when? how? who? and how long does those desperate kids and mothers on the ground need to wait for the delivery, while we in the diasphora sip our warm latte and enjoy in our borrowed comforts

One thread is implicitly inspiring and hopeful in its query on heroes. In *Supamans Super heros*, da-supaman recounts that he is frequently asked who his heroes are. So he describes them and then asks members to discuss their own heroes. Members respond, some with widely admired individuals such as Mohammed and other prophets. In response, da-supaman encourages people to think about everyday heroes. Several members mention their parents.

Somalinet also demonstrates an unexpected example of bridging social capital, in the way of MAD MAC, a Caucasian American citizen who served in Somalia with the U.S. Army. Member reactions vary; they may be baffled by his interest, threatened by his participation, or welcoming. He is accused of "trying to be something he isn't, Somali." To which he responds, "When did I ever say I was ANYTHING other than a US Army soldier? I'm white, I've never claimed to be anything else" (*MAD MAC ... why are u obsessed with us(Somalis)???*). *LETS BOYCOTT MAD-MAC TOGETHER, WE CAN* asserts that MAD MAC is an atheist and should be shunned in the name of Allah. MAD MAC responds that he is not an atheist but that it was within the initiator's rights to boycott him if he so chose. Several replies defended MAD MAC, emphasizing that his posts were interesting and better than other reading on the site. One post called him an "unsung hero," and some posts identified other members who were more offensive than MAD MAC. The degree of interest in the thread, 13 replies and 111 views (compared to the average 23 replies and 378 views), suggests that most members are accepting of or at least indifferent to MAD MAC's membership.

Other threads also explore MAD MAC and his contributions to Somalinet. After an initial exchange, the initiator of *"Black Hawk Down"* investigates MAD MAC's postings and highlights his project idea (posted elsewhere) for helping Somalia. The initiator concludes by encouraging others to join his efforts as she has pledged. In subsequent threads questions are directed specifically to this American Army member, including: whether another UN-peacekeeping mission could support the installation of a new Somali government (*The Next Battle for Mogadishu???*); a challenge to explain the foreign policy of President George W. Bush (*For Mad Mac: Talk to Us when Have Free thinking? Read this*); and a request to justify his interest in the cyber-community (*MAD MAC.... why are u obsessed with us(Somalis)???*). In turn, MAD MAC posts his own questions to the community, such as *Do most Muslims believe this?*, referring to the potential obligation to participate in jihad. In one thread MAD MAC posts as a coward and is then encouraged to post publicly, perhaps indicating the respect others have of his right to participate in the community (*The Next Battle for Mogadishu???*). Members trade insults with this member as they do with all members, perhaps confirming acceptance of his participation in the community.

Liberal Values

References to liberal values confirm hybrid identity within this diaspora. In a thread titled *ABDIQASIM BECOME DISAPOINTED AFTER HE ARRIVED*, members discuss the need to accept a president if that president is legitimately elected. In a more explicit discussion of American values, one member writes: "On the whole America is ahead on the individuals rights and freedoms, so instead of knocking it we should be using the possibilities that are opened to those of us who got the chance to live there" (*What is American Values*). The expression of liberal values and hybrid identity appears in purposive discussions related to the future of Somalia. One member relies on an American cultural icon, John F. Kennedy's famous statement, "Ask not what your country can do for you. Ask what you can do for your country." This member goes on to encourage hard work, as opposed to looting and welfare, reminiscent of the Protestant work ethic (*the former Somalia should be divided!*).

Several posts integrate liberal values with religious identity. One member stresses the danger of hatred and the power of equality, praying "may ALLAH PUT AND CREATE PEACE, LOVE, CARING BETWEEN THE AFRICAN PEOPLE IN AMERICA OR EUROPE OR IN OUR MOTHERLAND. PS. I LOVE ALL BLACK PEOPLE" (*THIS BLACK GIRL TOLD ME THAT I WAS STUPID BECAUSE SOMALIS ARE BLACK*). In response to the question *Is it compulsory to get married*, responses range from the purely Western feminist view, "FOCUSE ON YOUR CAREER AND YOUR GOALS EDUCATE YOURSELF AND YOU'LL LIVE A HAPPY PROSPEROUS LIFE" to a more subtle empowering message with reference to Islam:

Islam gives the same rights to a woman and a man. And for me, the first 'law' of Islam is 'be happy in your life.' ... So I think you have the right to be happy. If you don't find a man who will respect you or will make you happy don't accept the first man around because [of] traditions. ...

Examples of Conflict Mitigation/Rule Application

As described in Chapter 4, while profanity and personal attacks are accepted by the founder and often tolerated by members, occasionally members request that discussants refrain from name calling, whether as part of stated rules of engagement or general requests emerging from the discussion. In the research sample, such requests most often emerged in the context of substantive debates about Somali identity and options for the reconstruction of Somalia, the subject of approximately one third of the threads analyzed. In a thread titled *The Next Battle for Mogadishu???* a concerned member writes:

All the BS and name calling has to stop. And people from Puntland, Somaliland and Somalia have to work together. Perhaps they all remains separate states, or set up a Federation. Whatever makes it work. All rights must be protected and respected. All must be equal.

The member continues, making reference to U.S. history, indicating her/his identification with this host country.

There will always be some negative feelings. Just as there are Southern American who hate the Yankees for winning the Civil War. But at the end of the day, people get together, and work together. They defend their country together. When they disagree, they voice their opinion, and have enough respect to hear the other side.

The limits and perceptions of personal and clan attacks are continuously renegotiated in the context of individual threads. For example, in response to accusations of clannism, one member writes, "As far as I can see there is no clanism here but the telling of some harsh and uncomfortable truths. We are not here to give aid and comfort but to get people to think clearly and analyze the situation…" (*Entire City of GALCACIO … gets TAP water …. except BARXLEY {habr githir section}*).

In considering ways forward, members initiate various approaches to either deflect or resolve conflict, or emphatically state their interests, which are usually clan-based. Discussions often focus on the compatibility of Western models (e.g., democracy, federalism) with Islam and the particulars of the Somali context. Some of these attempted proposals seem more effective than others. One thread, *Shall we forgive each other or what?* received no replies and only twenty-eight views. Another similarly motivated thread *Would non-violence protest work in Somalia* received four replies and thirty-six views. The initial response was pessimistic, referencing the power of warlords, though examples of peace marches in various regions of Somalia were also noted. The thread ended with a proposal for every Somali citizen to disarm one "mooryaan" (variously defined as gunman, thug, or marauding youth). Other threads also demonstrated limited interest, for example, *Do You Think Somalia Needs A Foreign HELP?* (one reply and twenty-nine views), *How Can You Handle Such Fictitious Declaration? Speak Out!* (a call for nationalism and a verbal attack against one clan, 3 replies and 104 views), and *Sad news for Somalia* (a discussion of the possibility that an African peace-keeping force would bring HIV/AIDS to Somalia, 6 replies and 165 views).

Threads followed the developments of negotiations in Kenya during the research period and questioned proposals and prospects for resolution. Here, members demonstrate critical and analytic thinking in their commentary. For example, in *Peace Keeping for Somalia!!!!!!!!!!*, a member writes:

This whole federalism notion is full of more holes than Swiss Cheese. Questions that have yet to be answered before implementing a Federal system are grave:

1. What defines a Federal State? Will it be based on tribe? Regional map (if so, are we going to use the PreSiyaad Regional system or the Siyaad 18 region system)?
2. What is the nature of the relationship between the state and Federal Government?
3. How will each state contribute to the Federal government? Power, revenue, tax, laws etc.
4. How will power be divided among the States and vis-a-vis with the Federal Government?

I think that SOmalia is not ready to handle a Federal system due to the lack of economic resources and national identity. This whole Federalism talk is based on the arguement that a unitary system failed Somalia rather than bad management failed Somalia. The seeds of bad management are numerous and will grow in Federal states just as they did in a unitary state

In the same thread another member comments: "... the state that emerges from Mogadishu will take the revolution of 1991 into a conclusion. Somali people will make the decisions that shape their lives. ... Clans, regional pretenders, and imperialism will have no input in

Somalia's affairs." Both comments reflect an optimism in their orientation towards problem solving on the one hand, and pride and hope on the other.

Much interest was demonstrated in a purposive discussion of how to rebuild Somalia (*Reconstructing Somalia: Help Wanted*), with 49 replies and 749 views. Members focused on problem solving, reported on visits to Somalia, debated the role of clans in Somalia's future, and expressed guilt for not actively contributing to a solution. Specific purposive aims emerged. Members may indicate despair as expressed through angry exchanges, but still confirm a shared interest in future peace. In *The first medical school in Somalia for 12 years* a member communicates his view on the futility of such efforts since the doctors to be trained will be murdered "for simply wearing a nice shirt." After some angry exchange, the member expresses hope that the initiator may be right in his expressed optimism.

Among the most heated topics are the possible secession of Somaliland and the appropriate role of clans. Debates regarding secession tend to include significant name calling and graphic language. In one exception, *WE HAVE DONE OUR HOMEWORK*, the discussion was much more amicable, with a focus on practical issues, such as where to draw the border, whether or not refugees would be able to return, the name of Somaliland, and so on. Participants noted the pleasant nature of the debate several times, complimenting the primary debaters. When, after about a month, profanity started to appear one participant announced his withdrawal from the discussion. Despite the heated debate regarding the potential secession of Somaliland, the majority of participants appear to support a common future for a unified Somalia. Concern for what would come of southern Somalia is frequently expressed.

One of the most popular threads during the period of investigation (370 replies and 3,707 views) concerned clan relations (*Entire City of GALCACIO ... gets TAP water except BARXLEY {habr githir section}*). The discussion included personal attacks and some responses in the Somali language. One member contrasts the diaspora's manifestation of clannism with his perception of clannism in Somalia:

I don't think tribe will solve our problems. Just watch the forum and how some people are violently hateful. I don't think Somalis back home are to the level of doom some people in here talk about other tribes. I have hopes when I talk to people back home, and they seem to understand the futility of tribalism, perhaps they suffered the most while we enjoy driving nice cars in a well taken care of homes, that is why I don't take what people say here seriously. Somalis are Somalis at the end of the day.

That approximately 75% of these posts (not including the above quote) were entered as cowards may indicate the sensitivity of the topic.

Occasionally, potential conflict of another sort emerges, with an appeal to members' Muslim identity. In *Another Salaam Rushdi has risen*, a member identifies a book and author that profane Islam, urges Somalinet members to stop the book's publication, and encourages the assassination of the author. Respondents question this call to murder in the name of Islam.

Framing

The examples noted above and those in Chapter 4 illustrate how moderators and members frame issues for debate and discussion by establishing formal rules of engagement, proposing specific topics for exchange and debate, and establishing values-based criteria, often rooted in liberal values of self-determination, equal participation, freedom of speech, and tolerance for different views and perspectives. Much of the discussions are sense-making endeavors, whether with regard to identity and integration in an adopted home country, intergenerational stresses concerning that process, negotiating between hope and despair at Somalia's fate, and contemplating future prospects. In a seeming attempt to cope with atrocities committed, in one thread, *Afbiijo Atrocities and His future dreams*, a member adopts the personage of the clan leader Afbiijo in Puntland, "I slaughter, and I slaughter, and I slaughter...." Writing in the first person, the member describes what "he" has done with impunity. Other members reply directly addressing Afbiijo as if he were indeed the poster, appealing to him to "release the hostages" of Puntland and warning him that he will not succeed in his war against Somaliland.

Framing and specific proposals vary in their appeal and popularity. In *Do You Think Somalia Needs A Foreign HELP?* (one reply, twenty-nine views), a member posts a letter to Somalinet that reads like a "call to action" statement to the Somali diaspora community. The initiator addresses the letter to "all" and starts out by proclaiming that all of Somalia should be working together to forge a rebuilding strategy. She states that it is time for the diaspora community to ask the international community for help in the rebuilding effort. Another thread, *Combating Khat* (three replies, 42 views) solicits solutions to drug use in Somalia. A member asks the community what the best way is to fight the popular Somali narcotic, khat. One response communicates a feeling of disempowerment, stating there is little that can be done because of personal freedoms and the strength of the warlords.

AFGHANISTANONLINE

Like Somalia, Afghanistan is a pastoral society with a history of colonial contestation, and an even longer history of warlord and tribal rivalry. In unifying the country in 1880, despot Abdur Rahman crushed rebellions, killing thousands, resulting in a fragile harmony among Afghanistan's many ethnic groups and tribes. Weak central government and isolated rural areas enhanced the de facto governance of local warlords. Modest modernization began under the Amanullah regime when Afghanistan joined the international system of sovereign states in 1919 (Cramer and Goodhand 2002). Its first constitution in 1921 defined the rights of universal citizenship for the first time. Education and other reforms inspired by the revolution in Turkey were met with resistance by tribal and religious elites.

Rebellions led to Amanullah's replacement, by the Musahiban family (1929–1978), whose 1931 constitution acknowledged tribal powers, attempting to balance gradual reform with recognition of the formal role of tribal and religious leaders in government. The 1930–1960 regime, in particular, managed a delicate balance between these traditional powers and an emerging middle class and bureaucratic elite (see Cramer and Goodhand 2002: Oleson 1995). A "New Democracy" period, 1963–1970, sought to further distance the government from tribes and religious leaders through a more explicit modernization policy. A relatively democratic constitution in 1964 led to increasing political instability, which eventually led to the overthrow of King Zahir Shah in 1978. Subsequent coups culminated with the Soviet invasion in 1979.

Only with the invasion of the Soviets in 1979 were Afghanistan's diverse factions unified in common cause. But emancipation served to "open a Pandora's box of ethnic and tribal rivalries" (Curry 2001, 2), which yielded a full-scale civil war in the 1990s. The Taliban, whose members were trained in madrasahs in Pakistan, began fighting the local warlords in 1994 and seized Kabul in 1996, having vanquished all of the armed factions but the Northern Alliance. In 2002, the United States invaded Afghanistan, ending the Taliban regime and establishing the Karzai interim government, which continues to struggle with the balance of power among and with rival warlords as it seeks to establish national stability and reconstruct the war-torn society.

Marginalization

The years of Soviet occupation, civil war, and Taliban dominance yielded successive waves of refugees and immigrants. Many of these diasporans directly experienced violence and despair at Afghanistan's continuing struggle as a nation and a people. Discussion threads on AfghanistanOnline illustrate some of this frustration and despair. In *Gulbuddin Hekmatyar had links with KGB*, Zanburak posts an article about a dubious historical character from the time of Afghanistan's civil war. Following some discussion, he writes: "he killed my very intellectual uncle and lots of my colloquies. I like to kill him with my hand." The thread ends here, with no response from other members. Sometimes frustration is manifested in implicit shame of Afghanistan and its people. The discussion *Are the afghans serious of going back?* devolves into personal attacks sparked by reference to the "ordinary afghan" who "loves to be educated." A member responds:

This idea of "learning from life" is a bunch of crap and today's Afghanistan is a perfect example of how NO ONE learned anything from events of the past. Plus that fact that so many people put up with the crap of the Taliban and did not resist and bowed to their primitive and idiotic version of Islam is further proof that lack of education has haunted the nation for decades

This thread illustrates that the Afghan diaspora is not immune to the kind of shame and demoralization witnessed on Somalinet. The two original discussants return to the topic at hand, ignoring the personal attacks and frustration expressed in the meantime.

Overall, there seems to be much more hope expressed regarding Afghanistan's future than that found on Somalinet, though this optimism is far from universal. In response to *Good website on afghan Reconstruction*, a member replies, "Thanks for the post. It is good to see a record of POSITIVE developments for a change!!!!" Another member echoed this sentiment: "Thanks for providing this link. It was like a fresh windswept of hope and confidence in a time where some individuals are desperately trying to destroy our courage and optimism." He went on to accuse some members of the forum of deliberately undermining optimism and efforts to stabilize Afghanistan; their "evil," he wrote, is evident in "their type of writing and in their stubborn stupid opposition with any kind of reconstructions In our land." He also emphasized these members' sectarian views.

The Afghan diaspora seems generally prideful of their culture. In addition to the cultural defense mounted in *Afghan Dance* noted in Chapter 4, cultural pride is expressed in the initiation of *Afghan Recipes*: "I know that for many Afghans, 9/11 and the subsequent bombing affected them in different ways. Since I was generally in favor of 'regime change.' I decided to celebrate my culture by learning how to cook." This thread became the second most popular during the research period in terms of number of replies.

Cross-Categorical Identity and Bridging Social Capital

Like its Somali counterpart, AfghanistanOnline encompasses members who are keenly interested in the online community as well as the diaspora more generally. A member provides an analysis of membership diversity in *BAH!*:

This forum has a good number of Americans, a good number of Afghan Americans, several Afghan Canadians, several Afghan Australians, and some others. But none are living in the third world, and very few are rabid anti-American. Unfortunately, one al qaeda lover (kudos) tends to post enough garbage to make up for the lack in numbers. . . . You will also see a variety of views on world affairs. Zanburak supports the Iraq invasion, Kudos doesn't. JKabuli thinks Bush is a 'lunkhead,' Grace likes Bush and his administration. DanielRose thinks Sharon is the devil, Windswept thinks Arafat is the devil.

Very few sheep, and no religious fanatics.

Similarly, a member describes the community to a newbie in *Looking Ahead*:

threads easily go astray here and develop into personal exchanges without a connection with the original theme. I am a Finnish nerd and Hasanhh is an eccentric American who has converted into Islam. Both of us have little relevance for a real life Afghan constitution. But . . . Hafiz Baghan is our Grand Old Man, an Afghan ethnograph and definitely relevant for real life descriptions of what is going on in Afghanistan. We have other Afghan heavyweights as well and in all representatives of practically every political faction in Afghanistan

Tribalism is also present. In *Why!* a Tajik promotes Tajik nationalism and heated discussion ensues about ethnic sectarianism and racism.

These examples confirm the diversity of the AfghanistanOnline community, demonstrating potential for bridging social capital. Members try to bridge these ethnic identities by demonstrating respect across ethnic lines and emphasizing Afghaniyat, or Afghan-ness. In *Shari'a in Afghanistan* a member writes, "to my knowledge every ethnic group in Afghanistan has contributed in valuable ways to the national culture. And every group has engaged in ruining the works of the others."

Members also alternatively try to understand others' political views and then promote their own, with varying degrees of tolerance and personal attacks. In *Should the United States go home?*, Zanburak is very critical of the United States. Clare responds stating she has read his accusations very carefully; she asks him some specific questions about them, and then posts an article on "10 Reasons to Celebrate America." Zanburak replies:

Dearest love, you are one emotional American, I really like it some one defending their dignity and identity, but you don't know anything about reality. . . . You don't know what is going on in my land, I know better then you guys, because I am in tough with my people every day.

While this discussion begins as a somewhat amicable, if sarcastic exchange, soon the conversation again becomes personal developing into the "pro-U.S. involvements" versus the "cons."

Along with members' despair and frustration regarding Afghanistan's past and future, the dramatic changes in the political climate in

Afghanistan at the time of study led some members to be more hopeful, both about their own AfghanistanOnline community and for Afghanistan's future. A key component of this development was expressed hope for bridging among these various identities and interest groups. In a telling thread, *AOP Forum and the Afghan American Community*, Donna summarizes this perspective:

I believe that discussions and debates amongst Afghans in this forum have greatly improved from a few years back. Besides the obvious reason that Al-Qaeda/ ISI is no longer in power in Afghanistan, that we have more non-Afghan participants to share their views, and that we have tons more news and eye witness accounts to fuel discussion. . . . I feel that people are a little more at ease and familiar in discussion with eachother than from two years ago (it was really terrible before).

With respect to Afghanistan itself, the same member writes:

I think that when roads and airways link all parts of Afghanistan to eachother, when there is national media service and internet connection, the inter-Afghan dialogue will not only grow but it will repair relationships that have been very much abused throughout the decades of war inside Afghanistan.

Bridging social capital also extends between members of the diaspora and others seeking to understand Afghanistan and its culture, sometimes prior to serving there. In *Do Afghans have dogs as pets*, an American planning to live in Afghanistan for a year posts the indicated question. For the most part, the community sought to answer helpfully. A side conversation ensued about how worrying about dogs may discount the great human needs in Afghanistan. It was initiated angrily by one member who criticized Americans for the attention they lavish on dogs. The original poster stressed that he also wants to do all he can for the people of Afghanistan.

Like Somalinet's MAD MAC, AfghanistanOnline encompasses an unusual member, "a white American woman ... with a daddy who supported Duke and the klan" (*David Duke Going to the Pen*). She is also "the mother of a child by a Pakistani/muslim man." Because she posted as a "Newbie" another member responds, "Hey there, little gal. How come you don't gots no name and logo posted?" In encouraging her to adopt and publicize a username, this member implicitly welcomes her into the community, validating her participation. The original writer signs her message "Peace." In fact, Peace is a core member of the AfghanistanOnline community.

Liberal Values

As members try to bridge among these various identities and viewpoints they often embrace liberal values. For example, in *ai: Israel committed war crimes in Jenin*, a member questions the differential interpretation of violence against Palestinians and those against Israelis. He goes on to promote universal values, emphasizing we are all human:

At what point will the human race say ... I want a better life for my children and I will not hate my former enemies and teach my children tolerance and to treat everyone the way they want to be treated. We have to love people for the person they are and not because they are Muslim or jew. When we learn to practice the Golden rule (do unto others as you would have them do unto you) then the human race will start to make progress.... Only 'we' can stop the hatered and only 'we' can teach our children to hate people they do not know. ... We are all brothers and sisters on one small planet and you would think we could be smart enough to learn how to treat each other and be honest with each other

Similarly, Peace writes:

Open your heart and your mind . . . do not hate any people, and you will help your own self. If you want to change the world . . . start with yourself . . . love all people and don't judge them by their race or their religion. . . . Let me give you another example . . . if you are Muslim . . . and you go to heaven . . . and you are standing in front of God . . . and you look over and see a Christian or a Jew . . . will that make you wish for Hell? Or, if you are white and you look over and see a black . . . when you stand before God . . . will that make you wish for Hell? Can't you see, all the finger pointing towards any groups of people . . . cause us to have Hell on Earth.

In several instances, members draw from the experience of their host society, in this case the United States, demonstrating hybrid identity as they have internalized these societies' liberal values. One member opens his thread, *America's For-Profit Secret Army*, with a quote from Abraham Lincoln, implicitly encouraging U.S.

citizens to exercise their rights to question the privatization of security forces. He writes:

'This country, with its institutions, belongs to the people who inhabit it. Whenever they shall grow weary of the existing government, they can exercise their constitutional right of amending it, or their revolutionary right to dismember it or overthrow it.'

– Abraham Lincoln, 16th President of the United States, First Inaugural Address, March 4, 1861

Members also apply liberal values in expressing their opinions and proposals for what the future Afghanistan should be. In *Shari'a in Afghanistan*, a member writes:

Any time people base politics on arbitrary definitions, it is a license for the power hungry to redefine the rules of politics. More often than not, it is a precursor to war. The founding fathers of the US clearly recognized this, **so paradoxically, in order to protect religious life, we need to abolish religion from matters of the state.** Of course, we cannot abolish religion from society

Together, these examples demonstrate members' embrace of human rights, tolerance, the meaning and associated rights of citizenship, the separation of church and state (secularism in government), and the social contract as a basis for government. Liberal values are also demonstrated in members' attempts to mitigate conflict and apply rules.

Examples of Conflict Mitigation and Framing

Some threads center on the notion of social, political, and cultural tolerance versus politically charged on-line behavior. One member initiated a thread, titled *Bah!* in which he identifies himself as an American veteran home from fighting in Afghanistan. The message was inflammatory and prompted several heated responses. Another member stepped in as a peacemaker, declaring what she perceived as the appropriate norms of behavior, including a respect for diversity and a tolerance for others. She then tried to redirect some of the member's energies to a more constructive purpose from which all members could benefit:

It is a very diverse forum. And I'm sure we all would appreciate your views from 'having been there and done that'! Perhaps you could tell us some of your 'Adventures in Afghanistan'. The forum members who daydream about the good old day or of someday soon going back to their homeland would probably love to hear some of your stories.

In other threads, name calling and personal attacks seem to be accepted without question.

In the middle of a thread where a member hypothesizes our closeness to the "end times" (*My Quarterly Update*), two members engage in a discussion of math problems. Another member posts, "What the f___ are you people talking about?" This message is summarily ignored. Several posts later, another member finally responds to the initiator of the thread with a personal attack, calling him a "Cwazy Chwistian" and telling him to "Get a life . . . chwistian-twash!" This is followed by a response to the message to the mathematicians: "This is called *intellectual flatulence* . . . that's what they are babbling about!" The discussion of the math problems then continues, with a third member joining in. This thread demonstrates members' flexibility and tenacity in pursuing their own interests and ignoring dynamics with which they would prefer not to engage. Like Zanbaruk's expressed desire for violence noted above, the mean-spirited messages are summarily ignored.

Ignoring inflammatory remarks is a common response. Sometimes an inflammatory remark will signal the end of a thread. In other instances, the discussion may continue among other members as if the insult had never occurred. *Partying while Afghanistan burns* illustrates both responses. Members discuss the posted article of the thread title. After some exchange concerning opinions and checking of facts, one member asks another about where to acquire a DVD on Massoud (former leader of the Northern Alliance), whereupon another member responds with a sarcastic and vulgar attack on Massoud and, implicitly, this member.

Yet another member responds, "Once again the resident Dog of the forum ... [member name] the female claiming to be a manly man is BARKING about Ahmad Shah Massoud. I have finally found the best way to keep this dog (actually a pregnant dog) from barking." He goes on to introduce his notion of a "bark buster" product. More personal attacks are exchanged between the two members and then another member writes to the original DVD requester, "Don't waste your precious time on this insect ... he is on welfare, and has nothing else to do." This is followed by a message from the member who was asked about the DVD. He cuts and pastes the original request and simply posts where he acquired it. The thread ends with another attack and sarcasm from the member who was accused of being the barking dog, who posts photographs of dogs along with a fictional dialogue with Massoud indicated as one of the pictured dogs.

As this discussion indicates, emotions regarding ethnic divisions run high. However, not all responses end in personal attacks, and not all related threads resort to ignoring these. In *Karzai turns against Northern Alliance*, a member posts a news story by an Afghan correspondent. The story is potentially conflictive, highlighting favoritism of the Karzai government vis-à-vis various factions within Afghanistan. The members respond questioning the validity of the story and the source, to which the original poster states he is just posting information, not endorsing ideas.

Here and in other threads, members carefully check information and posts that are potentially conflict inspiring. The thread *Why!* on Tajik nationalism receives varied responses. A member responds to the posted webpage:

> Death To Talibism
> Death Nazism
> Death to racism
> Please please, your are extreemly bad influence on our Kids.
> Hope no Afghan kid or any kid comes across introduction of
> nazism in Afghanistan.
> You have no humanity in yourself.

Another member responds, first confirming their shared heritage:

> Me too ... I'm both Pashtoon and Tajik ... but don't you think that Mr Taher has a coherent argument there? ... with his site ... I was sad as well at first. ... but we should acknowledge ... his efforts for the information he has gathered in regard to tajiks and their background ... and etc ... he has a voice and it should be heard ... in some way ...
>
> I think His informative site is for equality in Afghanistan ... I think the site is ... trying to convey the message that every ethnic group in Afghanistan should be able to be proud of their background and heritage and should be able to put it in practice ... and etc. ...

This member appears to be encouraging tolerance and understanding before racing to judgment, and emphasizes the importance of recognizing the legitimacy of holding ethnic identities in addition to promoting Afghaniyat, implying that the two are not mutually exclusive. This argument is reinforced by a Newbie:

... this is EXACTLY how it should be! The different ethnics should be FREE and INDEPENDENT! A Hazara should be HAZARA first, a Tajik should be TAJIK first and a Pashtun should be PASHTUN first ... by giving them this freedom, you also give them a choice: the choice to live united in one country! ... You cannot compare Afghanistan to the US, as many people in here do ... when the US was founded, there were no 30 different ethnics, but 3 or 4 who were related to each other! All the others came later ... many years AFTER the US was already there ... in Afghanistan, it is different ... there are 30 DIFFERENT people who actually are NOT related to each ... and they were there BEFORE 'Afghanistan' was created ... The idea of a 'united Afghanistan' in which everyone has to submitt to Pashtun history, culture and tradition DOES NOT WORK ...

In this way, members try to reframe the issue, moving away from an either/or approach to redefining Afghan identity as ethnic *and* Afghan.

And by using Afghaniyat as the primary identity frame, members can scold each other for their ethnic discrimination. One member tries to challenge the Afghaniyat identity of another member whom he feels is violating the proper rules of treatment:

I am not upset with such insults. In fact I feel proud to read your comments because you have not any Afghan blood in your vains. If you were an Afghan you would not insult others. Either you are a Russian backed Khalqi or a Paki Talib

The member appears to justify personal insults by defining the boundaries of Afghan identity. Insults are to be tolerated when they extend beyond that identity but a true Afghan is presented as one who is tolerant of the many ethnicities comprising Afghanistan.

SOMALINET AND AFGHANISTANONLINE: ELEMENTS OF POTENTIAL CONFLICT PREVENTION

Both online communities exhibit a sense of marginalization, explore and promote cross-categorical identities, develop bridging social capital, demonstrate an embrace of liberal values as they negotiate shared norms of behavior, and frame issues to influence conflict potential.

Marginalization

The communities have a common homeland history of individualism, tribalism/clannism, external interventions, and systematic undermining of traditional/historical conflict intermediation institutions, with implications for perceived marginalization, shame, and hope for the future. However, the degree of felt shame seems to differ between the two diaspora communities. Somalinet members appear ashamed of Somalia's failed state and the tribal hatred that characterizes their homeland and sometimes their online community. The Somalinet community seems to agonize over the limited aspirations of Somali youth. Afghanistan Online's expressed shame appears to be more about not learning from the past, and rooted in some of their compatriots' embrace of the Taliban. Especially in *Are the afghans serious of going back?*, members seem to cope with their shame by distinguishing themselves from the "ordinary Afghan." Generally, though, the AfghanistanOnline community appears to be more proud of their shared heritage and relatively more optimistic about their homeland's future. This could reflect the dramatic political changes that occurred just prior to the research period.

Whereas on AfghanistanOnline members discuss and promote Afghan dance and cooking, promoting pride in their shared heritage, on Somalinet, cultural roots and manifestations are fiercely debated and often rooted in tribal identities and Islam. When Somalinomo is implicated, its acceptance is vague at best. One exception is the pride with which the Somalinet members tend to approach their poetry. This is a cultural artifact that links all of the tribes and members seem to share an intense interest in it, as demonstrated by the popularity of the thread, *Poems...... Love..... Hope..... Life.....* (620 replies, 9,091 views). These differences in targets and degree of shame and discrimination may reflect the origin and relative social class of participating diasporans. The Somali diaspora is made up largely of refugees, whereas the Afghan diaspora, particularly in North America, includes many of the best educated and higher social classes of Afghanistan.

Shame is also implicated in the communities' varied attitudes toward welfare and discrimination. On Somalinet, members alternately embrace or are shamed by Somali diasporans' reliance on welfare, whereas on AfghanistanOnline, welfare is used as an insult when a member is perceived as being unreasonable. Discussion of discrimination is a very prominent feature of the Somalinet community, with frequent comparisons to African Americans and, by extension, identity questions related to Somalis' African roots. Responses to the discrimination encountered by the diaspora seem to vary according to the context. Discrimination in Norway, for example, led several members to blame the Somali diaspora there for welfare dependency and lack of ambition (*Somalis= the most beautifull and most beloved people on earth*, discussed in Chapter 4). Discrimination in the United States prompted similar discussions but also inspired members to question their similarities and differences to the broader African diaspora, particularly African Americans. In both instances, the host society was held at least partially to blame. The North American Somali diaspora seemed divided; even those who sought to embrace an African identity still urged Somalis to distance themselves from the African-American ghetto culture. Discrimination is also expressed from within the Muslim community, for example, the Moroccan who claims that most muslims don't consider Somalis as "brothers."

There did not appear to be explicit discussions of discrimination on AfghanistanOnline. It is possible that Afghans encounter relatively less discrimination owing to their lighter skin color and that, unlike the Somalis, the diaspora does not appear to embrace or identify with ghetto culture (the sexually oriented personal attacks not withstanding). Alternatively, receiving societies may be more tolerant and accepting of the Afghan diaspora. Especially under the Taliban, an almost global sympathy for the plight of Afghanistan emerged, and this may have been particularly prevalent during the research period that followed shortly after September 11, 2001. Americans' attitude toward Somalia, on the other hand, is largely rooted in the killing of U.S. marines in 1993.

Cross-Categorical Identity and Bridging Social Capital

Both online communities are exceedingly diverse, with a variety of distinctions, including ethnicity/clan/tribe, political perspectives, religious fervor, and country of residence. In both communities, members often (though not always) engage in genuine efforts to understand opposing political views. When bridging among ethnic/clan/tribe identities, both communities appear to embrace an approach of subidentity first (i.e., ethnic tribe or clan), but national identity unifies (i.e., Somalinomo and Afghaniyat). Afghanistan's history supports this perspective. Its political history demonstrates a continuous approach of acknowledging the power of local warlords and validating their roles and identities, despite efforts to unify the country under a common nation-state governance structure and associated Afghaniyat identity. Unlike Somalia, Afghans experienced a taste of modernization and liberal values prior to more recent invasions and civil war, further supporting meta-Afghan hybrid identities. When members of the AfghanistanOnline community discuss ethnic/tribal identity, they criticize various groups' impact on their homeland but also recognize that each tribe has contributed. In contrast to Somalinet, this subtle complexity already implies a more hopeful/optimistic tenor regarding a future based on a hybrid Afghaniyat identity.

While the Somalinet community does make reference to Somalinomo, its historical roots and cultural artifacts seem more tenuous. Members challenge the very notion of Somali nationhood and secession of various territories are fiercely debated. Members at once promote the idealized notion of Somalinomo and confirm their tribal identities and mistrust of other tribal groups. Other members seem to struggle in their promotion of Somalinomo, promoting various proposals for how a unified Somalia would be governed. Several members highlight Somalis' shared experience; unfortunately, the experiences they share concern shame, discrimination, and violence. Hence, their bridging identity is one based on shame, and this extends to feelings of guilt for enjoying a diasporic lifestyle. Especially given this identity backdrop, Somalinet members are impressive in their tenacity vis-à-vis debating a hopeful future and discussing heroes and role models.

In both communities individuals who are technically outside of the diaspora seek to participate, for example, MAD MAC and Peace. These individuals assume a role of fostering better understanding among groups in the diaspora and between the diaspora and the host society, and channeling energy into considerations of constructive contributions. At times, both of them attempt to hide their identity from the rest of the community, perhaps suspecting that their participation would not be perceived as legitimate (MAD MAC) or that the divulsion of information about their true identity would jeopardize their continuing participation and, in the case of Peace, her role as peacemaker. Members of both communities prove them wrong by finding them out, seeking to better understand their motivations, and encouraging them to openly participate as full members of the community. These are extraordinary instances of bridging social capital that one might not have expected in a community centered on homeland identity.

Liberal Values

Both communities reinforce liberal values, notably with respect to government and political systems, religion, and universal humanity. Members of AfghanistanOnline confirm and support the legitimacy of an elected president even if it is not one's preferred candidate; the meaning and associated rights of citizenship are discussed; the separation of mosque and state (secularism in government) is promoted on both sites and sometimes fiercely debated on Somalinet; and the social contract as a basis for government is explored in both communities. Both sites underscore individual and human rights and freedoms, often with explicit reference to American culture; for example, members quote American political icons such as John F. Kennedy and Abraham Lincoln. Members also appeal to universal humanity on both sites, and both communities support religious and ethnic tolerance even as they include members of more extreme views.

Conflict Mitigation and Framing

Perhaps because the Somali diaspora has less history and shared Somalinomo experience, its conflict mitigation approaches are much more formal and structured than on AfghanistanOnline. In the first instance moderators outline specific rules of engagement in defined contexts of debate. On AfghanistanOnline no such rules are explicitly stated or recognized, though rules-in-use emerge concerning freedom of speech, voice, and exit, including the option to ignore inflammatory posts and continue with one's own communication priorities. In both communities norms are implicitly negotiated in the context of individual discussions.

Members attempt to frame identity as one that encompasses all subdivisions of the diaspora. On AfghanistanOnline, undermining optimism for Afghanistan's future and furthering inter-ethnic animosity is defined by one member as being "evil." In other instances, it is distinguished from true Afghaniyat. As noted above, similar attempts on Somalinet appear to be less effective.

Attempts to frame issues and actions concerning the future of these diasporas' homelands also vary in their effectiveness. Several attempts to promote or discuss ideas for peace and reconstruction in Somalia received very little attention, as did discussions of forgiveness and the prospects for non-violent protest. The lack of interest in these topics may be due, in part, to members' pessimism and sense of helplessness, as indicated by expressions of frustration and cynicism with regard to future prospects (e.g., *The first medical school in Somalia for 12 years*).

The discussions on both sites provide an impression of and appear to frame members' motivation to act as well as their perceived efficacy. Members appear to shy away from topics they deem unrealistic, but embrace more feasible activities, such as contributing to the development of a Somali Youth Confederacy, participating in specific project proposals (such as one promoted by the U.S. Army member on Somalinet), and donating to specific organizations and activities to *Help the Afghan Children*. In some cases, limited interest may be indicative of Friedman's (1994) and Esman's (1986) findings. That is, when social crises/issues are psychically overwhelming, diasporans may rely on their identity as American citizens or residents, living an American lifestyle, to distance themselves from the pain (e.g., *Do You Think Somalia Needs A Foreign HELP?*, *Sad news for Somalia*); they may view engagement of an issue as threatening to their American quality of life (*Are the afghans serious of going back?*); and/or they may simply view the potential rewards as too uncertain.

AfghanistanOnline demonstrates much less in the way of structured discussions around reconstruction. Most of the related threads are initiated with lengthy articles for which the posters have been accused of spamming. Arguably, by leading with long and complicated treatments (and many of them) discussion is discouraged. These discussions are intentionally initiated on Somalinet, with specific leading questions and rules of engagement. Keeping in mind that the average replies and views in AfghanistanOnline's General Discussion Forum are 11 and

129 respectively, there are a few threads related to the future of Afghanistan that receive significant participation. *Should the US Go Home?* Received 45 replies and 681 views; *Shari'a in Afghanistan* received 23 replies and 303 views; and *Partying While Afghanistan Burns* – which was initiated with the posting of an article – received 20 replies and 274 views.

The communities' norms enable members to express frustration and despair, even with anger, potentially resulting in healthy venting (e.g., on Somalinet, *The first medical school in Somalia for 12 years*; on AfghanistanOnline, *Are the afghans serious of going back?*). At the same time members self-regulate to encourage respect and rational debate. Arguably this self-regulation may expand the range of actors and skills development for facilitation and democratic practice. Subgroups, such as clans and tribes, are limited in their ability to manipulate the framing of issues and needs for their own self-interest or to foment further conflict. These limits derive from a culture of individualism, equality, and active participation that both communities share. Members hold each other to account by questioning the credibility of perspectives expressed and citing additional information and sources. Such questioning extends to calls for violence in the physical world, which may be quickly discredited, in the case of *Another Salaam Rushdi has risen* on Somalinet, or be summarily ignored, for example, on AfghanistanOnline, Zanburak's urge to kill expressed in *Gulbuddin Hekmatyar had links with KGB*.

DIGITAL DIASPORAS AND CONFLICT PREVENTION

Neither of these digital diasporas demonstrates much purposive action in the physical world, whether for peace or violence. However, they share the potential of other CGOs to politically mobilize marginalized groups, whether consistent with democratic policy processes, or for conflict/violence. Somalinet and AfghanistanOnline suggest several factors that may be more or less conducive to constructive contributions regarding conflict prevention, as opposed to destructive conflict promotion. Both communities have evolved somewhat of a balance of tolerating personal attacks but discouraging calls to violence. In embracing an extraordinary degree of diversity, they also manage to promote at least a vague notion, however real or imagined, of a common homeland identity that bridges ethnic, tribal, clan, religious, and political differences.

The communities differ in their demographics and origins, resulting in varying degrees of shame and implying different integration and identity construction strategies in their host societies. Somalinet reveals a relatively more profound shame rooted in the diaspora's dispersion origins and the homeland's continuing struggle; it also reveals a much higher tolerance for welfare reliance, and suggests a relative identification with a marginalized subculture in the host society. The AfghanistanOnline community, on the other hand, appears to be more hopeful given the definitive end of the Taliban regime at the time of study. The fact that many of its members are better educated and of higher social classes than their Somali counterparts may be one reason why welfare dependence is denigrated and used as an insult rather than tolerated and sometimes encouraged, as on Somalinet.

The two communities have evolved different framing approaches with respect to contemplating the future of their homelands. In this instance, Somalinet's greater structure and formality appears to be more effective than AfghanistonOnline's reliance on members' own interests and postings, some of which have been considered spam. And while freedom of speech is accepting of personal attacks, these are periodically discouraged or ignored, as are any references to or explicit calls to violence. The continuing conflict in Somalia and unresolved nature of its unified future may heighten the intensity of personal attacks among its members. Both diasporas seem to exhibit continuing angst and frustration related to the personal experiences of members or the ongoing suffering of their compatriots. Some members of AfghanistanOnline appear to be still processing the experiences, which led to their migration.

In sum, these CGOs demonstrate how digital diasporas use cyberspace potentially to prevent conflict by: providing a forum for expressing feelings of marginalization, exploring cross-categorical identities and developing bridging social capital, negotiating hybrid identity inclusive of liberal values and shared norms of behavior, and framing issues to explicitly avert conflict/violence. They illustrate alternative approaches to focusing and structuring debate about sensitive, potentially conflictive topics, and to presenting platforms for communal thinking about the future of the homeland. These are not gentle communities that skirt around difficult issues. Rather, members are blunt, challenging, and sometimes offensive – and with varying degrees of personal attacks and profanity. These cybercommunities afford diasporans the opportunity to express their subcategorical identities (e.g., ethnic, tribal, or clan), experimenting with related norms in ways that pose minimal risk for conflict in the physical world. Diasporans may experience frustration and even animosity owing to three sources: subgroup conflicts, the larger plight of their homeland, and their own experience of displacement. Through these cybercommunities, members potentially deflect this frustration and animosity through verbal as opposed to physical agitation and confrontation.

6

Policy Agendas, Human Rights, and National Sovereignty

When considering diasporas' political roles vis-à-vis the homeland state, policymakers, analysts, and homeland governments commonly fixate on diasporas' potential threat to state sovereignty and the potential security implications (for the nation, region, and, increasingly, globally). But diasporas may also support agendas consistent with liberal values, such as democracy and human rights, and these may be welcome to selected homeland constituents and the international community alike. Furthermore, diasporas may not threaten state sovereignty to the extent feared, and may even support it.

Digital diasporas assemble diasporans to consider issues surrounding human rights, assert their views on these, and debate policy options. This deliberation may occur exclusively in the digital world or more proactively, through political agendas informed and/or created by online discussions. This chapter analyzes two such cases. It revisits TibetBoard and explores its political debates, and it considers the case of the U.S. Copts Association and its physical world political agenda to improve the quality of life of Copts residing in Egypt. While much of the outside world does not consider Tibet a sovereign nation, the Tibetan identity and political community believes the Tibetan Government in exile is sovereign, and its subjects should not question its decisions. The religion and culture reinforce this deference. The U.S. Copts Association engages in the physical world in ways that may seem to threaten the Government of Egypt's sovereignty. I will argue the U.S. Copts Association may also reinforce it. First, I more closely examine perceived threats to sovereignty – migration, information technology, and human rights; and the role of IT in political mobilization.

DIASPORA POLICY INFLUENCE AND PERCEIVED THREATS TO SOVEREIGNTY[1]

Nation–states are sovereign from both internal and external perspectives (Krasner 1999). Internally, Westphalian sovereignty refers to the autonomy of domestic authority structures, or the absence of authoritative external influences; and domestic sovereignty concerns the structure of internal authority, as well as the state's effectiveness and control. Externally, interdependence sovereignty is the ability of governments to regulate transborder movement of goods, capital, people, and ideas; and international legal sovereignty refers to recognition by other states. Not all four facets are necessary for a state to be considered sovereign. For example, failed states (lacking domestic sovereignty) may be internationally recognized.

Scholars and policymakers have cast both migration and information technology as threatening to the established political order. The speed and volume of movements of people and information most obviously hinders states' external interdependence sovereignty – states' ability to regulate transborder movements. These movements may also have implications for states' internal control. Diasporas have become an additional external pressure on domestic affairs; through their lobbying efforts to host countries and the international community, they potentially influence international recognition of state sovereignty. Homeland governments may in some cases welcome diasporas' political engagement in domestic and international affairs on their behalf. In Armenia, for example, 69% of foreign direct investors 1998–2004 were diaspora-connected (Hergnyan and Makaryan 2007); from 1989–1999, at its beginning as a sovereign nation, fourteen diaspora organizations donated an estimated $630 million (Anonymous, 1999; qtd. in Gillespie and Andriasova 2008); and diaspora lobbying to the U.S. Congress has yielded disproportionate and significant volumes of U.S. foreign assistance to Armenia (King and Pomper 2004). Whether diaspora political efforts regarding the homeland are welcome

---

[1] The discussion of sovereignty draws from Brainard and Brinkerhoff (2006).

interventions or not, representation is problematic: Diasporans themselves often are not subject to the consequences of their preferred policy changes.

Migrants now cross state boundaries and bring their entitlements with them, whether these are related to their continued citizenship status in their home country, their ongoing affiliation with the imagined community of their cultural identity, or their recourse to universal values. The concept and experience of diasporas have evolved from one of victimization to challengers to the nation-state, as globalization creates "communities not of place but of interest" (Cohen 1996, 517). Organized diasporas may actively promote policy and regime change in their home territories.[2] When social groups perceive a threat to their identity, they are likely to develop an enhanced sense of solidarity, and are more likely to mobilize (Esman 1994, 1986).

Given that they influence human beliefs and perceptions, communication technologies are not politically neutral (Rheingold 1993). Not only do ideas represent social power, "we may think of ideas as causes of identities" (Philpott 1997, 23). Information technology holds the potential to influence the very way we perceive ourselves and enact our priorities, political or otherwise. For diasporans, some of these ideas and perceptions represent liberal values. These can inspire an individualistic and/or rights-based sense of empowerment, which may not have been considered prior to migration and/or IT access.

The Internet has fostered inexpensive, instantaneous global information sharing. Information technology not only increases the movement of goods and ideas across borders, it can circumvent national legal frameworks entirely. Not surprisingly, information technology has enabled the creation and enhanced the effectiveness of transnational movements to address key global public policy issues such as the Campaign to Ban Landmines and the World Commission on Dams.[3] Many of these movements base their work on and justify their challenges to governments according to universal moral codes rooted in liberal values. By linking transnational actors, information technology

---

[2] See, for example, Byman (2001); Cohen (1996); King and Melvin (1999/2000); and Shain (1994–1995, 1999).

[3] For the Campaign to Ban Landmines, see Cameron (1998); and Warkentin and Mingst (2000). For the World Commission on Dams, see Brinkerhoff (2002a).

can imply threats to the nation–state from both political and sociocultural perspectives.

Human rights present two types of potential threats to state sovereignty (Brainard and Brinkerhoff 2006). First, nation–states may be subject to influence and intervention based on universal codes, such as the UN Declaration of Human Rights, whether or not they are signatories. Second, nation–states may be influenced and expected to intervene in situations that may represent only limited perceived national self-interest. The responsibility to protect may be increasingly invoked, since people are most likely to suffer human rights abuses from their own government or its agents (Jacobsen and Lawson 1999), and these abuses may be linked to broader security concerns. Human rights are a rallying cry not only for transnational civil society groups, including diaspora communities, but also for other states and inter-governmental organizations seeking to justify impingements on state sovereignty.[4] Diaspora lobbying efforts in the host society and to the international community often invoke human rights and may even exaggerate the severity of the homeland situation in order to promote their agendas. Recent developments in international law and the International Commission on Intervention and State Sovereignty principle of responsibility notwithstanding, a strong sovereign state is still the most capable guarantor of human rights and international security (Fox 1997).

Diaspora influence on host-country foreign policy may be most effective when it corresponds with host-country national interest and values (Shain 1995, 1999). Diaspora organizations can reinforce, strengthen, and hold host-country governments accountable for their national identity. At the same time, through these efforts, diasporas can contribute meaningfully to socioeconomic development in their home territories (e.g., through lobbying for foreign assistance, economic remittances, and/or informing policy and programs), as the case of Armenia (described above) illustrates. These socioeconomic contributions potentially enhance their home-country government's ability to control internal sovereignty.

When combined, migration, information technology and the promotion of universal values (such as human rights) may be perceived as

---

[4] For an historical view of how human rights influence state sovereignty, and a normative argument for why this should be so, see Falk (1981).

a powerful threat to state sovereignty. Migration creates new cultural identities that ignore state boundaries. Information technology enables the organization of diasporas into associations and movements, as individuals selectively pursue information and interaction opportunities, reinforcing diasporic cultural bonds (Elkins 1997; see also Rowe 2001). Activity in cyberspace may have spillover effects in the physical world. For example, members of the Eritrean diaspora in North America debated the 1996 Eritrean Constitution in cyberspace on Dehai (news from home) at the same time as the constitutional committee debates. Some members of the latter presented their views on Dehai and others lurked to learn of different viewpoints (Rude 1996; qtd. in Koslowski 2005, 27). Opposition groups residing both within and outside of national boundaries are increasingly using the Internet to promote their agendas, particularly where censorship and other forms of repression are entrenched.[5] These agendas frequently include advocacy for human rights.

On the other hand, international interventions in domestic affairs – whether by diasporas or others, using IT or not – is aimed precisely to "produce stronger states, with a more inclusive political culture, with tolerance as the basis of strengthened legitimacy, and with internal disintegration less likely" (Hashmi 1997, 9). Specifically, the promotion of human rights and democratic processes is "designed to produce a broadly inclusive political process that the mass of citizens perceives as legitimate" (Fox 1997, 108). Threats to state sovereignty can be viewed as temporary efforts (in the case of interventions) and continuing accountability measures (in the case of transnational civil society organizations and their advocacy efforts) to create and maintain strong states, with liberal democratic principles, within a more stable international system.

When diasporas intervene to capture state power, they are obvious threats to national sovereignty. When their political influence, like other actors in transnational civil society, focuses on human rights and accountability they may be reinforcing state sovereignty, both of the homeland and for the international system.

---

[5] See, for example, Sharma (2002). In his treatise on the Falungong, Chung (2002) notes that the impact of such phenomena may be much more significant for reforming socialist systems that have been accustomed to near omnipotent regulatory powers. For further discussion of the role of information technology in promoting liberalization and democratization, see Kalathil and Boas (2003).

THE ROLE OF IT IN POLITICAL MOBILIZATION

The Internet facilitates the rapid exchange of information for the purpose of coordinating collective action. It reconfigures networks of communication, reinforcing and extending them, and influencing communication patterns and information access. The Internet facilitates the promotion of marginalized groups' political agendas (see, for example, Bennett and Fielding 1999; Dartnell 2003). At a minimum, cybercommunities may prepare members for political action even if they are not yet fully engaged in it.[6] It also facilitates the framing of issues through established social norms, the structuring of interactive components, and the rules regulating participation (see, for example, Warkentin and Mingst 2000). Information technology increasingly challenges public officials' framing of policy debates, both through the ability to post alternatively framed perspectives and through improved access to otherwise remote information (see Livingston 2003). And it affords opportunities to voice views that would otherwise jeopardize individuals' quality of life and political safety. For example, among others, gays and lesbians in the Iranian diaspora are using the Internet, viewing it as "a way of combating the confinement of opinions to private and inaccessible spheres enforced by the threat of persecution" (Graham and Khosravi 2002, 243).

No one contests that the Internet is a potentially powerful advocacy tool. But as it applies to developing countries, most research has focused on the impact of transnational IT-based advocacy efforts targeted to global public policies, which incorporate minimal participation of the local poor.[7] While the Internet is a powerful tool to fight tyranny, "if democracy advocates want to spur meaningful change, they must also recognize the Net's ability to change authoritarian regimes from within" (Kalathil 2003, 43).

But what of the so-called digital divide? Accessing the Internet requires supportive physical and regulatory infrastructure, as well as literacy and, at least some, English language proficiency. The digital divide concept in its pure form is increasingly challenged, largely

---

[6] Siapera's (2005) research on the websites of refugees in Britain reveals them to be "prepolitical" (500) in this sense.

[7] For example, efforts to promote democracy in Burma (Danitz and Strobel 2000). See also Keck and Sikkinck (1997).

because it is often associated with erroneous assumptions about the poor's capability, interest, and start-up costs for accessing the benefits of IT (see, for example, Prahalad and Hart 2002). The Internet alone may not be the only factor to consider when gauging communications divides. In Senegal, the Philippines, and the Democratic Republic of Congo, citizens combine low-cost voice communications with access to the Internet, making mobile telephones "a more empowering tool than the Internet itself" (Cabras 2002, 87). To truly assess the extent of digital divide, one would need to examine the efficacy of the available network of communications, which may combine a variety of technologies. People will use whatever communication resources are available in order to maintain contact and provide support (Wellman et al. 2001); obstacles to accessing one does not preclude others or combinations.

TibetBoard and the U.S. Copts Association challenge conventional notions of the digital divide and IT's challenges to state sovereignty; and they illustrate the power of digital diasporas for exploring and expressing political positions, sometimes with important real world implications.

TIBETBOARD

Dispersed and without a homeland, the Tibetan identity in diaspora is largely concerned with policy agendas and strategies to both re-secure the homeland and sustain a Tibetan cultural and religious identity in continued diaspora. As illustrated in Chapter 4, these two are not always compatible. This incompatibility yields a rich discussion concerning choice of political agendas, and how liberal values, including promoting human rights, are incorporated into these agendas. Assessing the extent to which any of these agendas or ideas are enacted in the physical world is beyond the scope of this study. We know that Dorjee Nudup's primary objectives in creating TibetBoard are: 1) facilitating political and cultural mobilization by acting as an announcement board for relevant activities, and 2) providing an open space for Tibetans to discuss, debate, and question official policies of the Tibetan Government in exile.

The very name of TibetBoard's most popular discussion forum confirms the political bent of the TibetBoard community: "Politics of the

People." Political consciousness is linked to discussions of hybrid identity. Members express concern that too much embrace of the hostland identity and lifestyle will lead to forgetting not only the Tibetan identity, but also its cause. Because of this danger, one member suggests Tibetans should be encouraged to stay in India instead of coming to America (*AMERICA...!!! IT'S NOT WHAT YOU THINK ...*). Others assert that learning from the hostland experience can help the cause: "its is not just about going there, but becoming a better human being and being on a better stand to support our cause" (*US Visa, why why*). Perhaps for this reason, public figures are expected to promote a "free Tibet." Recall that Yangchan Lhamo, a Tibetan singer who has gained acclaim among Western listeners, was criticized for being focused on her popularity and marketability as opposed to using her fame as an opportunity to promote the cause, or to serve the Tibetan people as Jetsum Pema does (*Who is the most Eligible Women?, Tibetan Entertainment*).

"Free Tibet!" is a frequently quoted call, and some member names reflect a related political agenda, for example, WakeUp_Tibet, tibetanwarrior, and Tibetan Liberation Front. Other usernames reflect alternative political perspectives, such as ChineseGuy. These particular individuals are core members, contributing frequently, and their posts reflect the politics implied by their chosen usernames. Members choose other usernames precisely to be misleading and provocative, such as Dali Llama, who expresses a pro-Chinese perspective and criticizes Tibetans for being backwards (for example, *FINAL SOLUTION TO THE CHINESE QUESTION!*).

Some make their political agenda very explicit, such as: "I want Chinese out from Tibet and Let Tibetan have their own country. I will even use violence to get my country back in the future (*Ban Chris! Ban all opposition to the HH Dalai Lama*). True to his name, Tibetan Liberation Front writes:

WE must act with resolve and determination! We must put the FINAL SOLUTION to the chinese problem into action! We tibetans are chosen by fate to eridicate Earth of this great evil that is all chinese! Kill them all and let God sort them out! We will kill them one at a time! If they fight us here, we will kill them here! If they run away like the dogs that they are, we will kill them there! We will fight them on the beaches, we will fight them on the shores! Death to all heathens! (*FINAL SOLUTION TO THE CHINESE QUESTION!*).

This post prompts several of the pro-Chinese members to respond, including Chris, hellfire, and Dali Llama, citing Chinese cultural superiority and possession of nuclear arms. This, in turn, inspires Chinese roaches! to urge others to "rise up and exterminate" these "roaches" (*FINAL SOLUTION TO THE CHINESE QUESTION!*).

Pro-Chinese members participate to promote their own political agenda. In *Are Tibetans Terrorists?*, Dali Llama discusses how China should improve security to prevent and punish "these criminals if they dare to split the country with violence." In *If I'm Chinese President . . .*, an interesting exchange emerges between ChineseGuy, who initiated the thread, and a self-identified, older pro-Chinese guest. The latter tries to encourage ChineseGuy, in a fatherly way, not to waste his time on the forum, but to study and "build the nation strong." He argues to ChineseGuy: "By causing the feelings of resentment among Tibetans, you are widening the gap between our two races." Consistent with liberal notions of rights and sovereignty, he goes on to argue: "You should not be encouraging them [Tibetans] to leave, cause then they'll always feel that you're illegally occupying their nation. In fact, that is illegal occupation if you force the natives out." At one point a non-Tibetan participant questions the identity of pro-Chinese Chris, warning the TibetBoard community that they should be suspicious of a non-Tibetan, pro-Chinese posting so frequently (147 times from April 1–May 11, the rough equivalent of twice a day as per the poster). He suggests Chris may be on the "job" monitoring TibetBoard for the PRC (*INDEPENDENT TIBET: REALITY OR FANTASY!*).

Not all political agendas are so neatly divided along pro-Chinese/pro-Tibetan lines. Sometimes efforts are made to promote understanding between the two sides. Occasionally, an ethnic Chinese will self-identify and promote peace and understanding. In one case, a member apologized for hurtful things the Han-Chinese have said to the Tibetans (*Misconception about the Chinese*). At the same time, this particular member maintains his own political agenda: "if you guys insist in separating Tibet from my motherland, we have the right to defend our sovereign" (*Misconception about the Chinese*). From the opposing side, a Tibetan tries to explain to ChineseGuy:

not all the tibetans want to kill the chinese . . . but u dont know the feeling of loosing a country and becoming a refuegee . . . we have hate because of what ur goverment did to us.. dont tell me that if u got beaten up or killed because u believed in a religion that u would turn your back and forgive them . . . so dont wonder y we have hate because it is pretty obvious . . . i am not any terrorist . . . i have no intentions of killing anyone . . . its just a bunch of talk and nothing more . . . it is the government not the chinese people that all the tibetans hate . . . so understand (*If I'm Chinese President . . .*).

Some members embrace a Tibetan identity but articulate and try to promote acceptance of the Chinese occupation. This argument may be made on religious grounds (as we saw in Chapter 4). Elsewhere, it is promoted as a matter of practicality:

There are many reason to hate the Chinese; but, we needed to learn to life with them. The Chinese are not that bad, all they want is for us not to separated, if we just work with them; then they will leave us alone (*IMO, It is wrong to hate..Let live in peace*).

The member calls attention to the money and employment the Chinese have brought to Tibet, arguing "the Chinese have done more to improve Tibet then the monks for thousand of years." The post received no replies and only twenty-nine views.

Still others are not certain of the appropriate political agenda and pose related questions, particularly with respect to incorporating violence into the struggle for independence. For example,

what i m starting to realize after watching the news of the world is that whoeva succeeds in creating a headline get noticed by the world and their message reaches out to more people. . . . All these questions lingers in my mind. It sometime sicken the dickens out of me and makes me reconsider the path we tibetans are taking(Nonviolence). . . . We Tibetans have always stressed about Nonviolence and being compassionate and loving. Is it really possible in this present world where everything is driven by greed and self benefit. . . . The call for independence by suicide bombers seem to gain more attention. We Tibetans had never resort to violence but isn't it high time we should try this path as well. . . . probably Independence isn't simply achieved by nonviolence. Sacrifices might be required (*What's there in Future for Tibetans?*).

In response, a member returns to the thread's opening question of what would happen in the absence of the Dalai Lama, and writes, "The peaceful approach have somewhat subdued the inner rage, and courage that is sometimes vital to our struggle" (*What's there in Future for Tibetans?*).

In another thread, a member asks, "IS TIBETAN INDEPENCE (and self rule) A REALISTIC REALITY OR A HOPELESS FANTASY?" (*INDEPENDENT TIBET: REALITY OR FANTASY!*). The member observes that the Chinese had occupied Tibet for forty-five years at this point, and "there is no sign of them loosing their tight grip over Tibet." A member responds with encouragement, stating that "It took Ireland 800 years to regain its freedom from occupation and still some part is ruled by the UK." This member later adds, "In light of the fact that no country has regained its independence WITHOUT some use of force or armed struggle the message is clear-don't give up the fight and keep all options open!" (*INDEPENDENT TIBET: REALITY OR FANTASY!*). The original questioner responds, "shouldn't use of violence be our last resort?"

Liberal values, such as democracy and human rights, are frequently invoked in three contexts: in support of the Tibetan cause, against traditional Tibetan identity and/or the political strategy of the Tibetan Government in exile, and in response to pro-Chinese agendas. In application to a "Free Tibet!" agenda, liberal values may include a call for and justification of violence, as tibetanwarrior argues:

anyone who supports violence is looked down upon the rest of the people and the government in exile treats that person with contempt. well if that is not a dictator in action than what.think about it. tibetans need a new political system where monks and lamas are banned then only true democracy and development will be possible (*Ban Chris! Ban all opposition to the HH Dalai Lama*).

In a Chinese member's efforts at appeasement (*Misconception about the Chinese*), the member invokes a "right" to defend sovereignty. In response, a Tibetan member invokes self-determination: "Don't you think it makes more sense to have the 'Tibetan people' to choose rather than you, a Chinese, decide who they are" (*Misconception about the Chinese*). In attacking the views of a pro-Chinese member, another member raises the issue of human rights: "Our pro-Chinese contributor ... is unwilling and unable to address the fact that Tibetans are denied civil. political and reproductive rights under communist Chinese occupation" (*INDEPENDENT TIBET: REALITY OR FANTASY!*). And even when a desirable political agenda is invoked, if it is not consistent with liberal

values, sympathetic members may challenge the writer. When Tibetan
Liberation Front, referred to here as TLF, initiates a post called
DISSENT AND OPPOSITIONS CAN NOT BE TOLERATED!!!,
a member replies: "hey ... are we Tibetans becoming communist ...?
are we Tibetans under dictatorship of TLF? TLF seems to be like NAZI
... " Another member similarly accuses TLF of being a fascist.

Liberal values are applied not only to political agendas, but to the
Tibetan diaspora community itself. For example:

Tibetans have to learn to express their individuality. That is the essence of
a healthy democratic society and we should not be swayed by all the 'negative'
influences that come with it. Instead when people are allowed to express
themselves this allows for –strangely a better platform for dialogue and understanding. Sadly the Tibetan community has a huge gap within – intellectually.
A part remains in the medieval mindset and a part western educated and aware.
Then there are the in betweens who are torn between these seemingly opposing
groups choosing to take sides when convenient (*wasted opportunity,
ignorance*).

In another instance, a member writes from inside Tibet, pointing out
that while there are problems for Tibetans in Tibet due to Chinese
occupation, there are also problems within the Tibetan community.
This member addresses Tibetans outside of Tibet:

You are free to say anything, cause you live in a democratic society. While HHD
suggests the 'middle way,' or for an autonomy, not an independent, Tibet, some
of you say that He is compromise too much. Independency never drops from
heaven. Do you really have the courage to fight for it? (*A Voice From Inside
Tibet, Think about reality and dreams*).

The member goes on to remind the Tibetan diaspora of the discrimination within their own community against recent arrivals from
Tibet.

Serious questions, including those referenced above, are often
greeted with personal attacks, empty rhetoric, or no response at all.
The highly controversial suggestion that Tibetans might take up suicide bombing to promote their cause was largely ignored. The first
respondent returned to earlier questions and reminded the poster that
most of those participating on TibetBoard are teenagers (*What's there
in Future for Tibetans?*).

U.S. COPTS ASSOCIATION[8]

The U.S. Copts Association is a diaspora organization representing Copts, the native Egyptian Christians. It incorporates interactive use of information technology in the service of an overt political agenda. The case description draws on personal interviews with the founder and CEO of the U.S. Copts Association, Michael Meunier, and secondary reports and literature. I also examined the Association's use of information technology and resulting interactions among members of the Copt diaspora. I reviewed empirical data and observed its webpage, e-mail digest, and discussion boards, covering the three-month period, January 1–April 1, 2003.

Egypt is considered a semiauthoritarian regime. Internet usage remains low, estimated at 2.86% in 2002.[9] Online, Egyptian newspapers are much more forthcoming about human rights abuses than their hard-copy versions. Self-censorship is likely the modus operandi of many websites, due to highly visible arrests for posting material critical of the Government of Egypt (GOE) or morally provocative.[10] Copts comprise a majority of the approximately ten percent of Christians in Egypt. According to the U.S. Department of State (2002b), "for the most part, members of the non-Muslim minority worship without harassment." In its 2002 "International Religious Freedom Report," the U.S. State Department (2002a) reports that the GOE has continued a trend toward "improvement in the Government's respect for and protection of religious freedom." Nevertheless, the report also details specific exceptions to this trend.

An Ottoman decree from 1856, and the 1934 Interior Ministry regulations require non-Muslims to obtain presidential permission to build places of worship. In carrying out these functions, the government must rule on the location of the site and the composition of the

---

[8] Unless otherwise indicated, sources of information are from interviews with the founding President and CEO of U.S. Copts Association, Michael Meunier, November 25, 2002a, and December 17, 2002b. Portions of the case description draw from Brainard and Brinkerhoff (2006).

[9] This refers to an estimated 1.9 million users as of 2002 and a population of 66.4 million (International Telecommunication Union, World Telecommunication Development Report and database; cited in World Bank 2004).

[10] See, for example, Africast.com (2001) and Howeidy (2001); qtd. in Kalathil and Boas (2003).

community in which the site is to be located. The president must also approve permits for church repairs. As a result of a December 1999 decree, the permission process for church repairs has been facilitated. However, Copts claim that local permits from security authorities still must be obtained and the approval process continues to be time-consuming and inefficient. Finally, the U.S. State Department reports that government discriminatory practices continue, including discrimination in hiring, as does a lack of cooperation with Christian families seeking to regain custody of their daughters who are forced to convert to Islam by Muslim men (U.S. State Department 2002a).

It is not clear how representative the U.S. Copts Association is of the broader Copt diaspora. Some argue that its actions may have serious repercussions for Copts still residing in Egypt (Ibrahim 1998; Rowe 2001). In the Egyptian press, the U.S. Copts Association has been accused of being "a relatively small group of well-financed and politically connected Copts" who are hostile to Egypt (Elgindy 1999).

Michael Meunier founded the U.S. Copts Association in the mid-1990s; it was formally registered as a U.S. nonprofit organization in 1996. Meunier remains the organization's president. Its mission is to promote the "advancement of Copts inside and outside their homeland" (U.S. Copts Association 2003b). Meunier also initiated efforts to establish a Coptic Information Center to focus on building and organizing grassroots efforts aimed at protecting Coptic rights. Much of his personal energy is geared toward mobilizing the Copt diaspora in the United States. He regularly delivers speeches and raises money within the U.S. Copt community.

The U.S. Copts Association's antagonism toward the GOE is clearly demonstrated by the opening "Flash Intro" of its webpage (U.S. Copts Association 2003b). This introduction, accompanied by Coptic singing, opens with the phrase, "Egyptian authorities punish the Christian victims." Following is a list of allegations against Egyptian police and others, concerning incidents over the last twenty years of torture, murder, riots, and the burning of Copt villages. The appeal seeks to reach not only Copts and members of the Copt diaspora, but also the global Christian community. The Flash introduction ends with an appeal for Christians around the world to pray for religious freedom, human rights, and equality in Egypt. Furthermore, it implies a commitment to work on behalf of all Christians; its concluding phrase is "Copts.com Demanding equality for Christians in Egypt and around the world."

Specifically, the U.S. Copts Association has nineteen key demands connected to its pursuit of equality for all Egyptian Christians. These focus on the need to end discrimination against Copts, increase Copts' access to government services and roles in the government, and respect the basic human rights of all Copts. The Association demands that the government acknowledge and discontinue discrimination against Christians applying for jobs, requesting promotions, and enrolling in public schools. It insists on equal air time on government-controlled TV and radio stations, inclusion of Coptic history in school curricula, and fair representation in the Egyptian Parliament. Finally, the U.S. Copts Association seeks acknowledgment of Copts' basic human rights. It demands fair prosecution and compensation for crimes against Copts and seizure of Coptic land, and the basic freedom to choose and practice the religion of their choice.

According to its mission statement, acts of discrimination and atrocities targeted against the Copts "are perpetuated and perpetrated, intentionally or through denial and neglect, by the Egyptian government as well as some misguided and misinformed Muslim individuals" (U.S. Copts Association 2003b). Despite these allegations, the mission statement also confirms: "We firmly believe that what is good for the Copts is good for Egypt and what is good for Egypt is good for the Copts, as their past and future were and shall remain inseparable" (U.S. Copts Association 2003b).

Simultaneous to the establishment of the U.S. Copts Association, Meunier launched the website (www.copts.com) to distribute news and information. The website is publicly available and requires no registration. It offers a range of material benefits to members, including relevant "top stories" concerning discrimination, church, community, and more general news. It provides background information on the history of the Copts, their church, and ancient Egypt. There is also a substantial listing of Coptic martyrs, with some photographs and biographies. While martyrs are an important element of Coptic history and culture, emphasis is given to the modern martyrs. This includes a compiled list of anti-Copt atrocities from 1972–2000 (courtesy of the Ibn Khaldun Center for Development Studies, Cairo, Egypt). Press releases regarding the activities of the U.S. Copts

Association, as well as from other Coptic and human rights organizations, are included.

The site is also available in Arabic. According to Meunier (2002b), the site is "geared to educate the Copts in Egypt about their rights ... things they would never hear about in Egypt," including the atrocities committed against Copts in Egypt and efforts to prosecute the alleged perpetrators. The U.S. Copts Association relies on a range of communication technologies to educate Egyptian Copts, gather information, expose atrocities and discrimination as it occurs, and facilitate individual participation in the organization's goals. Meunier maintains a telephone network, and depends on local-level sharing of information. Some Egyptian villages, for example, may have only one computer, but the articles and information available on Copts.com are shared much more broadly through word of mouth and hard copy printouts. Meunier estimates that for every one to two computers, another thirty to forty people receive the distributed information. Meunier also relies on a network of people on the ground in Egypt to funnel out information and documentation (such as photos) of human rights abuses to the United States. This involvement of a substantial number of Egyptians "lends a credible air of authenticity" to the U.S. Copts Association's agenda (Rowe 2001, 91).

In March 1996, Meunier incorporated a set of interactive electronic components into the Association's efforts. These interactive components take two forms. One consists of a set of discussion boards, which are accessible on the website. To participate in the discussion boards, one must register (which is free of charge). Meunier intentionally developed the discussion boards to offer an opportunity to Copts residing in Egypt to "participate and communicate and feel part of a community" (Meunier 2002b). As a consequence, the content of the discussion boards is more cultural than political, ranging from science and technology issues to Coptic history, Egyptian studies, religion, and civil society. Meunier intended the boards to be as inclusive as possible and posters include people representing the grassroots as well as, for example, famous Egyptian poets (who include their poetry on the boards). Most of the discussions are in Arabic.

The second interactive component consists of a listserv, the "Copts Digest." As with the discussion boards, to participate (that is, to receive the Digest and contribute postings) one must register. Unlike the discussion boards, however, the Digest is distributed primarily to English speakers and so it is predominantly in English. According to Meunier (2002a), there are at least 10,000 recipients of the Digest, and among these are "a lot of influential people, so not only Egyptians, but also Egyptian officials, embassy, and media centers, and ministers of information." Topics addressed range from religion, to political action, to theological doctrine.

To participate, one agrees to adhere to certain etiquette rules, which obligate members to refrain from using, in Meunier's words, "foul language to describe other people or religion." Because of press censorship in Egypt, Meunier is very sensitive to maintaining members' ability to openly express their views in the Digest; every effort is made not to censor messages. Besides the etiquette rules, other rules require registered users to respect a diversity of viewpoints and an array of ideological positions. Beyond these rules, Meunier and his website moderators attempt to ensure that postings do not specifically target Egypt with hostile actions. Meunier and his moderators do not tolerate and, therefore, refrain from allowing, postings that contain a call to arms against Egypt. Meunier argues that he would not want to prompt a GOE backlash against Copts living in Egypt. This policy also buttresses his view that what is good for Egypt is good for Copts (and vice versa).

In some instances, Meunier will allow a posting to be distributed on the Digest but will weigh in with the position of the U.S. Copts Association relative to the post. One member suggested that Copts should be advocating for a separate state, a clearly inflammatory remark given the participation in the Digest of high level GOE officials. Vigorous debate ensued in which other members expressed disdain for the original post and hopes for a unified Egypt in which people of all religions could live in freedom. Meunier, in his role as president of the Association, also contributed to the debate, reminding everyone that "... our struggle for equality in Egypt is a peaceful one. We have never at any point encouraged or even entertained any separatists ideas or thoughts, since we believe Egypt is a blessed land for all Egyptians" (U.S. Copts Association 2003a). Meunier sees the Digest as a central forum for rich debate, but cognizant of the fact that Egyptian officials receive the Digest, also attempts to maintain both decorum and moderation.

The interactive components of Copts.com have become a central forum for debate and/or expression about human rights issues.

Discussions concerning the El-Kosheh massacre demonstrate. On December 31, 1999 an argument between a Coptic shopkeeper and a Muslim customer erupted in two days of violence in which 21 Copts were killed and 260 Coptic homes and businesses were destroyed. Members of the Copts Digest debated whether to wait for the Egyptian courts to process the case or whether to present the issue to the International Criminal Court (ICC) at The Hague. In December 2002, Meunier went to The Hague to gather information on how to proceed with a case. In February 2003, ninety-three of the ninety-six defendants were acquitted. By March 2003, the listerv was lighting up with members expressing horror at the acquittals and seeking directions from U.S. Copts Association on how they could take personal action on behalf of facilitating the presentation of the case to the ICC.

Beyond an exclusive Internet and e-mail presence, the Association operates a multifaceted communication network. In November 2002, Meunier received a Federal Express package from Egypt with pictures of a church whose renovation had been stopped by local Egyptian authorities. A family from the local village has a relative living in Belgium who, following a telephone conversation with them, posted information about the problem to the Digest and e-mailed Meunier the priest's telephone number. The priest gathered information regarding all of the paperwork, permits filed, and photographs and passed them to a Copt in Cairo, whom Meunier trusts, who then sent it to the U.S. Copts Association. Meunier subsequently arranged a meeting between the priest and the GOE, resulting in formal permission to resume the renovation.

The U.S. Copts Association also directs a lot of energy at the U.S. Congress, in an effort to influence diplomatic interventions to improve the plight of Copts in Egypt. In 1998 the Association lobbied Congress for a "Freedom of Religious Persecution Act," which called for trade sanctions against states violating religious freedom (Ibrahim 1998). According to Meunier (2002a), it was due to his efforts with members of Congress that President Mubarak was pressured to facilitate the permission process for church repairs, resulting in a 1999 decree. Meunier occasionally testifies before Congress and has been asked to hold joint press conferences with members of Congress. Meunier, representing U.S. Copts Association, also participated in strategy sessions with President George W. Bush regarding the case of Dr. Saad Eddin

Ibrahim, head of the Ibn Khaldun Center for Development Studies. Ibrahim had been imprisoned in Egypt on alleged corruption charges. His case sparked an international advocacy effort, which argued that he was being harassed due to his work on human rights.[11] In this session, Meunier strongly advocated for the $150 million cut in U.S. foreign aid to Egypt that was offered as an incentive to release Ibrahim. In May 2003, Meunier made an intervention to the United Nations Human Rights Commission.

DIASPORA POLITICAL AGENDAS, HUMAN RIGHTS, AND IT

TibetBoard and the U.S. Copts Association both play important roles in shaping members' beliefs, perceptions of reality and self-perceptions, and ideas. Members embrace this function by explicitly asking others to discuss perceptions and potential political agendas, sometimes sincerely posing questions rather than proclaiming agendas. Meunier's explicit aim for the Arabic portions of his site are to "educate" Copts residing in Egypt, shaping ideas and perceptions that may lead to political participation. Both cases also concern the political debates, agendas, and influence of marginalized groups who, without access to information technology might not otherwise have the opportunity to explore and enact political agendas. While TibetBoard and its political consciousness are primarily enacted through debate in cyberspace, it may very well shape ideas that can influence future action in the real world. Some of that action may take place through the activities and events advertised on TibetBoard. U.S. Copts Association more explicitly pursues an action agenda; limited evidence is available to support its results.

That both diasporas and the communities they've created expect respect for human rights is clear. At TibetBoard, Tibetans argue for self-determination (*Misconception about the Chinese*) and use accusations regarding the violation of human rights in Tibet by the Chinese as a rationale for their fight for freedom (*INDEPENDENT TIBET: REALITY OR FANTASY!*). Ironically, democratic values are applied

---

[11] The Ibn Khaldun Center for Development Studies focuses on human rights in Egypt generally but, as a consequence, publishes reports that are specific to the Egyptian Copts. In December 2002, a retrial was ordered and Dr. Ibrahim was released; he was acquitted of all charges in March 2003.

even to question the disallowing of considering a violent alternative (*Ban Chris! Ban all opposition to the HH Dalai Lama*). On their part, pro-Chinese members similarly invoke expectations rooted in liberal values. A Chinese member extends an olive branch, yet asserts that if Tibetans insist on independence, the Chinese will have the "right" to defend their sovereignty (*Misconception about the Chinese*). And an older Chinese member explains to a younger one that he shouldn't encourage Tibetans to leave Tibet, else the Chinese presence in Tibet might be viewed as illegal in the international arena (*If I'm Chinese President...*). Tibetans also apply liberal values to their own community. Some members argue for tolerance for dissent generally, both with respect to political agendas (*DISSENT AND OPPOSITIONS CAN NOT BE TOLERATED!!!*) and regarding relations within the Tibetan diaspora between more traditional members and modernizing ones (*wasted opportunity, ignorance*). Equality and an end to discrimination are also called for with respect to newcomers in the diaspora (*A Voice From Inside Tibet, Think about reality and dreams*).

The U.S. Copts Association is obviously explicit in its expectation of human rights. It seeks their enforcement through behind the scenes maneuvering in Egypt, more publicly in the international arena by seeking redress in the International Criminal Court, and with Meunier's testimonies to the U.S. Congress and the UN Human Rights Commission. Among the U.S. Copts Association's nineteen demands are the acknowledgement of Copts' basic human rights, including freedom of religion. The Association itself seeks to embody liberal values in its practice and to promote them among its membership. Freedom of expression is highly prized despite some content rules for the E-mail digest and discussion forums. Members are entreated to respect a diversity of viewpoints and ideological positions. Through outreach to Copts residing in Egypt, the Association also promotes these values. Its "education" agenda implicitly aims to politicize these members by informing them of their rights and of instances of abuse.

As for information technology, it is clear in both cases that IT has shaped, reinforced, and extended the networks of the two diasporas and other interested parties. TibetBoard brings together those who are interested in questioning and debating official Tibetan Government in exile policy and traditional values, but who might otherwise not have an opportunity to learn of each other and express these ideas. Within the Tibetan diaspora there are those who are more religious in their Buddhist practice and those who are relatively more secular. Tibet-Board links these individuals and perspectives. It also assembles Tibetan and Chinese advocates who might otherwise have no occasion to meet or at least to engage in debate without immediate physical world implications. Membership includes non-Tibetans and interested Westerners. While the membership may be primarily of teen age, as implied by some of the posts, there is inter-generational dialogue on occasion. A final, perhaps less expected example of an extended network, which also challenges the assumption of a universal digital divide, is the participation of a Tibetan claiming to reside in Tibet. He also invokes liberal values when he highlights the diaspora's access to freedom of speech and questions whether or not the members are using it to fight for Tibetan independence (*A Voice From Inside Tibet, Think about reality and dreams*).

The U.S. Copts Association more actively shapes, reinforces, and extends networks of communication. The Flash Intro of its webpage seeks to engage Christians beyond the Coptic community "in Egypt and around the World." Its cyberpresence, email digest, and physical world activities seek to link: Egyptian Copts with the diaspora; social classes within the Copt community; and diaspora members across countries of residence. By engaging a network of varied communication technologies, the Association further connects individuals who would otherwise always remain on the periphery of these discussions, debates, and actions, challenging the notion of a simplistic and universal digital divide.

Digital diasporas' political influence and engagement has potential significance, as it shapes ideas and agendas, raises political consciousness, and provides forums and links for dispersed and heterogeneous communities. Created communities debate different perspectives, boldly challenge accepted wisdom, and potentially consider action in the real world. The political consciousness and specific agendas emerging from this deliberation may be enacted in the physical world, either through individuals' participation in other organizations and networks, and/or through the bricks-and-mortar components of the organization. By encompassing and promoting liberal values, and by seeking political inclusion, digital diasporas may broaden perceptions of the legitimacy of their causes both within and outside of their respective communities.

Do the Copt and the Tibetan diaspora potentially threaten the state sovereignty of their homelands? The U.S. Copts Association, for all its advocacy, explicitly frames debate and agendas so as not to promote a separate state or violence against the GOE. It holds the GOE accountable for its own laws and does so under the radar screen, allowing GOE to save face in terms of domestic and international legitimacy. In the case of the violated Church repair regulations, the U.S. Copts Association exposed the GOE's limited capacity to enforce its rule of law locally. By intervening, the U.S. Copts Association supported the GOE's effectiveness and hence its domestic sovereignty.

While most Tibetans seek a separate sovereign state, TibetBoard demonstrates disagreement regarding whether it is possible and by what means to pursue this agenda. Members of TibetBoard seem to question the sovereignty of the Tibetan Government in exile – challenging the sometimes assumed effectiveness of the traditional rule of Tibet both historically and in exile, and questioning its methods. It seems the majority of TibetBoard members are teenagers. Despite the imagined violent confrontation and eventual autonomous Tibet, as a collective, they do not appear to be mobilizing for political purposes; they are exploring and imagining other possibilities, as they freely express themselves. At least one member directly acknowledges this: "i have no intentions of killing anyone.. its a bunch of talk and nothing more" (*If I'm Chinese President* ...). On the other hand, the inclusive deliberation and the sustenance of a Tibetan identity, albeit a hybrid one, may provide the basis needed to support the Tibetan Government in exile in the long run.

7

Helping the Homeland

Chapter 6 examined digital diasporas' political engagement, regardless of whether it becomes mobilized in the physical world. This chapter more explicitly analyzes identity mobilization, in this case, for contributing to socioeconomic development in the homeland. I investigate several examples, beginning with a CGO, Rebuild-Afghanistan. Moving beyond cyberspace, I then describe three physical world organizations whose mission it is, at least in part, to serve the homeland. These are two diaspora philanthropy organizations with different degrees of professionalism – Afghans4Tomorrow and Coptic Orphans, and one transnational business, Thamel.com, which was introduced in Chapter 3. I first review how identity is mobilized for purposive goals.

HOW IS IDENTITY MOBILIZED?

Three types of factors inform diasporas' mobilization to influence the homeland, those related to: their ability, the enabling environment, and their motivation (see Esman 1986). IT can contribute to each of these.

Ability to Mobilize

The most commonly identified factor necessary for effective mobilization is the creation of a sense of solidarity and community identity: "When colleagues see the world together, they are likely to share the same

understanding of the world. This makes collective action possible"
(Navarro 2003, 138).[1] A dense network of relationships, or bonding
social capital, can engender trust (Coleman 1988, 1990) and generate
the shared identity required for collective action (Ostrom 1990).
Furthermore, with more intense interaction, participation in collective action is more likely (Dutton and Lin 2001).

Community identity enables the harnessing of diverse resources
and capacities. These include material resources, skills, and organizational resources. To effectively mobilize, diasporans must possess
capabilities (personal and interpersonal skills and experience) and
confidence. Diasporans' specific skills and capacities (whether as individuals or associations) inform both the mobilization process and the
nature and impact of their contributions to the homeland. Bringing
these material resources, skills, and capacities together requires an
organizational or networking base (see Klandermans and Oegema
1987), which enables diasporans to contribute their sometimes
unique perspectives, skills, and resources to the collective effort.
A networking base also affords diasporans opportunities to reach
beyond their own capacities to pursue heterogeneous networks,
where individual actors act as bridges between diffuse sources of
information and resources (Burt 2000).

Enabling Environment/Opportunity Structures

Opportunity structures must be available for diasporans to mobilize
for particular agendas (Esman 1986). These opportunities may be
present, or not, in the host society, homeland, and/or internationally.
They may include: availability of economic opportunities; at least
neutral regulation of diaspora activities generally and with respect to
specific agendas; access to necessary infrastructures (political, technical, informational/communication); host-country government proactive support of the diaspora through targeted service provision for
integration, and potential reliance on the diaspora for input and action
in support of its foreign policy vis-à-vis the homeland; a home-country
government that is neutral or actively solicits diaspora participation

---

[1] See Pratkanis and Turner (1996); for diaspora-specific discussions see King and Melvin
(1999/2000), and Shain (1999).

and contributions; and private sector actors who recognize the market diasporas represent for both home- and host-country business opportunities.

Opportunity structures are highly dependent on diasporans' access to power resources. There are five types of relevant power resources: economic, social (social status based on social roles or on complying with socially valued criteria), political (ability to influence the exercise of authority), informational, and moral (i.e., the perceived legitimacy of decision makers) (Uphoff 1989, 2005).[2] Related questions for assessing an enabling environment for diaspora contributions include:

- Does the regulatory environment support economic opportunities?
- Can diasporans access positions of authority and respect within society, both for influence and for obtaining these positions for themselves?
- Can they access and influence decision makers?
- Can they access the information necessary or supportive of their effectiveness for a particular agenda?
- Is their cause perceived to be legitimate?

Opportunity structures available in the home or host country can be complex. Home-country governments may at once solicit diaspora participation and/or contributions and provide disincentives (such as taxation or excessive regulation) or interfere in their application. In the host country, diasporans may experience xenophobia and reprisals against diaspora identity expression in the same countries where they experience facilitated networking through accessible telecommunications technology (Butler 2001).

Motivation to Act

Diaspora groups and individuals may be more or less inclined to concern themselves with quality of life and policies vis-à-vis their home countries. Much will depend on "their inclination or motivation to maintain their solidarity and exert group influence" (Esman 1986, 336).

---

[2] While Uphoff (1989, 2005) includes physical power (i.e., coercion or violence, depending on perceived legitimacy of applied physical force), this chapter focuses on development contributions, which do not include the use of force, legitimate or not.

This is largely dependent on integration processes and members' implicit assessment of the relative benefits of identity options. The higher the cost to status and security in their adopted country, the greater the likelihood that the diaspora community will split and/or fail to mobilize (Esman 1986).

Diaspora communities mobilize, in part to express their identities, and these identities can be reinforced through activity on behalf of the homeland or in support of quality of life in the host society. For some, expressing the homeland identity is a means for creating a sense of belonging. Diasporans also express their identity through adherence to cultural obligations and expected behavior vis-à-vis both the homeland and the host society. These obligations and norms are primarily rooted in family relations and responsibilities, and they may be modified through the identity negotiation process and the context in which that occurs. The felt need to actively express identity may derive from various forms of marginalization (social, economic, political, or psychic), confusion and a sense that the homeland identity will be lost without proactive expression (e.g., when overwhelmed by pluralism), or simply in response to social reinforcement and perhaps pride.[3] For many, mobilization becomes an expression of a hybrid identity, which may encompass liberal values. Ideally, pride in hybrid identity gives rise to an embrace of basic freedoms and rights and psychological empowerment, reflecting a belief that these diasporans can effectively work to advance, protect, and embody these rights for themselves and potentially for the homeland.

Homeland crisis may awaken a homeland identity and motivation to mobilize in support of the homeland, whether among older diasporans who have long since integrated into the host society, or among youth who may have never seen the homeland first-hand. For example, a Pakistani diaspora organization (DO) in Britain raised $25 million for relief in the aftermath of the 2005 Kashmir earthquake (Özerdem 2006). The end of the Taliban regime in Afghanistan spawned the creation of new DOs to support its reconstruction (Kerlin 2008), and

[3] Whether intentional or not, religious diaspora groups who pursue purposive objectives concerning quality of life in host and home territories are likely to experience a deepening of their traditional faith and culture. Haynes (1997) argues that secularization occurs, "*except when religion finds or retains work to do other than relating people to the supernatural*" (emphasis in the original) (713).

mobilized many second generation Afghan Americans for the first time (Brinkerhoff 2004). Homeland tragedy may also become the basis of the diaspora's very identity, as in the case of Armenia (see, for example, Shain and Barth 2003).

Process factors also influence diasporans' incentives to mobilize. Some coordination and consensus on the direction of collective energy, including what is acceptable and what is not, is necessary (Snow et al. 1986). Organizations and their members frame issues in order to develop the consensus sufficient for collective action. This framing includes shaping perceptions of the problem/challenge, the most appropriate means to tackle that challenge, and the group's ability to do so, including the opportunity structures available and confidence that it can be done. The latter requires a sense of efficacy and subsequent impact, which can sustain the mobilization beyond one-time efforts.[4] Inspiring confidence in the group's ability to enact change is achieved, in part, by referring to past as well as future successes.

To be motivated a diasporan must also feel psychologically empowered. Related individual traits and organizational capabilities, include (Uphoff 2005): confidence, the capacity to aspire (Appadurai 2004), and energy and persistence. These, in turn, require objective resources (including the necessary competence), positive emotions, and feelings of self-efficacy. Psychological empowerment is closely related to subjective well-being, or "people's positive evaluations of their lives, including pleasant emotions, fulfillment, and life satisfaction" (Diener and Biswas-Diener 2005, 125; see also Diener 1984); an important component is a sense of meaning and purpose. Positive emotions contribute to feelings of sociability, self-confidence, energy, engaged activity, altruism, and creativity; and people prefer these to be based on valuable experiences, rather than produced artificially (Diener and Biswas-Diener 2005).

Individuals and groups are unlikely to pursue their goals without optimistic expectancy that they will achieve them (see Bandura 1997). Success leads to positive emotions, which is likely to yield continued energy and action. Empowered feelings and successful action tend to form a self-reinforcing loop. The opposite is also true: repeated failures and resulting negative emotions can lead to

---

[4] See Hinkle et al. (1996); Kelly and Kelly (1994); Klandermans (1997).

depression, resignation, and a sense of helplessness (Diener and Biswas-Diener 2005).

Group norms may influence individuals' perceptions of and responses to initial conditions, including beliefs of self-efficacy vis-à-vis an individual's context. Diaspora origin may inform diasporans' motivation and sense of potential efficacy, that is, their perceived ability to integrate in the host country and/or influence the home country. Context includes the diaspora community and its framing, the diaspora origin, and the host society. Context will determine available experiences, which may yield perceived successes or failures, and result in varying degrees of psychological empowerment.

IT and Mobilization

How does IT enhance mobilization for purposive benefits oriented to the physical world? IT facilitates mobilization through the organizational and networking resources it represents (i.e., bridging social capital, among other things), as well as the forum it provides for solidarity and collective identity, which results in valuable experiences that produce positive emotions, contributing to psychological empowerment. IT also facilitates access to other economic, political, and informational resources; enables efficient and sometimes enforceable issue framing within groups; and assists in cultivating a sense of efficacy through information dissemination about progress and success in achieving collective objectives.

The Internet offers hard to reach populations access to information beyond their particular location and enables these populations to "bring those resources to bear on real and immediate problems" (Mele 1999, 305). As noted in Chapter 6, it may be particularly important for small, marginalized groups, facilitating their networking and the promotion of their political agendas. And the Internet reconfigures networks of communication, reinforcing and extending them, and influencing communication patterns and information access (see, for example, Dutton and Lin 2001). The Internet can link dispersed individuals to decision making arenas, enabling them to make claims and represent a broader, albeit dispersed community. It can be used to report on progress and success, inspiring sustained effort and calling others to action. In short, the Internet provides an organizational and networking base, facilitates information dissemination related to generating a sense of efficacy and impact, and links both like-minded and diverse diasporans, forming an intense but heterogeneous network of social capital.

As we have seen in other chapters, CGOs provide forums for members to discuss and debate purposive goals, but these communities may or may not mobilize to enact them. Mobilization may occur among individuals and subgroups of these communities and not necessarily be discussed in the context of the broader cybercommunity. Such organizations may post links to other sites with purposive objectives vis-à-vis the homeland and provide forums for discussing action agendas and sharing information in support of the homeland (for example, AfghanistanOnline and Somalinet). Some digital diaspora organizations may be created with the sole intention of fostering purposive objectives vis-à-vis the home country. Like all organizations, their effectiveness in doing so varies. Rebuild Afghanistan, Afghans4Tomorrow, Coptic Orphans, and Thamel.com illustrate.

REBUILD AFGHANISTAN[5]

Abdul Meraj started Rebuild-Afghanistan (www.rebuild-afghanistan.com) in the aftermath of September 11, 2001. The site's mission was to "serve as a virtual place and point of contact among all who are willing to participate in rebuilding of Afghanistan." Rebuild-Afghanistan (RA) provided "a neutral, non-political medium" for Afghan and non-Afghan professionals alike. Working with a committee, Meraj conceptualized what RA would be and then worked primarily with one other partner to manage the site and provide content. Meraj was born in Afghanistan and stressed that his motivation was not political, but rather to feel better about the tragedies in Afghanistan by trying to help in any way he could.

In its first two months, RA received an average of 37,766 hits per month, reflecting the intense interest in rebuilding Afghanistan after September 11, 2001. From August–November 2002, the average hits numbered 16,159. Because of its explicit focus on rebuilding

[5] This case description builds from Brainard and Brinkerhoff (2004). The discussion draws from Meraj (2002, 2003). The empirical data for Rebuild Afghanistan cover the life of the organization up to September 12, 2003.

Afghanistan, Meraj was asked to be listed as a "cooperating organi-zation" on the Development Gateway Foundation's webpage on Afghanistan Reconstruction (www.developmentgateway.org). RA provided audio and print news, and information and advertisement regarding specific programs, such as: organized tours for Afghan professionals returning home, how to donate books to Kabul University, how to send other goods to Afghanistan, learning to speak Dari or Pashto, and how to build earthquake resistant shelters. Links on the homepage included: the Afghan Assistance Coordination Agency, a statutory body of the Afghan Interim Administration, responsible for coordinating external assistance to Afghanistan; Afghana, an Afghan web directory, which in turn maintained a links page specific to organizations active in Afghanistan reconstruction; and Afghans4-Tomorrow (described below).

A prominent feature on the home page was a job and resume database. Meraj believes this was a primary reason the Development Gateway contacted him. However, other than this link there was no further contact from the Development Gateway and no exchange of information regarding jobs and job seekers. The database was not very active. At the time of investigation, there were no jobs posted, and only eighty-nine resumes were posted in the areas of health (six); engineering (twenty five); oil and gas exploration (one); mining (one); education (two); finance, economics, and banking (ten); computer science (twenty six); agriculture (one); communications (nine); and sales and marketing (eight).

RA's homepage also provided an opportunity for discussion. Meraj created and structured the original discussion topics. All of the threads pertained to specific challenges related to rebuilding Afghanistan: education, health care, the economy, and government reform. Also included were pages for engineers on reconstruction, important news, and computer donations. Additional threads encouraged visitors to send letters to Afghans, including to leaders and, through the "Kids Corner," to children (the Kids Corner included children's posts of pictures and fables they had created). Contributors did not have the ability to modify these topics or add new threads. Once members posted, their e-mail addresses became publicly available. RA may have provided a networking opportunity among members, who then inter-acted outside of the discussion boards.

Individuals primarily used these discussion forums to post announcements. However, a few threads were relatively more active. Under "Afghanistan Education Reform," a thread on "basic school supplies" began December 27, 2001 and ended October 1, 2002. It mostly concerned people wanting to help and not knowing where/how to send supplies or adopt a school in Afghanistan. In January 2002, one person wrote about having $4,000 worth of picture books translated into Farsi and not knowing where to send them. In July 2002, a member of the Afghan diaspora responded stating that these books could assist in a project he had in Afghanistan. The last post was in October 2002 and identified two website links to NGOs that accepted books and donations for schools in Afghanistan. One of these, the Academy for Educational Development, is a frequent contractor for the U.S. Agency for International Development.[6] Many participants appeared to be teachers and not necessarily diasporans. Others identified themselves as members of the Afghan diaspora either directly, or their identity could be deduced from their name, reference to having lived in Afghanistan, and/or language. A broader, though similar, discussion appeared under the thread "Education Assistance." Here, the cochair of a project of a local UN Association shared that the U.S. Air Force would fly books into Bagram Air Force base in Afghanistan. Under "Job Openings" an official from the International Organization for Migration advertised its "Return of Qualified Afghans Programme" and indicated where individuals could apply.

An additional, less structured discussion page, afforded members the opportunity to express "Opinions, Thoughts, Questions, Even Jokes"; share "Stories from inside Afghanistan"; and discuss rebuilding Afghanistan, how one might help in the rebuilding effort, and travel to Afghanistan. Members could add new threads, but their e-mail addresses were not publicly available.[7] Many of the threads were posts of articles or previously published commentaries on subjects relevant to rebuilding Afghanistan. However, a few posts were more personal and purposively directed to support the rebuilding

---

[6] This particular project was supported by a consortium of educational and Afghan-related NGOs and professional associations.
[7] Meraj adopted a newer technology in 2003 that hid e-mail addresses to prevent their use in spamming (Meraj 2003).

effort. For example, *Volunteering* (May 11, 2003) included the following offer:

> I would like to volunteer my services in two ways:
>
> 1. to help new Afghans settle in the Toronto and Durham area
> 2. go back to Kabul for two weeks this summer/fall as a volunteer aid worker. I have medical and dental experience as well as a good knowledge of the city, having lived there for 6 months in 1973.

Another thread, titled *Deforestation* (June 9, 2003), offered:

> I was interested in starting a non-profit organization to raise money or 'tree' donations for reforestation. I could work at this end but would need local conservationists in Afganistan to forge an agreement with me to facilitate and network those resources in a highly effective way. Any thoughts about such an endeavor?

Most of the posts, including these, received no response. The website ceased to exist some time in 2004.

AFGHANS4TOMORROW: A COMMUNITY OF ACTION[8]

Afghans4Tomorrow (A4T) was established in 1999 and formally registered as a 501(c)3 in 2001. It is a "non-political organization dedicated to the reconstruction and development of Afghanistan ... [that] provides essential services to its people through the expertise, knowledge and dedication of Young Afghan Professionals abroad." Its vision and connection to an Afghan community of identity is affirmed on its website (www.afghans4tomorrow.com):

> We have committed ourselves to this organization, more importantly we have committed ourselves to each other. Brothers and sisters with one goal, with one vision. Making a difference in the lives of every Afghan is our goal and mission.

---

[8] The description draws from Brinkerhoff (2004) and takes data from our personal interview with Mayel and Associates (2003) and other organization reports. Descriptions from these sources were updated in 2006 based on available information posted to the webpage.

Its logo – found on its reports and t-shirts that are prominently worn in all their project photographs – underscores its perspective on service and principles of operation. Accompanying the organization's name and a bicolored whoosh are the words: moral obligation, knowledge, expertise, strategy, vision, and trust.

A4T has become a vehicle for members of the Afghan-American diaspora to take leave and vacation time from their jobs in order to go to Afghanistan and make contributions of time, energy, and expertise to the rebuilding effort. Its welcome message clearly targets the Afghan diaspora:

It is time for Afghan Professionals from around the world to **mobilize** and help in the reconstruction effort. . . . Find out what we have been doing, how you can **do your part**, and how **together** we can **rebuild** the foundation of our great past [emphasis in the original].

This mission is not just about serving the needs of Afghanistan, but also assisting diasporans who want to participate in some way. According to the acting President and Director of Public Relations,

Afghans in general are very dedicated people. They have lived their lives thinking back about Afghanistan. They want to give whatever they can; it's just a matter of strategizing them. There are a lot of projects of development agencies that need Afghans to go back; some of them are rigid in their requirements. . . . That's not always realistic for Afghan-Americans. We try to put those two together and help as many people as possible go back (Mayel et al. 2003).

In 2003, approximately thirty volunteers occupied formal roles in the organization, with additional periodic and informal volunteer support from other members of the Afghan-American diaspora. Each formal volunteer commits at least ten hours per week to the work of the organization, with significantly more as needed, during more intensive project implementation. This is especially true when members travel to Afghanistan (using vacation time from their jobs) to do needs assessments and project implementation. As the number and range of projects has increased, the volunteer staff residing in Afghanistan has also increased. As of 2003, approximately half of the volunteers were living in Afghanistan, as well as the president of A4T. Some of the staff in Afghanistan formally work for other organizations focused on the rebuilding efforts and volunteer for A4T on the side. Staff members are frequently asked to speak at a variety of events related to rebuilding Afghanistan and at conferences and events of their own making. They use these opportunities to solicit and recruit additional volunteers and staff.

While it is a purely voluntary organization, whose expenses are supported through staff donations, A4T is a structured nonprofit with a board of directors, officers, and department (program area) directors. In 2003, departments included agriculture, commerce, education, energy, health and human services, housing and urban development, land management, transportation, finance, and treasury. A4T seeks affiliate organizations for each of its departments, "in order to build strong networks for the betterment of the Afghan people," and to ensure access to requisite expertise. Listed affiliates include the American Society of Afghan Professionals, Engineers without Borders International, and the nonprofit Humanity in Crisis. A Project Methodology section of its webpage includes a project description template and a statement on "Participatory Project Planning." The latter credits A4T's participatory and inclusive approach for its successes. It uses a school building project as an example, where the idea came from the community, and the entire community was convened for its input and participation.

Among its early projects in Afghanistan, A4T implemented: Seeds for Afghanistan (which continues to operate as a separate NGO in cooperation with A4T), Ministry of Finance (MOF) training and staffing support, and support to schools. The Seeds project solicits seed donations from the webpage and other public outlets.[9] From October 2001–March 2003, Seeds for Afghanistan distributed 200,000 packs of vegetable and flower seeds (Heath and Shapiro 2003). A4T delivers these seeds to farmers and widows in Afghanistan. The Seeds program partners with PARSA (Physiotherapy and Rehabilitation Support for Afghanistan), a Kabul-based NGO that helps widows and orphans through income-generating projects. The program provides cucumber, tomato, beans, broccoli, lettuce, and medicinal herb seeds for widows' gardens. The program director also delivers planting training.

---

[9] Donors are instructed to donate seeds that would grow in the same climate as Colorado, where the donation site and program director are based.

In the early years of the Karzai Government, staff of A4T worked directly with the Ministry of Finance (MOF) to provide training in Microsoft Office software, and assisted a USAID contractor in staffing the MOF with qualified diasporans. Once on the ground in Afghanistan, A4T asked those it recruited to the MOF to volunteer for local A4T projects. A4T also provided basic school supplies, books, and teacher salaries, sometimes adopting selected schools. It solicited donations for its school programs on its webpage. In these early years, A4T partnered with the NGO Global Exchange, who provided support for shipping and distribution, as well as donations to support requests for specific supplies and equipment for A4T-supported schools.

The organization has grown in its sophistication and strategic focus. In 2005, the webpage announced that some departments were no longer active, leaving agriculture, education, and health and human services as the only operational project areas. Also in 2005, it completed four major projects: two school projects, one in Kabul, the other in the Wardak Province; a water improvement project; and the first greenhouse in Farza (A4T 2005). It also completed the construction of a medical clinic in Wardak that was scheduled to open in early 2006. A4T now operates a guesthouse in Kabul that can accommodate up to fifteen guests, and continues to organize and host delegations of Afghan Americans who come to learn and serve. A4T partners with other organizations, responds to local needs, and introduces innovative technology. For example, the German company DISCOBED provided twenty water cones (filters) for A4T's schools. With these solar energy devices, water is distilled, reducing gastrointestinal diseases (A4T 2005). A4T worked in partnership with Engineers Without Borders International (EWB-I) to conceptualize and execute a water improvement project in the village of Bustan.

In building schools, A4T employs its participatory methodology and seeks to introduce new technologies, as appropriate. It initiated this approach at the start of its school building efforts. For example, the Education Director's March/April 2003 report recounts a visit to a village in Farza, where an international development NGO contracted an Afghan construction company to build a new school. According to the report:

The school resembled a prison, cold, without chairs and tables, and roofs that within just a few months of construction were already leaking mud and water. As a result the whole school was dangerously humid, and teachers and students complained about back pain and lack of light (Omar 2003).

During the same visit to Afghanistan, the A4T team visited a leading USAID contractor in Afghanistan to demonstrate new roofing technology, courtesy of its partner, Engineers Without Borders International. According to the report, the contract for building 100 new schools had already been sub-let to "well-known NGOs" with a plan to replicate the school in Farza. This portion of the report concludes, "The idea of the new roofing technology impressed every one but bureaucracy and planning will not give it a chance. Our own project will be a unique engineering design using local labor and local materials" (Omar 2003).

A4T works closely with the Ministry of Education, whose protocol officially recognizes A4T schools. High-level ministry officials participate in the school openings. The ministry asked A4T to help establish The Afghan Academy, a network of twenty small regional campuses to provide remedial education to those who have not had education access for some years (A4T 2005). A4T already operates two vocational and training centers in Kabul.

A4T is primarily engaged in the physical world; its staff views its cyberpresence as essential to their organizational effectiveness. First, it is a primary mechanism for linking members of the Afghan diaspora to information and opportunities regarding Afghanistan reconstruction. Second, it is the most cost-effective means for disseminating information about A4Ts work, recruiting volunteers, and soliciting donations. A4T places a high priority on transparency and trust building within its extended community. It uses the website to communicate as much as possible about each project. According to the acting president and public relations director, the website is "the voice of our organization. It's our trust. It's everything ... because the work we do is read about through the website" (Mayel et al. 2003).

On its webpage A4T provides relevant links for most of its departments, all of which concern information about reconstruction and development in that sector.[10] Many of these are links to formal donor,

---

[10] The link analysis was conducted in 2003.

government, nongovernment, and private sector development actors. Donor links include various agencies of the United Nations, World Bank, and the Asian Development Bank. It also posts links to U.S. agencies, including Commerce, International Development, and Agriculture. Among the nonprofit links are: Future Harvest, International Committee of the Red Cross, National Peace Corps Association, and Save the Children. A separate links page lists the Afghanistan Directory of Expertise, an initiative of the Development Gateway that was assembled by an A4T staff member as part of her job at the World Bank; Federal Funding Opportunities; and an Afghan foundation for children and youth. The main page provides "quick links" to recent reports on Afghanistan, and a link to Afghanistan's Official Donor Assistance Database, administered by the United Nations Development Programme.

COPTIC ORPHANS [11]

During a two-year tour of duty to Egypt with the U.S. State Department, Nermien Riad, an engineer by training, visited a Coptic orphanage in Cairo. She was moved by the children's predicament and when she lamented it, the sister replied, "Why do you say 'Poor things'? You should see their families!" Riad then learned that the orphanage was filled with children who were not orphans but whose families could not afford to feed them. The sister took her to visit one such family so she could see directly their poverty and dismal quality of life. Riad was moved to provide a small donation – the equivalent at the time of U.S. $10.

This set the stage for what giving and service mean to Riad and laid the foundation for the creation of Coptic Orphans, her life's work. Today, Coptic Orphans (CO) implements four programs in Egypt: child

---

[11] Data is drawn from the Coptic Orphans webpage, annual reports, and interviews. A field visit to the Cairo office and the Valuable Girl Project in Cairo in January 2004 afforded an opportunity to meet with some of the Egyptian staff. Interviews include then Egypt Director, Wafaa Sorial, as well as the Virginia-based Executive Director, Nermien Riad, and the International Program Director, Phoebe Farag. Unless otherwise stated, the source of information is from the latter two personal interviews (January 21, 2004).

assistance (the Not Alone program), the Valuable Girl Project, Serve to Learn, and 1001 Tales.

The Programs of Coptic Orphans

CO's primary activity is child assistance, through the Not Alone program. Of its four programs, Not Alone covers the largest numbers and geographic area in Egypt. The program begins with a request to a church to nominate a representative to serve the children within the geographic scope of the congregation. The volunteer representatives (or reps) must be educated (college degree preferred) and become responsible for identifying needy children who have lost one or both parents. CO trains reps to be child advocates who visit each child on a weekly basis. Through child sponsorship the children receive school assistance, food, and other necessities, approximately $12 per month per child. Reps provide mentoring to ensure literacy and general development, including hygiene training. One emphasis is cleanliness. Under threat of losing the assistance, households are encouraged to keep their homes clean, regardless of their level of poverty: "Being clean takes you a little bit away from poverty I think. It's like a step above your current class situation" (Farag 2004).

The mentorship reaches beyond the children to the families as a whole. Surviving parents and guardians are encouraged to comply with the requirements of the program in order to maintain the assistance; over time they come to change their priorities about what is important, valuing literacy, for example. As Riad (2004) reports, "The mothers know our policy more than the reps. If the kid doesn't know how to read, they're not going to get any more assistance. ... When we go and visit the children, the mother would say, 'Come, my son is reading! Come see!'" Riad credits this as CO's biggest impact: "Our ability to change people's thinking. ... Poor or not poor, this is what matters most. Not that we bought them food or we got them clothes – big deal, they're still illiterate. [Our impact is] to be able to change their minds and their thinking and then to make that come out in changes in the children."

CO is establishing partnerships with other Egyptian NGOs in order to identify additional needy children, recruit volunteers, and reach into new geographic areas in Upper Egypt. However, it will not extend child assistance to Muslim children. As a Christian organization, it works with Christian volunteers, as Riad explains:

For a Christian to be entering the home of a Muslim on a consistent basis, we fear that it might be viewed as apostasy, or trying to covert, which is punishable by death according to Shaaria Law. . . . We figure the only time that we would be able to assist Muslim children is when we say, 'This is the program we have. You come to us.'

The Valuable Girl Project is the brainchild of Phoebe Farag. She launched the program with CO while she was pursuing her MA in International Education. It began with a pilot in Upper Egypt, was extended to Cairo, and as of 2005 the program was serving 500 girls in twelve different sites in Egypt. The program is modeled after the big sister concept, pairing older girls with younger girls who receive academic support and benefit from having a role model. Big sisters receive a small stipend that they can use at their discretion, though it is often applied to their own school fees (Sorial 2004). The Valuable Girl Project is the only one of CO's programs that has received external government grant support, in this case from the U.S. Embassy in Cairo (in both 2003 and 2004).[12]

In its expansion to Cairo, the Valuable Girl Project took on an added dimension. The Cairo suburb that The Valuable Girl Project serves was selected based on poverty levels and Coptic residents, at the suggestion of the local Coptic Church. Residents are a mix of Copt and Muslim families, who suffer from similar challenges of poverty and illiteracy. When the Valuable Girl Project was announced, it so happened that a roughly equal number of Muslim and Christian girls requested to participate. The Project paired one Muslim girl with one Christian girl for each big sister. The affection among the girls, regardless of differences in religious beliefs, was immediately visible. Religion was not the focus of discussions, but it did emerge in discussions of other topics. For example, conversations about cheating lead to the discovery of common values expressed in the Koran and the Bible. Participation in the Cairo program grew such that as of this writing each big sister is

---

[12] In 2004, CO also received an ExxonMobil Summer Internship Grant (Coptic Orphans 2004).

assigned one little sister regardless of religion, often yielding mixed religious pairings.

Serve to Learn specifically targets diaspora youth. CO launched the program in response to the many requests it received from young donors who wanted to do more to help. Beyond education objectives, a supplemental focus of Serve to Learn is "to maintain the identity for the younger people that are here [in the United States]. They have no reason to go to Egypt. All the family is here already. They've done the sightseeing. What more is there to do?" (Riad 2004). The program provides service opportunities to Arabic speaking volunteers to teach a summer English course to Egyptian children. Among the latter, priority is given to orphans already participating in CO's programs; other children are welcome to attend the summer course for a fee. Volunteer applicants must write two essays explaining why they want to serve. Opportunities are also competed based on Arabic proficiency and teaching experience. The demand to serve comes from beyond the Coptic community. In response to the popularity of the program, by both volunteers and beneficiary children, the program has expanded from eight volunteer positions to sixteen to twenty and the course was expanded from three to six weeks. Noting their children's enhanced appreciation for their heritage and improved Arabic, even the parents of the volunteers express gratitude to CO.

Finally, the 1001 Tales is modeled after the U.S. program Reading is Fundamental. Communities with high educational risk are targeted for book fairs, where children are allowed to select and keep one book each.

CO Donors

In 2004, 96% of CO funding came from the diaspora Coptic community, and diasporans provided almost 88% of CO's funding in 2005. In 2002, diaspora funding topped U.S. $1 million, surpassing all Coptic organizations in the United States, including the official church charity. By 2006, CO was raising over U.S. $2 million a year (Riad 2007). CO benefits from ready-made structures for community gatherings: churches and church services, and Coptic youth conventions. Presentations are made at churches, reporting on the challenges, progress, and results and requesting congregants to join the mailing list. Similar presentations are made at Coptic youth conventions, including a music video featuring contemporary music by a Christian nu-metal band, P.O.D. Images of children are juxtaposed with human development statistics, tales of discrimination, and other personal vignettes with the lyrics, "We are, we are ... youth of the nation."

Farag believes that one reason CO is so successful in its fundraising is because its staff is young and these targeted donors identify with the young professionals, who are typically the ones presenting at these conventions: "We don't talk with an accent. We're much more like the younger professionals who are now bringing in an income. In this sense CO is appealing to the first and second generation Copts in diaspora who are expecting a more American-style of professionalism."

A key motivation of donors remains identity. When asked about Coptic identity among the youth, Farag replied, "I think it's created differently, but it's created. It's not the same identity that our parents have. ... I think part of it is because there is a network." In her own experience, she observed, "Seeing a poor Egyptian is different from seeing a poor anybody else. ... Seeing a poor Egyptian is seeing somebody who is just like me, but living in poverty." Coptic youth conventions reinforce this identity and encourage youth to seek each other out and support each other, for instance, when they move away from home and start college. Some of this comes naturally, as Farag reports:

You're such a minority. You're a minority in Egypt; you're a minority in America; you're a religious minority, even though I'm Christian in America. Just to find somebody who grew up as you grew up and knows a little bit about what it's like to be who you are. It's really important when you're going to a new place.

Riad emphasizes the importance of religious identity in this process. The Coptic community focuses on creating its own churches rather than integrating with other existing Christian Orthodox churches; and upon their creation, services are available in English, as opposed to Coptic or Arabic, which could alienate younger generations. The church is proactive in trying to sustain this identity among the youth. Churches regularly organize youth tours to Egypt so youth can visit the monasteries, see their history, and learn their heritage. The church also encourages service and charity to the Coptic communities in Egypt. Service is an important component of the Coptic faith.

CO appeals to both first generation Coptic diasporans and the older generations. As Riad reports,

> I can speak fluent Arabic, I could use the same language that the older generation can understand and I can shock them with things that I know will shock them, versus the younger ones that I use totally different stories to get them. The older ones, all you have to do is you say, 'The father converted.' With the younger ones, I have to explain what that means.[13]

These donors can also be distinguished in part by differing expectations. One set has no interest in any recognition: "Take my money, but don't thank me. Don't tell me where it's going because it's based on the biblical verse of 'Don't let your right hand know what your left hand is doing. ... I don't want to know who I'm helping. I want to just help someone so I can get my reward up in heaven.'" In contrast, Riad reports that the younger generation wants more reporting and accountability.

The Keys to Coptic Orphan's Success

Riad credits CO's success to "having one foot in two cultures." That is,

> our identity, our faith, our being Copts, and then having gone through education here [in the United States] and worked in other professional organizations. So those are my expectations. I've never worked in Egypt. I don't know what it's like there. So I'm modeling after what I've seen here.

This American professionalism has posed some challenges to CO as well. Riad and Farag both note a resistance from Copts in Egypt and the United States to consider supporting an organization with professional staff who receive salaries. Similar to the persistent challenges in the nonprofit sector worldwide, there is an expectation

---

[13] Upon a father's conversion to Islam, the wife and children may be financially disowned if they do not also convert. Legally, the children are required to convert with their father. According to Riad, some such families prefer to hide in order to maintain their Christian faith.

that donations should never – or only minimally – support organization overhead.

Hybrid identity has been essential to CO's success. Being an American and not knowing how things are expected to work in Egypt prompts Riad to ask, "Why not do it this way?" As she puts it,

Had I been raised there, number one I wouldn't have been exposed to that idea to begin with. Number two, I wouldn't have asked for justification of why or why not. There, it's a given, 'We don't do that.' So, thank God we don't understand, we don't have the same thinking ways so that we can begin to question why do we do it this way?

Farag points out that while some of these ideas may be implemented in Egypt already, and certainly there is a long history of valuing literacy and education, class differences create a sense of fatalism. American culture and socialization place far fewer limits on expectations and possibilities for those born into less fortunate circumstances. This extends to differing perspectives on justice: "The American thinking is 'I see an injustice, therefore I'm going to do something about it.' Whereas in Egypt, the Egyptian thinking is more, 'I see an injustice. That's the way life is'" (Riad 2004).

When CO staff learned of the massive illiteracy in the Egyptian school system, tackling this problem became a priority. Many children pass from one grade to the next and remain illiterate. In order for children to pass exams and enable them to keep their jobs, teachers provide answers to national exams and teach memorization instead of reading. According to Riad, "When we saw this, we said, 'We've got to do something about this!' Some of the reps said, 'That's the government, what can we do? That's the way it is.' And we said, 'No! You *will* do something about it!'" Riad made clear that if participating children were not literate within a year, they would be expelled from the program and it would be the responsibility of the reps. Over 600 children were made literate in one year.

Drawing on her engineering background, Riad is fierce about documenting all processes – she cowrote a manual for all representatives with the Egypt Office Director – and maintaining a database that affords opportunities for monitoring and reporting on results. Initially, Egyptians criticized CO for being overly bureaucratic. For example, they will not accept forms from the reps if they are not correctly filled out. Over time, with demonstrated results, this emphasis on accuracy and efficiency has come to be valued by beneficiaries, reps, and donors alike.

This professionalism extends to CO's use of technology. CO maintains a database on all of the programs, including the weekly reports of all assisted children. The database is accessible on a secured server to CO offices in Egypt, Virginia, Canada, and Australia. CO invested in establishing DSL service with the Cairo office, and the Virginia and Cairo offices now share a telephone area code, making all phone calls local. So, when a donor called to ask about his sponsored child, Riad phoned Cairo who reported back the rep report from the day before. The CO webpage, www.copticorphans.org, describes its programs, provides an opportunity to begin sponsorship and join the mailing list, and posts annual reports since 2002. It's current financial information (total revenues and program and administrative expenditures) is posted directly under "About Us," along with an announcement that the audited financial statement is available upon request, a description of how CO keeps its administrative costs low (e.g., through in-kind donations), and a link to CO's Guidestar Report.[14] The Serve to Learn program application process is entirely web based.

This professionalism would not have the same impact without the Coptic connections. This was something Farag learned first hand. Farag had previously done volunteer work in Tanzania, driven by a call to serve. When she moved to the Washington, DC, area, she began volunteering in CO's Virginia office, having learned of the organization through a Coptic youth convention in the United States. She knew girls' education would be the focus of her graduate studies, but she had initially thought "Egypt was too complicated. There's the religion thing, my Arabic is not that strong. ..." She had previously visited Egypt with a church tour trip. After she started The Valuable Girl Project in Egypt, a professor asked her, "How did you negotiate culture?" It was then that Farag realized,

there's something special about me doing this versus somebody else. ... I realized I'd done training in this rural part of Egypt where not even my parents

---

[14] Guidestar is an independent nonprofit watchdog, reporting information on nonprofits to ensure transparency and accountability.

have been, yet they accepted me as one of them. They knew I was from America, yet I spoke to them in their language. I went to church with them. I took communion with them. ... That's actually when I started to appreciate this whole idea of being motivated to serve my home country.

Beyond the identity affinities, CO's success is due to its partnership with the Coptic church in Egypt. This partnership begins with the identification of the reps who then identify the children. The Not Alone program has established relationships with the communities, which enables the successful introduction of new programs. When Farag launched the Valuable Girl Project, she reports,

Coptic Orphans had a relationship with the community prior to my project and we needed to know stuff about this community in order to do it. The project would not have been so successful the first time around if we didn't have such a close relationship with the schoolmaster, who paved the road with gold for me. Without the schoolmaster, we could not do the project. He opened up the school. He opened up the library. He's a well-known figure in the village.

These Coptic links are as important in the United States or Australia as they are in Egypt. Riad emphasizes the importance of taking mass together, wherever you are. Such organizational and faith-based links led to the creation of the CO office in Australia.

The hybrid identity of CO and its staff and volunteers is illustrated in its annual reports. In addition to interspersing biblical quotes, the 2003 Annual Report, for example, includes the following quotes from CO's adopted country:

'Let your heart feel for the afflictions of everyone, and let your hand give in proportion to your purse,' George Washington, the first U.S. President.

'None of us has gotten where we are solely by pulling ourselves up by our own bootstraps. We got here because somebody bent down and helped us.' Thurgood Marshall, former U.S. Supreme Court Justice.

THAMEL.COM

In 2003, the World Summit on the Information Society recognized Thamel.com as one of three businesses in the world that are "most contributing to poverty alleviation" (Katauskas 2004). For his socially responsible business outlook Joshi credits a sociology class on the impact of advertising on society (Lewis and Clark College 2005), and his family edict to "use your talents and trade to make a difference in the lives of the people around you" (qtd. in Henke 2002–2003). As mentioned in Chapter 3, Joshi's efforts to support Nepal began with his creation of Nepal's first national lottery, with support from His Majesty's Government (HMG) of Nepal and private investors, including a major contribution from an American businessman. The lottery, with a 2 million rupee prize per week (approximately $40,000–$45,000), was organized on a rudimentary IT platform. It employed teenaged "runners" who took orders manually and then input them into one of over a hundred cable modem terminals set up for that purpose (Henke 2002–2003; Joshi 2004b).

The objective was to fund the South Asian Federation Games (for which HMG had pledged $6 million), and at the same time generate employment throughout the country. The lottery employed approximately 1,500 people, some directly as runners, and – an unforeseen development – others working on commission, who represented the business establishments that hosted terminals. At one point, the lottery was estimated to be generating over $1 million per month. Joshi proposed to HMG that after the first year the lottery would be used to fund social development and infrastructure. Unfortunately, the lottery's success attracted the attention of a new government administration, and individuals' demands for kickbacks led Joshi and his investors to close up shop.

After the demise of the lottery, Joshi became deeply concerned about the bright, young, skilled people who had organized its information system. Labor migration has long been a source of subsistence for rural families. Increasingly, Nepalese find their way to the Gulf States, where they can earn more money with manual labor than in applying any technical skills they may have (see for example, Seddon 2005). Having raised their expectations for what was possible in Nepal, despite the digital divide, Joshi was not surprised when several of his former employees urged him to try something new. Based on the success of U.S. dot coms, they suggested an information portal on Nepali businesses, which eventually grew into Thamel.com, marketing locally produced goods for both local and diaspora consumption, and providing remittance services to the diaspora, as described in Chapter 3.

Gift and gift certificate delivery requires locally knowledgeable staff, as many streets and numbers are not formally marked. Delivery staff carry cell phones to communicate delivery status to headquarters in Katmandu. Joshi acknowledges, "In Nepal we don't have good infrastructure, so we have to create this delivery-supply chain. To deliver an item, we have to make sure the right amount is there and we have to verify the address, but often there is no address." Gift delivery is an event with a ritual all its own, where family members assemble in formal clothes to enjoy the gift together. If it is a cake, the delivery person is invited to join the celebration. Despite initial concerns, when the deliverer is from a lower caste, he does not encounter any stigma or difficulty from the gift recipients. According to Joshi, "the delivery person takes on the identity of the person sending the gift. ... They actually become a surrogate." Digital photographs confirm gift receipt and build trust.

As noted in Chapter 3, by 2003, Thamel.com employed 50 full-time staff in Nepal, maintained over 500 business affiliates (ranging from the largest businesses in Nepal to street vendors with annual revenues under $1,000), served 18,000–20,000 people in 25 countries, contributed over U.S. $1 million a year in revenue to the local economy (Joshi and Granger 2003), and generated $1.3 million annual revenue (Joshi 2004b; Katauskas 2004). According to Joshi, "Everything that you see on our site today – except for the payment processing, that gets done in the States – everything, the software, the literature, the whole concept of the whole IT infrastructure, was totally made in Nepal." Beyond these economic figures of employment and revenue, Thamel.com makes more specific contributions to economic development in Nepal through its business development and remittance services.

Thamel.com's business development services derive both from its earliest intentions to promote local businesses, and in response to demand from its customers. "Like E-bay ... Thamel.com is an intermediary in that it connects orders but it takes those to the extent of actually buying those products and reselling them to the end recipient" (Granger 2004). This opens a door with the local businesses to assist them in improving product quality, consistency, and timely production. Thamel.com maintains various relationships with its affiliates. It has a wholesale relationship, offers options for nominal fee-based advertising on the website, and provides an annual membership opportunity. The Khukuri affiliate – a cooperative – is an annual membership relationship where Thamel.com provides all of the marketing, money transfer, and delivery services and retains 15% of the sales.

Some of Thamel.com's business affiliates have not been able to respond to the new demands, especially in high demand periods, such as Father's Day. One affiliate proposed a cake with a particular design that proved too labor-intensive to meet the high-volume, short-timeframe demand. This led Thamel.com to be more selective with its affiliates and products, and also inspired a broader range of business development services. These include product design and consulting for quality control and e-commerce export.

Thamel.com offers remittance services for 2.4–3%. This has become a popular service, but as Joshi notes, "We don't want to be known as a money transfer company. We do not want to be out of focus from our core strength: creating value for our business partners in Nepal and vendors in Nepal." Thamel.com leverages money transfer into products and services in partnership with producers and banks (with some profit sharing). Chapter 3 described how Thamel.com enables diasporans to set up bank accounts in Nepal for specific purposes, or with restricted access (to make sure the money reaches the intended beneficiary).

Unlike his experience with the lottery, in the case of Thamel.com, HMG's attention to Joshi's success yielded positive synergies. Thamel.com acquired international acclaim through Joshi's receipt of the 2003 Tony Zeitoun Award at the World Summit on the Information Society in Geneva, where he was televised in Nepal wearing traditional dress. This prompted a letter from the prime minister's office saying, "good luck kids and continue to do whatever you have done" (qtd. in Joshi 2004a). Joshi was also invited to participate in an International Trade Commission seminar in Nepal, again receiving kudos from HMG. He now serves on an advisory board to HMG for the design of appropriate IT policies.

IDENTITY MOBILIZATION FOR HELPING THE HOMELAND

The four diaspora organizations represent varying degrees and locales of community solidarity. Rebuild Afghanistan provided very little sense of community identity and solidarity. Requests for guidance and support for initiating new activities beyond monetary and material donations were left unanswered, as strangers speaking into a void. Perhaps as a consequence, future visitors were discouraged from participating in discussions. RA's experience suggests that shared goals are insufficient for mobilization purposes. Also needed is a structure for discussions that would facilitate community building, such as an ability to create new topic areas and threads, discuss personal experiences, and share emotions.

Even though it does not foster an online community, Afghans4Tomorrow makes a very personal and emotional appeal that likely sparks the initiation and creation of communities offline. The webpage immediately expresses common identity, shared experience, and a sense of responsibility for the homeland. The overriding framing of RA's purposive goals seemed to have attracted a highly diverse membership whose motivation to potentially help in the rebuilding of Afghanistan likely varied a great deal. Serving as "a virtual place and point of contact among *all* who are willing to participate" [emphasis added] is probably not as inspiring to a deeply committed potential core as "Brothers and sisters with one goal, with one vision. Making a difference in the lives of every Afghan."

CO frames the issues and the response but still connects its donors emotionally, emphasizing a shared identity and faith, and providing volunteer opportunities to younger generations. Its webpage and marketing materials are highly emotional, incorporating juxtaposed images of poverty (Egypt) and opportunity (United States) and emphasizing donors' hybrid identity and shared community. Its annual reports further underscore hybrid identity. Church services and youth conventions endorse CO's work and provide an even stronger foundation for community solidarity for its programs.

Thamel.com relies primarily on the market as opposed to the development of community solidarity. However, its marketing and service delivery encompasses the emotional element that ties consumers to its business. As a member of the diaspora, Joshi understands his customer "viscerally," and he aims to provide a value experience (Prahalad and Ramaswamy 2004). Thamel.com creates experience opportunities that can become highly personalized. The gift delivery ritual provides an important value experience for recipient families, inclusive of Thamel.com's delivery person. And despite their long-distance absence, diasporans enjoy a personalized experience when they receive the digital documentation of the event. The Father's Day quote (Chapter 3) illustrates the depth of this personal meaning.

The organizations benefit from a range of organizational networks and resources. Rebuild Afghanistan provided links to other organizations but did not establish relationships with these organizations. Rather than partner with established mechanisms for meeting his objectives, Meraj aimed to be the sole or at least a competing service provider. For example, his job and resume database replicated similar efforts already underway (and longstanding) by the United Nations and the Development Gateway. The most promising opportunity for partnership could have been with the Development Gateway, because its organizers had reached out to Meraj, though this relationship was not activated in support of mutual aims. Afghans4Tomorrow benefits from conferences and events on rebuilding Afghanistan, organized by others as well as themselves, to promote their work and solicit contributions, including new project ideas and volunteers to champion them. It proactively seeks organizational partnerships to access expertise, as well as complementary efforts to maximize impact. Coptic Orphans has a ready advantage in its partnership with the church. In addition to representing the basis for community solidarity (faith), the church provides ready audiences at church services and youth conventions, and identifies and selects representatives and targeted families in Egypt.

Regarding opportunity structures, all of the organizations described cater to diasporas for whom economic opportunities are available. At least some of the members of targeted diasporas reside in middle income or developed countries, and represent a ready skills-base for volunteer and professional contributions. These subgroups face minimal regulation of their homeland-related activities. While increased scrutiny of all potentially Muslim diaspora organizations occurred after September 11, 2001, neither Rebuild Afghanistan nor Afghans4Tomorrow reported any implications for their work. All four of the organizations also capitalize on their access to IT infrastructure, though to varying degrees. They all provide services that are socially and morally acceptable and even laudable.

The enabling environment in the homeland may be a greater issue. Afghans4Tomorrow faces security issues on the ground in Afghanistan, particularly outside of Kabul, but reports a comparative advantage vis-à-vis other development actors who do not know the language and culture and/or who cannot blend in as well. Coptic Orphans operates somewhat under the radar screen of the government of Egypt. It filed to register with the Ministry of Social Affairs in 2003 (a legal requirement of all NGOs), and proactively followed up with both the Ministry of Foreign Affairs and the Ministry of Social Affairs; as of May 2007, there was still no response (Riad 2007). Despite its faith-based mission, and even its inclusion on occasion of Muslims, it has not attracted attention from the authorities or the press in Egypt, nor does it seek it. The difficult relations between Copts and Muslims in Egypt, however, influences selected strategies and targeted audiences for some of its projects, for instance, preventing them from including Muslims in the Not Alone program. The 2006 unrest in Nepal was a natural concern for Thamel.com, but they continued delivery even during the peak of protests, posting pictures of this perseverance on their website.

Given the relatively supportive environments in which most of the targeted diasporans reside, there is not likely to be any risk to their quality of life in the host society by participating in these supportive activities. All of the organizations make expressing identity as easy as possible. Participation is for the most part not very taxing or visible, as it often concerns financial donations, product purchase, and/or information exchange. Afghans4Tomorrow is particularly innovative in reducing the costs to labor contributions by framing opportunities for the short term, potentially implemented during vacations from full time jobs or school in the adopted country.

The three physical world organizations proactively target diasporans' interest in identity expression. This was not a specific focus in the framing of Rebuild Afghanistan, though it did attract diasporans. A4T and CO connect diaspora identity with solidarity and duty and use the homeland's suffering to inspire a sense of responsibility and even guilt. The ability to tap identity expression as a source of motivation is predicated on the identity's sustenance. A4T, CO, and Thamel.com all aim to "keep the dream alive" as examined in Chapter 3. A4T and CO, in particular, may sustain the homeland identity in younger generations, who otherwise could lose interest in the homeland.

Through a variety of means, A4T, CO, and Thamel.com inspire confidence and a sense of efficacy. Methods include dissemination of success stories on the webpages, visual and verbal presentations to diaspora gatherings, and digital photographs. These resulting artifacts foster psychological empowerment – the belief that these contributions matter. Rebuild Afghanistan may have had the opposite effect as unanswered requests and minimal participation were visible over a long period of time, likely discouraging new participants.

IT enables the mobilization of volunteers, donors, and clients; and it affords opportunities to inspire confidence, as above. It is a central resource in the day-to-day operation of both Coptic Orphans and Thamel.com, and is the primary vehicle for information dissemination and recruitment for A4T. As in the many other cases described, IT is used in all four organizations as a means to link both homogeneous and heterogeneous participants. For purposive objectives, in particular, the ability to post links to other purposive sites may be invaluable for members/visitors to these websites. The purposive outcomes for these individuals cannot be known. The experience of RA confirms that for the organization, these links only generate purposive benefits when they represent active relationships.

The three physical world organizations successfully capitalize on diaspora identity to promote purposive objectives targeted to and/or resulting in socioeconomic development in the homeland. They effectively harness a range of resources from diasporas, including time and information, labor, and money in the form of donations or purchase. Taken together, the four organizations represent three degrees of professionalism: 1) good intentions but not necessarily skills (Rebuild Afghanistan); 2) good intentions, voluntary skills, and working in partnership with other actors to enhance available expertise (Afghans4-Tomorrow); and 3) high professionalism, represented by a nonprofit with paid staff, some voluntarism, and long-term formal partnerships (Coptic Orphans); and a profitable and acclaimed transnational business (Thamel.com). These organizations demonstrate what is possible, and in very effective, emotional ways, where a digital photograph may say it all.

8

Digital Diasporas: A New Avenue for Peace and Prosperity?

Whether exclusively in cyberspace, or engaged in the physical world, as the organizations featured in this book demonstrate, digital diasporas: 1) create hybrid identities, potentially inclusive of liberal values; 2) manifested in communities and organizations with various types of social capital and generated benefits; which in turn, 3) may support integration and security in the host society and peace and socioeconomic development in their homelands. The Internet facilitates each of these outcomes. In support of hybrid identities, it provides dialogical space, a forum for storytelling, tools for issue framing, and a context for nonhierarchical norm development and experimentation with liberal values. The Internet fosters: bonding social capital, by providing a safe space for anonymously sharing trauma and identity struggles; bridging social capital, by assembling sub-groups from the diaspora and across host societies; and bridging-to-bond social capital, by bringing together dispersed and isolated diaspora groups to enable bonding. The Internet contributes to mobilization by facilitating shared identity, issue framing, and confidence building; acting as an organizing/networking tool; and providing a vehicle for information and referrals.

As demonstrated by MyCopticChurch and TibetBoard, the storytelling and sharing the Internet affords provides logistical and community forums for disseminating information about the homeland faith and/or culture; and for reinforcing and/or recreating that identity in ways that can make it more relevant and sustainable across generations in diaspora. As Thamel.com illustrates, diasporans can also use the Internet as a tool for linking and participating in homeland relationships, festivals, and economic growth. AfghanistanOnline and Somalinet illustrate how the interactive components of the Internet enable the creation of cybercommunities that produce both bonding and bridging social capital. As seen in AfghanistanOnline, Somalinet, and TibetBoard, CGOs create bridging social capital among segments of homeland society, and between diasporans and homeland compatriots and curious host society representatives. Deliberation in these communities reflects diasporans' embrace and experimentation with liberal values. Members' interaction may deflect conflict engagement in the physical world and provide opportunities for members to express ideas, frustration, and conflict in cyberspace, potentially diffusing a need for its expression in the physical world. The case studies suggest support for McCormick's (2002, 12) hypothesis that "if the Internet can provide a canvas upon which nations can paint their social, linguistic, cultural, and political beliefs, then perhaps the physical struggle for safe cultural havens and borders may no longer be as necessary for their preservation or evolution."

These activities and opportunities may also lead to more proactive engagement in the physical world. TibetBoard and the U.S. Copts Association illustrate how digital diasporas consider and may enact policy influence efforts. They potentially incorporate liberal values into their discussions and policy agendas; and they may use these values to inform and promote the direction of these agendas and/or the process of their pursuit. Digital diasporas also include traditional nonprofit organizations and businesses with more direct implications for socioeconomic development in the homeland. Afghans4Tomorrow, Coptic Orphans, and Thamel.com inform their socioeconomic development agendas – reconstruction, education and child assistance, and small business and economic development, respectively – with their own negotiated hybrid identities, inclusive of professional skills and experience attained in diaspora, liberal values and psychological empowerment; and sensitivity, commitment, and understanding of the homeland, its identity and needs.

This final chapter analyzes the interdependence of these processes, the relevance and efficacy of digital diasporas and physical diaspora organizations (DOs), and the likely evolution of this organizational sector. In closing, I elaborate policy recommendations for host- and homeland governments and international development policymakers and analysts, and practical implications for diaspora organizations.

DIGITAL DIASPORAS' REINFORCING OUTPUTS, PROCESS, AND OUTCOMES

Regardless of the diaspora origins and context of reception, the Internet can facilitate identity expression, contributing to integration and possibly security. The case studies' five home countries represent diasporas with different origins and reception experiences. The Somali diaspora may face the greatest challenges, owing to members' association with African Americans, subjecting them to similar discrimination in American society. Tibetans endure the hardship of a total loss of the physical homeland. Both comprise majority memberships with refugee status. Somalinet and TibetBoard, in particular, illustrate that in cyberspace, diasporans can freely express their homeland identity without risk to how they are perceived and potentially treated in the host society and within the physical world diaspora community where they reside. The relief of identity stress, and identity negotiation more generally, can yield security implications both for the adopted country society and the homeland. Digital diasporas can deter marginalization and identity stress, which might otherwise make these individuals vulnerable to recruitment from destructive sources of alternative collective identity. Furthermore, migrant integration can be eased when diaspora members have opportunities to express their hybrid identities collectively.

The various outputs of diaspora organizations – identity negotiation, community, bonding and bridging social capital, and organizational resources – all of which can be IT-enabled, combine and reinforce one another to facilitate outcomes with potentially important implications for quality of life of diasporas and their compatriots in the homeland.

Identity Negotiation

The Internet provides important opportunities for creating a sense of identity and solidarity around a shared cultural heritage and diaspora

experience. Digital diasporas provide identity support, enabling diasporans to integrate new ideas, values, and experience into their identity frame of reference, testing the boundaries for what it means to their
homeland identity as well as a potentially more modern and individualistic adopted-country identity. As members continuously negotiate
their own identity, they provide examples and further fodder for others'
identity negotiation processes. As communities, digital diasporas may
evolve a moving consensus on shared hybrid identity.

Digital diasporas enable members to sustain their identification with
the homeland and to bond with others who share that identity. Tibet-
Board members credit the community for "making me more Tibetan
than I was before" (*Time to Move on...*). And MyCopticChurch enables George Andraws (and others like him) to connect with those with
whom he most identifies: "people who are just like me: other Egyptian
Copt families who have immigrated" (Andraws 2003). Several of these
diaspora organizations promote pride, or at least a sense of affinity
with broad identity concepts rooted in the homeland, making explicit
reference to, for example, Afghaniyat, Somalinomo, and Tibetan-ness.
These organizations enable members to question elements of their
homeland identity even as they seek to sustain it. Some CGO communities may promote a relatively stricter adherence to the traditional
identity, such as MyCopticChurch, while others simultaneously sustain
and challenge traditional elements of homeland identity (e.g., Tibet-
Board). Physical world diaspora organizations also help members to
sustain their homeland identities. These organizations enable disposr-
ans to retain their adopted country lifestyles yet still support and connect with the homeland through volunteering and donations (A4T,
Coptic Orphans) or through the marketplace (Thamel.com).

Members of these organizations, as well as their founders,
self-identify as "diaspora."[1] They sometimes use this term as a basis
for explicit identity discussions, and highlight their "in between-ness"
in using this identity label. Hybrid identity negotiation processes provide support for identity challenges, potentially relieving the identity
stress from encountering new cultures, obligations, expected behavior,
and affinities. On Somalinet, members discuss the reliance of the Somali

---

[1] In all the discussion threads analyzed, never once did CGO members refer to themselves or others like them as "migrants."

diasporans on welfare systems, question their association with African Americans and the ghetto culture, and acknowledge a love-hate relationship with the homeland. Members seek to reconcile their preference for the adopted homeland with their allegiance to a suffering homeland (for example, *What would you miss?*), with all the guilt (*Any Hope for Somalia?*) and self-interest (*PEACE & Your POCKET: Good for your $$$$*) this may entail. On AfghanistanOnline, members sustain their memories of a more peaceful Afghanistan, and express their angst for its future.

The case study organizations encompass liberal values and other features consistent with an increasing identification with the adopted country. The interactive components of these communities present opportunities for diasporans to learn, explore, and enact liberal values. On Somalinet, members experience the market mechanism first hand: "Sadar said, if the post is popular it will stay afloat if its not popular it will sink like the titanic" (100th *post of the forum! Some stats so far*); and they value the "wonderful forum's" freedom of speech opportunity: "This is the closest to a true free-speech dialog opportunity that I have ever encountered" (*Forum Down?*). On TibetBoard self-determination, rights, and sovereignty are invoked by supporters of both sides of the political divide (e.g., *Misconception about the Chinese*). In considering adopted country values and experience, in two of the CGOs, members make explicit reference to John F. Kennedy's famous inaugural speech, "Ask not what your country can do for you. Ask what you can do for your country." They apply it as a call to serve not their home of residence where it was inspired, but the now distant homeland.[2] Coptic Orphans employs similarly inspiring quotes from famous Americans in history.

By relieving identity stress, providing identity support, enabling experimentation, and eventually incorporating hybridity, digital diasporas support integration. Identity negotiation creates organizations. These and the hybrid identities they represent can be mobilized for purposive objectives. Hybrid identities inform what these objectives will look like and how they may be implemented.

---

[2] This famous quote seems to have broad appeal across many diaspora groups. It was also quoted by a Haitian diasporan in a discussion concerning "Haiti's Diaspora: Can it Solve Haiti's Enduring Social Conflict?" (Washington, DC, U.S. Institute of Peace, July 25, 2006).

Communities/Organizations

Through the interactive processes of identity negotiation, community norms emerge. Members provide correction to each other both in terms of shared identity and acceptable behavior. Community members explicitly seek clarification on aspects of the homeland identity and seek advice on how to reconcile it with Western lifestyles. While related exchanges can be found in all of the case studies, this is an area in which MyCopticChurch particularly excels (e.g., *'my religion is the right religion'*; *Diaspora, relations before marriage*). On AfghanistanOnline members convey that nothing but pride in the Afghan culture would be tolerated in the community (*Afghan Dance*). Somalinet members were similarly quick to condemn calls for violence (*Another Salaam Rushdi has risen*). On their part, TibetBoard members demonstrated their willingness to risk criticizing a relatively shared identity construct (Free Tibet) in order to establish democratic values as a core identity construct (*DISSENT AND OPPOSITIONS CAN NOT BE TOLERATED!!!*). More subtly, members may provide feedback and correction regarding identity and behavior simply by voting with their mouse. Posts deemed to violate community behavior and identity norms may be ignored. For example, on Somalinet, *How Can You Handle Such Fictitious Declaration? Speak Out!* was a call for nationalism and a verbal attack against one clan; it received only three replies. Posts considered spamming on AfghanistanOnline are ignored entirely.

The communities created through and representing hybrid identity negotiation represent various types of social capital and provide a range of benefits. Bonding social capital is manifested in the solidary and identity benefits members receive as they cope with the diaspora experience; threads where members support each other through identity stress are particularly moving. Through these communities members combat feelings of marginalization, as described above. These communities also yield bonding social capital among the different factions and locations of the same diaspora and even between diasporans and host country representatives. The Internet thus becomes an important tool for bridging-to-bond social capital.

Bridging social capital is not a static outcome, where the simple assembly of diverse diasporans, sometimes together with host society representatives, is sufficient to deem it so. Rather, bridging social

capital is what these communities live and seem to thrive on. Members
eagerly engage each other in debates, arguments, and sometimes verbal
attacks, as they negotiate their identities as individuals and communities. Somalinet provides the most explicit examples, where members
formally structure debates among the various political factions (*A
Dialogue Between A Nationalist DALMAR and Islamist Nur*) and
clans (*Tribalism, Religion and Nationalism: The Future of Somalia*).
TibetBoard similarly engages Free Tibet and pro-Chinese factions, as
well as explores cross-generational issues (*If I'm Chinese President . . .*),
and even links members still residing in Tibet with the diaspora (*A Voice
From Inside Tibet, Think about reality and dreams*). AfghanistanOnline links chronological generations, diaspora generations, and various
tribes.

Given their minority status in host societies, it may not be surprising
that diasporans would seek common identity cause on the Internet,
despite the various subgroups comprised in the diaspora. What is perhaps more surprising is the bridging social capital one finds on these
sites that links diasporas with interested members of the host society.
Somalinet includes MAD MAC, participating due to his personal
experience with the U.S. Army in Mogadishu; AfghanistanOnline
includes Peace, who became connected to the Afghan diaspora through
her child, born to a Pashtun; and TibetBoard includes Chris, who
became interested in the Free Tibet cause.

In each of these communities, these members become representatives not only of themselves but of their society and its values. These are
active members. Their intensive participation may reflect their personality and degree of interest. These would already need to be significant
for them to enter these communities at all, especially as they subject
themselves to criticism and potential ostracism. In fact, some community members propose ostracizing these members, for example, MAD
MAC on Somalinet (*LETS BOYCOTT MAD-MAC TOGETHER,
WE CAN*); and Chris on TibetBoard (*Ban Chris! Ban all opposition
to the HH Dalai Lama*). And these members sometimes posted anonymously before they were encouraged to participate as legitimate members, for example, MAD MAC (*The Next Battle for Mogadishu???*),
and Peace (*David Duke Going to the Pen*). Yet they make crucial contributions to the identity negotiation process. Diasporans are able
to pose direct questions and the curiosity of both sides seems

genuine. Diaspora organizations in the physical world may also include nondiasporans, who share the interests and support the missions of these organizations, and want to contribute. The founder of the Seeds for Afghanistan program with A4T is a non-Afghan American, and non-Coptic Americans seek to participate in Coptic Orphans' Serve to Learn program.

Each of the benefits these communities provide also serves to inform identity negotiation and becomes an important input for mobilization. The solidary benefits described above largely emerge from identity support (cultural identity benefits), as well as interaction and values experimentation with other subgroups or host society representatives. Material benefits are crucial to sustaining the homeland identity, not only through reporting the historical record and particulars of traditions, but also disseminating news and information about the homeland today.

Together, these benefits eventually yield the shared identity necessary to collective action. This shared identity becomes the foundation for psychological empowerment. While the challenges of the homeland may seem daunting and irresolute for an individual diasporan, discussing options and demonstrating agreement, even if only online, can inspire confidence that peace may one day be possible, for example, in Somalia. Collective agreements on issues, agendas, and sometimes action, empower individual members to believe in the possibility of change and their potential role in making it happen, together. Alternatively, when the feasibility and/or probability of proposals seem particularly doubtful, members fail to mobilize even just to respond online. Examples on Somalinet include *Shall we forgive each other or what?* and *Would non-violence protest work in Somalia.* Members also use these benefits to frame issues and action. The community norms supportive of solidary benefits, and the cultural identity benefits that support a degree of consensus on this shared identity become important resources for conveying what subject matter is open to discussion, which priorities are shared, and which agendas might be pursued and how.

Mobilization

The collective expression of hybrid identity increasingly occurs through activities in support of the homeland. Hybrid identities inform political considerations and action agendas vis-à-vis the homeland, whether they pertain to potential conflict within the homeland and/or among subgroups of its society, or human rights, quality of life, or partisan political agendas. Issues of freedom of speech, democratic values, self-determination, and human rights are readily applied to Somalia's interclan conflict and failed state, Afghanistan's tribal conflict and reconstruction, Tibet's political impasse with China and aspirations for a free and independent Tibet in the future, and improved quality of life and human rights for Copts residing in Egypt.

These hybrid identities become the foundation for collective action; they are enacted in the mobilization process, as reflected in the networks created in and by these communities. Afghans4Tomorrow explicitly embraces and promotes its allegiance to both Afghanistan and the United States as it links to diaspora experts and other development actors to contribute to Afghanistan's reconstruction. Coptic Orphans builds upon its faith community and the organizational resources of the Church at the same time that it incorporates professionalism and an American can-do attitude to redress educational injustices in Egypt. And Thamel.com similarly builds upon its technical and business expertise, acknowledging the Nepali diaspora as having a particular identity with its own needs and desires, including links to the homeland.

DIGITAL DIASPORAS: INTERESTING ANECDOTES OR POTENTIAL IMPACT?

The true extent of digital diasporas' impact on diaspora and homeland quality of life is impossible to measure. Because so much occurs in the fluid environments of cyberspace and human psychology, we will never know how many ideas expressed are actually mobilized in the physical world, nor will we be able to get inside the hearts and minds of participating individuals to assess their psychological well-being. As Vertovec (1997) warns, we should be cautious in assuming diaspora behavior is based on rational choices (see also Edgerton 2000). Like all human behavior, myriad factors combine to urge action in one direction or another. Some of these factors may be subconscious. For that reason, it is important to proceed cautiously when seeking to explain and measure diasporan behavior and motivations, and it is crucial to include psychological considerations, that which may not be readily apparent, even to these individuals.

Research confirms the importance of community, solidarity, and identity support to psychological well-being, even absent a diaspora experience. How much more, then, are these factors essential to those who face the psychological trauma of reconciling two lifestyles, two identities, and potentially involuntarily (i.e., as a consequence of forced migration)? Community, with its bonding social capital, solidary benefits, and identity support may be challenging to create for societies that are, by definition, dispersed. Information technology presents a resource of miraculous importance to diaspora communities precisely for its support of these advantages: the communities one can create there, inclusive of bonding social capital, bridging-to-bond social capital, and solidary benefits; and the opportunities and freedom to negotiate identity.

Internet organizations are somewhat famous for their proliferation and reverse proliferation, with few having a very long shelf-life. In the diaspora arena, Meyer and Brown (1999) identified forty-one diaspora networks. In 2004, Lowell and Gerova revisited these and added twenty more. Having identified an inactivity rate of 34% (twenty one out of sixty one) (which they defined as the absence of a website or a website that had not been updated for two years), they question the importance of the Internet "in fostering linkages between expatriates and the homeland," arguing that a reexamination of these networks "gives some reason for pause" (24).

This performance might indeed give pause to those in search of the purposive benefits of such networks for facilitating mobilization, and form may matter for purposive objectives such as those discussed in Chapters 6 and 7. However, in matters of community and identity support, it is the function of CGOs, not the form that is most important. Specific organizations may come and go, but the basic infrastructure and its function can almost certainly be found anytime for any diaspora group. In the discussion forums I examined for this study, CGO members frequently referenced other CGOs, sometimes with a sense of pride in their own community and competition with the others, and often indicating their own current or past participation in these.

King (2003, 180) argues that without accounting for the "political," the "imagined communities" (Anderson 1991) created online are irrelevant to international affairs. Even when the potential physical world efficacy of digital diasporas cannot be systematically determined, this study shows that digital diasporas are highly salient to international affairs. Digital diasporas provide **identity support** (and relief of identity stress) and **solidary benefits** to combat marginalization, which together create a **collective identity** that can inspire **psychological empowerment** and **may be mobilized** to support integration and/or contributions to the homeland. These outputs are achieved as members **negotiate their identities** and **experiment with liberal values**. Even if ideas grow no feet (i.e., the community does not mobilize in the physical world), other important needs and objectives are being met solely through the discussion of these possibilities. These outcomes have security implications, as they may change the cost-benefit analysis that might otherwise leave individuals vulnerable to recruitment into violent activities.

Although we cannot know the correlation of participation in these CGOs and real world engagement for the homeland, we can surmise that there may be a connection for selected members. In fact, prior to her engagement with Coptic Orphans and the creation of the Valuable Girl Project, Phoebe Farag participated in Coptstalk from 1996–2000, starting when listservs were relatively new. Farag credits this community for "expand[ing] my horizon of Coptic people that I could interact with and later on try to engage in Coptic Orphans' cause" (Farag 2007). Joshi laments that such discussion forums were not available before he launched Thamel.com. Today, he uses these discussion forums to look for ideas: "We go after how people are feeling and how we can offer services and product[s] that cater to their needs. Forums have played a strong role in formalizing [our] product development concept" (Joshi 2007). These examples suggest that with the increased availability of discussion forums, CGOs may at once shape ideas for diaspora entrepreneurs of the future, and represent important resources for mobilizing diasporans today. Like other grassroots organizations, CGOs may represent latent capacity. In a review of grassroots organizations' participation in policy processes internationally, Coston (1999) highlights their latent capacity, which can be mobilized on an as-needed basis.

CGOs may be "pre-political" (Siapera 2005), preparing members for political action in the future. Some digital diasporas explicitly organize offline (physical world) community meetings, organized in multiple cities where members reside. In the case of British Chinese Online and Dimsum, these meetings have generated collective action in the physical world, for example, to protest racism, support cultural representation, and/or promote media coverage (Parker and Song 2007). Through these social gatherings and the mobilization they generate in the physical world, these digital diasporas "change the terms of engagement between these ethnic groups and the wider society, and they have considerable potential to develop new forms of social action" (Parker and Song 2006, 575).

Many of the organizations in this study are CGOs, existing only online. Research confirms that digital communities have difficulty translating ideas into real world action.[3] Purposive action may require CGOs or members thereof to tap into broader networks, inclusive of physical world diaspora organizations. Since most diasporans belong to more than one and multiple types of diaspora organizations, this finding may not be as pessimistic as it may seem.

We need to understand diasporas, identity and transnational engagement in a broader context, beyond single organizations and interventions. Diasporans are likely to belong to more than one diaspora organization, joining each to fulfill different needs and purposes. As Sheffer (2006, 244) puts it:

[diasporans'] need to make consequential decisions concerning identity and contacts with their homelands motivate them to establish multiple organizations to deal with their particular interests and concerns. Hence, significant new features of all existing diasporas are the multiplicity and scope of those organizations and their dedicated pursuit of the strategies they adopt vis-à-vis their multiple protagonists: host societies and governments, other ethnic groups in host countries, homelands, regional organizations, and other segments of the same ethnic nations.

The same individuals who participate in negotiating their identities in CGOs may also be leading project efforts through formal diaspora organizations, whether philanthropic or business oriented, or may be working for other business, political, or development organizations with projects in their homeland. Diasporans do not live in virtual communities (Sheffer 2006, 245). They may participate in them and their

---

[3] See, for example, Adams Parham's (2004) study of the Haiti Global Village Forum.

physical world behavior may be influenced accordingly, but they engage with physical world organizations in their daily living. While not all CGO members are likely to be engaged in purposive activities directed to the homeland, those who are likely benefit from these online opportunities, especially in terms of solidary and identity benefits.

The Internet is relatively young. And we know that youth tend to be more active in its digital communities. Younger generations of diasporans tend to use the Internet to connect with others exclusively online; while older generations may use it to supplement their existing physical space networks (Ven den Bos and Nell 2006). As these younger generations age, they may become more engaged in purposive activity in the homeland. One would expect that these activists will have benefited in some way from the maintenance of homeland identity, the negotiation of hybrid identity and its experimentation with liberal values, and the psycho-social support these diasporans received online in their youth, as Phoebe Farag's example suggests.

Regarding diaspora organizations' real world impact, studies of these organizations remain in their infancy. Selected hometown associations have been examined, indicating limited but promising results for homeland quality of life.[4] Other studies offer some evidence of impact, though this impact is acknowledged to be limited, and future potential is almost always highlighted among the key findings. For example, in a Department for International Development (DfID)-commissioned report, AFFORD (African Foundation for Development) studied thirteen UK-based African diaspora organizations and found contributions that included raising funds to: build hospitals, maternity wards, vocational centers, and bridges linking remote areas to services; provide clean water and electricity; supply books and computers to schools; and support income generating activities – all "overhead free" (Ndofor-Tah 2000). While the report notes a relative modesty in these contributions, it underscores their significance in neglected and remote areas. It also observes that these organizations are volunteer led and members struggle with juggling multiple responsibilities.

---

[4] E.g., for Mexico, see Orozco (2003), and Orozco and Lapointe (2004); for Guatemala and El Salvador, see Popkin (2003); for Ghana, see Henry and Mohan (2003); for Zimbabwe, see Maphosa (2005); for China, see Dahles (2004); and for Turkey, see Hersant and Toumarkine (2005).

A study of the UK-based Ghanaian diaspora concludes that while the diaspora is mobilizing funds for national development through community development projects, the resources come in small amounts, and are sporadic and unorganized. Nevertheless, "this activity could form a key plank for a national development strategy given the appropriate policy and institutional framework" (Zan 2004, 3). Many of the UK Ghanaians' initiatives are founded on personal networks and are of "questionable" sustainability (Zan 2004). Another DfID-commissioned study warns that while the contributions of the six UK-based diasporas studied can be significant, diaspora groups may engage for differing purposes, including self-advancement, the advancement of their particular sectarian interest, or even to support or agitate for continued unrest (Van Hear et al. 2004).

Even if we assume at least a potential for these organizations to have constructive homeland impact, one may wonder if this is a first generation phenomenon that is likely to dissipate as diasporans eventually integrate in host societies. In fact, once a "dual orientation" is established – that is, a simultaneous focus on the ancestral and adopted homelands, it is hard to dismantle (Vertovec 2004). The traditional, linear model of assimilation, where with new generations roots are eventually forgotten and a new identity is adopted, is no longer assumed. Rather, we know that diasporans more proactively select a relative balance of ancestral and adopted homeland identities based on an implicit cost-benefit analysis.[5] CGOs, as we have seen, can facilitate this process and make the representation of the ancestral homeland identity more possible. Perhaps counter-intuitively, recent studies of selected U.S.-based Latin American diasporas suggest that the longer diasporans have been in the United States, the *more* likely they are to engage on behalf of the homeland (Guarnizo, Portes, and Haller 2003; Portes et al. 2007). This engagement is also more common among the highly skilled (Lowell, Findlay, and Stewart 2004).

The case analyses in this book demonstrate a variety of ways that identity can be managed – intentionally or not – in order to sustain an ancestral homeland identity and potential affinity and contributions to the homeland. Some CGOs may be created with the explicit intention

---

[5] For example, Matute-Bianchi (1991), Portes and Zhou (1993), Sánchez Gibau (2005), Suarez-Orozco (1987), and Waters (1999).

to sustain ancestral identity in diaspora. This was most evident in MyCopticChurch and TibetBoard. Afghans4Tomorrow's mission explicitly emphasizes a conception of hybrid identity that encompasses a commitment to serve the homeland, indeed a "moral obligation" according to its logo. A4T and Coptic Orphans proactively solicit the participation of diasporans in supporting the homeland, either through donations or volunteerism. CO is even more proactive in reaching out not only to Coptic congregants of all ages, but specifically to youth. Using the church and youth conventions as vehicles, CO seeks to educate youth about their heritage and link that education to serving Copts in Egypt. In addition to these education efforts among youth, CO successfully markets and provides a ready vehicle for diaspora contributions. CO sustains remittances across generations and from families who may no longer have relatives in Egypt, and channels these remittances to development objectives (see Brinkerhoff 2008b).

Similarly, Thamel.com takes for granted that diasporans may have a desire or a sense of obligation to stay connected to the ancestral homeland and provide support for their family. This is Thamel.com's market and they make it as easy as possible for diasporans to achieve these objectives by purchasing Nepalese goods and services and channeling remittances to longer-term investments that may eventually reduce family dependency on diasporans. Conexion Colombia, a Bogatá-based nonprofit, represents another approach. It operates like a United Way for the diaspora, soliciting and channeling diaspora contributions to selected Colombian charities (Portes et al. 2007).

Even without interventions, ancestral homeland identity may resurge when the homeland experiences a crisis. Research shows this to be the case for the U.S.-based Afghan diaspora (Kerlin 2008), for instance. Abdul Meraj's creation of Rebuild Afghanistan is one example. Disasters may be necessary to galvanize diasporans who are more individualistically settled (Guarnizo and Diaz 1999; qtd. in Portes et al. 2007). The ancestral identity may be more sustainable when it is created or recreated around a crisis event, such as in Armenia (Esman 2008). In the latter case, diasporans and diaspora organizations, themselves, may be the most important protagonists in shaping and sustaining this conception of ancestral identity.

The relationship between these efforts to sustain identity across generations and resulting hybrid identity may or may not translate into purposive efforts vis-à-vis the ancestral homeland. We can state with greater certainty that with respect to quality of life for diasporans, CGOs provide important functions supportive of community and identity, which may potentially combat marginalization and psychological vulnerability. While the enabling features of the Internet do not, themselves, guarantee that some portion of the ancestral identity and its potential mobilizing force for the homeland will be sustained, these examples suggest that the Internet can be a powerful identity management tool, and one that diaspora organizations, businesses, and homeland governments might do well to acknowledge and potentially utilize.

THE FUTURE OF DIASPORA ORGANIZATIONS

In his historical review of immigrant associations, Moya (2005, 835) warns of a tendency to focus attention solely on the larger and/or more institutionalized associations when, in fact, those with the most significance to the daily lives of immigrants themselves are small associations that represent "the most common form of immigrant sociability outside of the family." These include hometown associations, which may be active in improving quality of life in both home- and hostland. It also increasingly includes CGOs.

Other than continued proliferation and "come-and-goes" (organizations with a limited lifespan), what is the future of CGOs? On the one hand, more settled diaporans may take their communities to new platforms, such as Facebook and MySpace. Alternatively, or additionally, these organizations may increasingly combine advantages of CGOs with elements of physical world organizations, and vice versa. For example, Joshi (2007) is in the process of developing a "Platform for Delivering Social Remittances," which will provide a matching function between the needs of the social sector and businesses in Nepal and diasporans. Pope Shenouda, the Coptic Patriarch, launched in 2008 "Coptic World" (www.copticworld.org). The site plans to assemble links for a variety of Coptic websites and communities, and will include interactive components (Farag 2007).

Why do diasporas create so many associations? Curtis and associates (2001) posit that volunteerism tends to be higher, the longer a country has experience with democratic institutions and the higher its national economic development level. This finding suggests that individuals who have no experience with associations and volunteering may acquire an interest and develop capacity once they settle in such countries, as in North America. While Moya (2005) cites several studies noting such proliferation even within homeland cultures whose adherents previously might shun associational life, he concludes that such "association mania" may be more a function of the diaspora experience than any characteristics of the receiving country. Indeed, much of this organizing has its roots in the functional needs of the migrants. Civic/cultural organizations are the most common diaspora organizations, and this holds across diaspora characteristics, including origins, reception in the host society, and relative dispersion of settlement (Portes et al. 2007).

What we know of physical world diaspora organizations to date is: They are highly varied; most tend to be volunteer based and relatively unsophisticated; and they achieve results, if any, on small scales, through very personalized networks. Diaspora organizations are "typically all-volunteer groups with minimal administrative skills and minimal organizational structure" (Dade 2006). A comparative study of diaspora organizations from Colombia, the Dominican Republic, and Mexico found that less than half of these were registered as formal nonprofits and four-fifths of them had no paid staff. Still, 45% did have legal status and some of the diasporas were more organizationally sophisticated (Colombia, followed by the Dominican Republic) than others (Mexico) (Portes et al. 2007).

Whether aimed at quality of life in the home- or hostland, many diaspora organizations are likely to suffer from various forms of voluntary failure. Salamon (1987) outlines four voluntary failures: 1) philanthropic insufficiency, rooted in NGOs' limited scale and resources; 2) philanthropic particularism, reflecting NGOs' choice of clientele and projects; 3) philanthropic paternalism, where those who control the most resources are able to control community priorities; and 4) philanthropic amateurism. However, just as these failures apply less-and-less to the NGO sector as a whole,[6] so, too, are we likely to see an increasing sophistication and capacity within the diaspora organization sector.

---

[6] See Brinkerhoff (2002b); Brinkerhoff and Brinkerhoff (2002); see also Hulme and Edwards (1997).

This already occurs somewhat naturally as individual diaspora communities evolve. One of the few studies of diaspora organizations finds that more established immigrants prefer more formal and institutionalized initiatives (Portes et al. 2007). Sometimes these are reflections or extensions of traditional American nonprofits, such as Lions and Kiwanis clubs. Historically, the growing variety of associations that developed in diaspora led to increased specialization of these organizations (see Ross 1976; Smith and Freedman 1972; qtd. in Moya 2005). More generally, as grassroots organizations increase in age, size, and in their purposive activities, there is a tendency for such organizations to become more complex in their structure and function (Brainard and Brinkerhoff 2004; Smith 2000). Along with the specialization of a diaspora community's organization sector, as immediate needs related to the migration experience decrease, diaspora organizations may turn their attention more toward the homeland.

The sophistication of individuals' participation is also likely to increase with progressing integration. According to the literature on voluntary associations, membership increases with education, income, and professional employment (Moya 2005). As diasporans progress educationally and economically in the adopted homeland they, too, may join more associations. As individuals are increasingly entrenched in the societies and economies of the hostland, they may still join associations organized for constructive ends targeted to the homeland (see, for example, Guarnizo et al. 2003; Portes et al. 2007). The more educated among these diasporans are also more likely to organize for homeland interventions (Lowell et al. 2004) that are national in scope (Portes et al. 2007).

I argue that the evolution of the diaspora organization (DO) sector as it pertains to homeland development is currently on a par with NGOs' development starting in the mid 1980s. At that time, Korten (1987) wrote a significant piece on the evolution of the NGO sector, delineating three generations (see also Korten 1990). These generations mark an evolution of the sector as a whole. Today, they continue to be descriptive of particular NGOs and many NGOs combine features of the three. The first generation is marked by a relief and welfare strategy focused on relieving shortages of goods and services in the immediate term for individuals and families. The second generation adopts a local self-reliance strategy focused on self-help initiatives in neighborhoods and villages with a time frame based on the life of individual projects. The third generation is the most strategic in its management orientation, focusing on creating sustainable systems. These NGOs seek to address policy and institutional constraints, largely through advocacy, with a longer-term time frame.

Applying this framework to diasporas suggests that most DOs can be described as first generation. Remittances typically begin with a focus on one's own family and, through hometown associations and other philanthropic NGOs, the scope may be expanded to communities. The strategy is largely one of welfare with short-term aims, even when applied to infrastructure projects. Diaspora medical missions are similar in their orientation. The sophistication of some diaspora philanthropy organizations is increasing and many efforts are now aimed at microenterprise and community development initiatives, which might be viewed as second generation endeavors. Coptic Orphans is a second-generation DO, with its emphasis on education and compensating for the Egyptian Government's literacy failures.

The most advanced DOs are wedding such activities with a third generation strategy that seeks to improve policy and institutional frameworks in support of both targeted homeland communities/populations and diaspora contribution efforts. For example, the Zacatecan Federation of Hometown Associations in the United States orchestrated matching programs with the Mexican Government and spun off a political arm to lobby on both sides of the border, for an improved migrant investment environment (Jiménez 2004). In India, diaspora members have contributed significantly to the IT sector, through direct investment (approximately 16%), brokering investment relationships, and proposing and promoting necessary changes to the legal framework in order to improve the investment climate.[7] Other diasporas have organized for regional and national development, inclusive of partnerships with the homeland government, yielding new government programming and policy reforms.[8]

---

[7] See Margolis et al. (2004) and Saxenian (2002a, 2002b).

[8] See, for example, Iskander (2008) for the case of rural electrification and road infrastructure in Morocco; and Fontaine with Brinkerhoff (2008) for national development in Dominica.

With growing capacity and sophistication, DOs will likely increasingly assume the service delivery advantages attributed to the NGO sector more generally (see Brinkerhoff and Brinkerhoff 2002). Economic models suggest that nonprofits fill gaps left by standardized service packages (responding to government and market failures), resulting in a greater diversity and customization of services (Weisbrod 1975), increased competition, and greater efficiency (Hansmann 1987). From another perspective, nonprofits are seen as more trustworthy than government and private service providers, thus solving principal-agent problems related to contract failure.[9] DOs have the potential to tailor services to the particular needs of specific homeland communities and populations. They have greater incentive to reach areas for which the government may lack capacity or political will, filling gaps in public service provision (see Ndofor-Tah 2000).

In the short run, however, DOs are likely to continue to suffer from voluntary failures. Whether or not service delivery will come with enhanced efficiency will depend on the organizational capacity of individual DOs; especially in the short term, many of these organizations are likely to continue to suffer from voluntary amateurism. The trust factor is also dependent on the degree to which these DOs genuinely represent or are consistent with the stated needs of targeted communities. Given the complexity of diaspora communities and factions this will not always be the case. DOs may be organized based on sectarian homeland identity, potentially enhancing their particularism in terms of what services will be provided to whom (see Van Hear et al. 2004). Furthermore, and especially in the first generation of organizational development, DOs are likely to be paternalistic in the design and implementation of homeland projects and services. For example, the trajectory of hometown association projects often begins with church repair and renovation, health and education, then cultural and sports projects. Does this pattern reflect the stated needs and desires of the communities? Or does it reflect the DOs' own well-intentioned but possibly misguided perceptions and priorities? That DOs may continue to suffer from philanthropic insufficiency is largely contingent on their aspirations for what they seek to accomplish. The more advanced DOs are pursuing support for their work from government and international

---

[9] See Douglas (1998); Mansbridge (1998); Lipsky and Smith (1989–1990).

development agencies, but these DOs struggle to put together or respond to requests for assistance on their own (Dade 2006). On their part, funding agencies are limited in their ability to fund nascent organizations with weak or no track records.[10]

POLICY IMPLICATIONS

Given digital diasporas' potential – some of it realized, some of it evolving – for individuals and communities' quality of life in the adopted country and in the homeland, what should governments and other public actors do? Despite the growing visibility of homeland governments and donors in the diaspora and development arena, in reviewing the experience and research to date, as Portes and associates (2007, 253) put it:

all empirical evidence indicates that economic, political, and socio-cultural activities linking expatriate communities with their countries of origin emerged by initiative of the immigrants themselves, with governments jumping onto the bandwagon only when their importance and economic potential became evident (see also Portes 2003).

Indeed, diaspora identity expression and transnational engagement occurs with or without policy interventions.

Yet more can be done to maximize the potential contributions of digital diasporas to diasporans' quality of life and integration into the host society, and to improved policy and standards of living in the homeland. To that end, I make seven recommendations for policy and practice, targeted to host governments, homeland governments, the international development industry, and diaspora organizations.

Host Governments

Understanding hybridity is crucial in the consideration of social policies. Given hybridity, affirming the homeland identity and even talk of return does not mean that diasporans do not value or embrace their

---

[10] Oxfam-Novib has provided Dutch diaspora organizations training for proposal writing, and supports many of these organizations' work through grants originating from the Dutch Ministry of Foreign Affairs.

adopted country and society. An improved public awareness of this complexity could encourage tolerance and, ideally, incentives to seek improved understanding of particular individuals and communities.

Portes (2006) examines three practical theoretical stances or policy orientation options vis-à-vis migrants in receiving societies. Hard assimilation seeks to completely assimilate migrants to the exclusion of a homeland identity by the second generation. Permanent culturalism emphasizes the homeland identity, sometimes to the exclusion of an adopted country identity. It can lead to ethnic enclaving, which, in turn, can isolate immigrant communities, potentially sending them down a path of downward assimilation, where the second generation and beyond experiences a downward spiral of economic and educational opportunities (see Rumbaut and Portes 2001; see also Waldinger and Feliciano 2004). Soft assimilation tolerates ethnicity but promotes the ultimate goal of integration. It encourages knowledge and respect of mainstream culture, laws, education, and language. It typically leads to gradual and voluntary integration. Minimal requirements for its success include knowledge of the adoptive country language and observance of its rule of law. It is this model, Portes argues, that leads to the American tolerance and even encouragement of hyphenization.

Promoters of multiculturalism should take caution that its implementation not lead to de facto permanent culturalism. This is an argument eloquently made in Amartya Sen's treatise on *Identity and Violence: The Illusion of Destiny* (2006). Sen paints a picture of history and contemporary identity maps that defy categorization on singular dimensions and challenge notions of normative hierarchies and a clash of civilizations. Since forcing hard assimilation can lead to substantial identity stress, and permanent culturalism risks downward assimilation, the preferred path is soft assimilation. Soft assimilation celebrates hybridity. It is supported by the digital diaspora organizations and experiences recounted in these pages.

Beyond general strategies to promote understanding, tolerance, and embrace of hybridity through a soft assimilation approach, I make two policy recommendations for host governments. Policymakers and analysts still grapple with what integration into a host society means, though the consensus in the scholarly community is moving increasingly towards a sense of belonging based both on socioeconomic achievement as well as identity (see Thomson and Crul 2007). The two do not always coincide. For example, analysis of British-Chinese diasporans' discussions in online communities, reveals that while they may be economically successful in British society (e.g., highly educated and skilled, with high employment rates and salaries), they still do not feel that they "belong" in British society (Parker and Song 2007). Through online discussions they express their collective concerns about social marginalization and "invisibility" (Parker and Song 2007, 1057). Successful integration requires both a supportive receiving context and an integrated identity, which may manifest in diasporan participation in the host society, either through activities that bridge the diaspora and host communities, or directly and independently in the host community/society.

Recommendation 1: IT regulation should maintain privacy and access in order not to interfere with opportunities for exploring identity and representing liberal values.

In this study, I have primarily focused on the identity component. The Internet is an ideal resource for examining identity stress and identity negotiation. First, one can read the shared thoughts of research populations. It is surprising how much CGO members will share that may be personal and profound. Some of this candor may be credited to the Internet's anonymity. Second, interaction patterns, including frequency and shared interests can be observed, as can other social dynamics, such as deference/leadership. Third, these observations can be made unobtrusively. These discussion forums are in the public domain. Participants can reasonably expect that they are being observed, though the observer can monitor discussions imperceptibly.[11] Fourth, because these sites assemble dispersed populations, they allow for qualitatively different comparative discussions than what could take place and be observed in the physical world. Fifth, members join around a shared diaspora identity; the nature of the discussions inevitably turns to identity negotiation and thoughts of the homeland. Rarely can researchers observe these types of discussions.

Despite the use of the Internet for recruitment and dissemination supportive of terrorism (as discussed in Chapter 1), the Internet's

---

[11] For this research, the founders of all of the organizations studied granted their permission for this observation; the research methodology was also IRB approved.

advantages to a democratic society should be protected. Most of the regulation under consideration would not prevent cyberterrorism, just as efforts to prevent it to date have been unsuccessful (see Weimann 2006). A panel on "Democracy, Terrorism, and the Open Internet" at the 2005 International Summit on Democracy Terrorism and Security concluded that "interfering with the democratic freedoms offered by the Internet would probably damage democracy more than it would harm the terrorists ... the Internet's positive effects in connecting people, for example far outweigh the possibility of abuse" (Safe Democracy Foundation 2005). The Internet is a "technology embedded with democratic values" (Safe Democracy Foundation 2005).

Beyond its inherent democratic characteristics, the Internet's conducive features for identity negotiation and representation of liberal values (in both form and function) are important contributors that should be sustained and protected. As detailed in this book, the motivation to express identity is natural and common to all human beings. As Friedman notes, "cultural identity is not a mere game for those engaged in it, but a deadly serious strategy of psychic and social survival" (1994, 245). Whether addressed in cyberspace or in the physical world, diasporans face a psycho-social need to develop and express their hybrid identities and to experiment with the integration of values and conceptions alternative and additional to those from their homeland, including liberal values. Diasporans may feel constrained to express, explore, experiment, and reevaluate their cultural identities in the physical world, whether due to social pressure from their families or physical world diaspora community, or in response to discrimination and other subtle social cues from the host society. The Internet is a low-cost, efficient means for diasporans to fulfill these crucial psycho-social functions.

What we learn from these identity negotiation processes and their significance in the physical world leads to my first policy recommendation: IT regulation should maintain privacy and access in order not to interfere with opportunities for exploring identity and representing liberal values.

Recommendation 2: Policymakers can focus on changing the stakes for identity mobilization, enhancing the possibility of constructive directions by creating an enabling environment for a high quality of life and community for diasporans.

Diasporans make implicit cost-benefit analyses with respect to both identity orientation and identity mobilization and its direction. Policy-makers can influence the terms of this analysis by attending to the "context of reception." This is typically defined according to three factors: "the state policies directed at a specific migrant group; the reactions to and perceptions of the immigrants by public opinion; and the presence or absence of an established ethnic community to receive the immigrants" (Grosfoguel and Cordero-Guzmán 1998, 357). The importance of a receiving ethnic community is consistent with the arguments presented here in terms of the need for solidary benefits stemming from a shared, collective identity; it further high-lights the salience of digital diasporas' contributions.

Focusing on the context of reception represents the institutional approach to integration. Instead of focusing only on the diaspora groups themselves to maximize the potential for successful integration, it is necessary to consider the role of institutions in promoting or inhib-iting immigrants' progress in the host society. Rudmin's (2003) histor-ical review of acculturation literature and theory yields important overlooked findings. He concludes that typologies of acculturation (e.g., Berry 1997; Rosenau 2003) reify and emphasize individual traits and erroneously may serve to reinforce assumptions that little can be done to influence acculturation patterns. He cites earlier studies that emphasize situational factors. For example, Seelye and Brewer (1970) found that situational factors such as job circumstances are more pre-dictive of acculturation processes than individual attributes (e.g., atti-tudes and personality). Supportive institutions become the opportunity structures that may help integration as well as mobilization.[12]

This leads to my second policy recommendation: Policymakers can focus on changing the stakes for identity mobilization, enhancing the possibility of constructive directions by creating an enabling environ-ment for a high quality of life and community for diasporans. Such an enabling environment might include, for example, access to small busi-ness and home ownership loans, and support for access to vocational training and higher education. Grosfoguel's and Cordero-Guzmán's (1998) review of the Cuban diaspora experience confirms the

---

[12] For a discussion of the institutional approach in transnational comparative context, see Thomson and Crul (2007).

importance of both social networks – internal community solidarity – and "broader social structures that constrain or enable access to capital, information, and resources by members of a specific community's micro-networks" (355) for integration and success in the receiving country.

While the context of reception can support integration and facilitate identity mobilization, identity mobilization can, in turn, support integration. Identity mobilization represents psychological empowerment that can lead to constructive contributions to societies. Mobilizing in support of constructive contributions – whether to the homeland or in the hostland – can reinforce liberal values. It is through such mobilization that diaspora communities further experiment with liberal values, both in the definition of political and programmatic agendas and the processes of pursuing them.

Homeland Government

What might a homeland government do to more effectively capture diasporas' mobilization for development? So-called "sending" governments are increasingly recognizing the importance of their diasporas. Many are reviewing their definitions of nationality and citizenship, with a growing recognition of ancestral lineage (*jus sanguinis*) in an effort to sustain linkages of subsequent generations to the homeland (Hammar 1990; qtd. in Koslowski 2005). Some states are even promoting dual citizenship, in order to capture the potential benefits of their diasporans' lobbying in their adopted countries for more favorable foreign policies (Koslowski 2005). As of 2000, approximately eighty-nine countries allowed for dual citizenship or included migrants as official members of their political communities (Renshon 2000). Some states, seeking to retain loyalty to the homeland, are making it easier for nonresident citizens to vote in absentia (e.g., India). The opportunity to vote in the homeland may be increasingly viewed as a right. While this may seem questionable to some, Koslowski (2005, 28) raises the question: "If their remittances and investments support whole communities and contribute a significant share of the home country's GDP, would denying them the vote be tantamount to 'taxation without representation'?" In countries recovering from conflict, governments have reached out to their diasporas to participate in national planning and reconstruction, for example, in Afghanistan and

Liberia. AfghanistanOnline included a thread from the interim Government of Afghanistan soliciting the diaspora's feedback on its draft constitution.

From the perspective of home country governments, there are three broad policy options for addressing migration: migration management, the diaspora option (Meyer et al. 1997), and democracy and development (see Lowell et al. 2004). Policies for democracy and development remain the backdrop (though not always a requirement) for the realization of diaspora contributions to development. The diaspora option seeks to engage diasporas for remittance capture, and includes diaspora networking, and diaspora integration (see Gamlen 2005). Diaspora integration policies are those described above – policies extending citizen rights, as well as general diaspora outreach, such as the organization of diaspora summits, and diplomatic visits to diaspora communities and organizations.

Remittance capture entails not only increasing the volume and productivity of remittances, but also policies that seek specifically to encourage diaspora economic investment. Home governments are increasingly soliciting remittances and offering policy incentives (e.g., dual citizenship, tax-free investment opportunities, and matching funds) and investment options.[13] The latter include remittance-backed bonds, foreign currency accounts, investment tax breaks, exemption from import tariffs on capital goods, duty-free shopping bonuses, and free passport issuance (Gamlen 2005).

The diaspora networking strategy encompasses activities that provide intermediary functions in addition to programs and policies that incentivize and facilitate knowledge exchange, business/investment, and diaspora philanthropy. As mentioned in Chapter 1, examples include Mexico's 3x1 program (see Orozco with Lapointe 2004), and Mexico's Institute of Mexicans Abroad, housed in the Federal secretariat of Foreign Relations (see Ayó n 2006). The government of the People's Republic of China pursues a diaspora networking strategy through institutional structures, policies, program activities, and official websites (see Biao 2006). Policies target skilled overseas Chinese professionals (OCPs), for example, providing high quality of working and living conditions during OCP returns, including national level

---

[13] See, for example, Lowell and De la Garza (2000), Orozco with Lapointe (2004), Pires-Hester (1999).

benefits (e.g., support for purchasing a car), and local government benefits (e.g., priority phone installation). Funded programs include short-term visits, collaborative research projects, OCP research projects conducted in the PRC, and contractual professorial and research chairs in the sciences. Other program activities include visiting delegations, business venture conventions, scientific conferences, and industrial parks targeted to OCP-initiated ventures.

Are such policies always helpful and effective? A recent review from Asia confirms mixed results (Brinkerhoff 2006a). Welcome and effective policies depend on the particulars of the actors and context. Levitt and de la Dehesa (2003) argue that "the size and organization of the emigrant community vis-à-vis its homeland, the capacity of state institutions to make and implement credible policies, and the unique role of political parties have an impact on the form, timing, and effectiveness of state policies towards communities abroad" (589). Since contributions are likely to occur with or without government intervention, sometimes the best policy may be simply getting out of the way. Some policies may promote and expand diaspora homeland development initiatives, but government policies can also compromise their viability through attempts at co-optation and manipulation (Portes 2003). On the other hand, government policies may strongly impact the goal direction of diaspora mobilization vis-à-vis the homeland, if they move beyond symbolic appeals (Portes et al. 2007).

Recommendation 3: Homeland governments should use digital diasporas to solicit and possibly influence diaspora contributions; disseminate information about homeland developments, perhaps seeking endorsement; and stay connected to their diasporas, acknowledging them in ways that may encourage diasporans' further engagement in support of the homeland.

Experimentation with diaspora networking policies is in its infancy; it is still unclear whether or not diaspora integration strategies outweigh their investment and potential risks in terms of diaspora engagement in the homeland. Governments face a steep learning curve. There is a considerable need to identify specific policy options, codify alternatives, and assess effectiveness. The promise of such policy options, though, remains contingent on government policy regimes that are weak in both capacity and coordination (see Global Commission on International Migration 2005). Nevertheless, continued experimentation and government capacity building for such policy design and implementation are necessary.

Digital diasporas represent a relatively harm-free, low-cost opportunity for homeland governments to explore and experiment with relationships to their diasporas. This leads to my third policy recommendation: Homeland governments should use digital diasporas to solicit and possibly influence diaspora contributions; disseminate information about homeland developments, perhaps seeking endorsement (e.g., for post-conflict draft constitutions as in the case of Afghanistan); and stay connected to their diasporas, acknowledging them in ways that may encourage diasporas' further engagement in support of the homeland.

International Development Community

A final policy arena to consider concerns the international development community, or the industry funded by Official Development Assistance. Where do diaspora contributions fit in the formal policies and programs of official development assistance? Globalization has exacerbated many of the challenges to effective development assistance (see Florini 2000), including a declining capacity of national governments, changing private sector and NGO roles, and weak and outmoded global institutions (Brinkerhoff 2004). In response, Lindenberg and Bryant (2001) call for a new global NGO architecture, including networks and virtual organizations. However, they conclude somewhat pessimistically, that "... none of the globalizing organizations from any part of the world have a fresh vision of how more genuine, multidirectional global networks for poverty alleviation and conflict reduction might be most realistically developed" (Lindenberg and Bryant 2001, 245). On his part, Dichter (2003) notes some positive advancements outside of the development industry, notably the growing promise of telecommunications and economic remittances from diaspora communities. Diasporas may be one source for addressing the industry's challenges of relevance, representativeness, and responsiveness (see Brinkerhoff 2004).

Recommendation 4: International development practitioners should tap digital diasporas to solicit information, and cultural and technical expertise; disseminate information about their programming for the purpose of

constituency building and coordination; and seek intermediary support in order better to reach the diaspora, and target communities and those with requisite skills and experience.

To date, most diaspora-related initiatives originating from the donor
community concentrate on research, brain drain, and, increasingly, enhancing the productive benefits of remittances. Isolated experimentation and experiences are accumulating, wherein DOs are more engaged
in the interface with formal development institutions, including providing technical assistance, intermediary services, and even as implementing partners (see Brinkerhoff 2004). Diasporans have individually
been engaged in formal development assistance for some time. Yet even
this experience remains relatively unexamined. A recent review of an
experience recruiting from the diaspora for the reconstruction of Iraq
(Brinkerhoff and Tadesse 2008) is one exception. Here, too, a more
systematic review of options and experience is needed, and particularly
with the increased role of official development assistance in postconflict
reconstruction, where societies have largely lost their human capital to
war and forced and elective migration.

Just as with homeland governments, digital diasporas are a relatively
harm-free, low-cost opportunity for the international development community to explore and experiment with integrating diasporas into development programming, potentially using them to respond to the industry's
challenges of relevance, representativeness, and responsiveness. This
leads to my fourth policy recommendation: International development
practitioners should tap digital diasporas to solicit information, and cultural and technical expertise; disseminate information about their programming for the purpose of constituency building and coordination; and
seek intermediary support in order better to reach the diaspora, and target
communities and those with requisite skills and experience.

Recommendation 5: Given diasporas' voluntary, low-cost contributions and
their infusion with liberal values, host governments and international
development actors should consider building their organization capacity in
support of supplementary or partnership approaches to development, much
as they did for the young NGO sector.

If the evolution of DOs continues as I predict, we may very well see
expanded contributions of DOs to development objectives, and in ways

that are consistent with the relevance and purported advantages historically attributed to the nonprofit sector. However, development agencies will have difficulty supporting and partnering with organizations with weak capacity and little, if any, track record (Dade 2006). These potential contributions can be accelerated with capacity development support.

When considering diaspora contributions to development, policymakers primarily see the volume of remittances. On their part, DOs tend to be weak organizationally and may sometimes lack the sensitivity required for effective development processes, and the understanding for developing effective sustainable strategies. Until these two sides can interact more and talk with each other, we may remain at an impasse, despite the tremendous opportunities represented by diaspora resources (including cultural, social, and human capital). Building the capacity of the DO sector can contribute to its organization capacity, its knowledge of development and development processes, and its ability to speak the language and understand the thinking of traditional development actors so that DOs and traditional development industry actors can more effectively work together. International development actors made similar investments in U.S.-based NGOs and the fledgling NGO sector in developing countries in the mid- to late 1990s.[14]

This leads to my fifth policy recommendation: Given diasporas' voluntary, low-cost contributions and their infusion with liberal values, host governments and international development actors should consider building their organization capacity in support of supplementary or partnership approaches to development, much as they did for the young NGO sector.

In promoting an increased role for diasporas in international development, two caveats are in order. First, there remains a risk that homeland governments may overrely on diasporas to stimulate their economies and develop targeted communities and regions. Several scholars warn that diasporas should not be considered responsible

---

[14] For example, from 1994–2001, the U.S. Agency for International Development supported the Global Excellence in Management (GEM) Initiative. The goals were to: "(1) Promote organizational excellence in development organizations in the U.S. and abroad; (2) Create new forms of global cooperation; and, (3) Sustain excellence, develop capacity to continually learn, adjust and innovate over time" (Appreciative Inquiry Commons 2007).

for the development of their homelands, nor should governments' perceived responsibility be diminished based on diaspora development activities (see Levitt 2001; Mahler 2000; Vertovec 2004).

Second, diasporas are not homogeneous, and so contributions must be examined in light of the subgroups comprising them. In some instances, these contributions may be welcomed by homeland compatriots and governments alike; in others, the contributions may exacerbate tensions between compatriots and the homeland government; and in still other instances, diaspora contributions may be unwelcome by all but a small minority in the homeland. The latter occurs, for example, when a diaspora mobilizes for its own brand of political and cultural reform. The legitimacy of diaspora influence on the homeland may be questioned, even if homeland compatriots and governments are in agreement with its intention.[15]

In the development arena, as DOs gain in their sophistication and experience working with the international development industry, one can hope that they will overcome the voluntary failures of philanthropic paternalism and philanthropic particularism, and that they will also learn the lessons of participatory development and respect for self-determination. These are elements of the liberal values some of the CGOs examined appear already to embrace when contemplating the future of their homelands.

Diaspora Organizations

As DOs do not make policy, here I set forth two recommendations for their continuing and expanding practice. Both of these concern learning from the experience of development NGOs more generally.

Recommendation 6: Diaspora organizations that seek to make socioeconomic contributions to their homelands should retain control over the labels that

---

[15] For example, after the destruction of the Babri Masjid mosque in Ayodya, India, a group of "concerned non-resident Indians" took out an advertisement in the *Indian Express* (one of India's largest English-language daily newspapers) urging the "restoration of common sets of values and laws based on the 6,000 year heritage," to which a group of "Indian citizens in India" responded with an advertisement in the same paper: "Is it not presumptuous of the Indians who left 'mother Bharat' and caused a severe brain drain to dictate how we Indians, who remained behind should run our country?" (see Lal 1999, 150 and footnote 20).

describe them. Specifically, "diaspora organization" will confer greater perceptions of potential relevance and sophistication than "hometown association."

Much as occurred in the NGO sector, if DOs are to realize their potential in the world of official development assistance, pursuing collaborative opportunities and benefiting from capacity building support and policy influence, they face a need to strategically assert themselves in these processes. Historically, NGOs were considered insignificant – of small scale and very limited capacity. Today, aside from the cumulative, though for the most part uncoordinated power of individual remittances, diaspora initiatives for development are similarly viewed as small scale and limited in their capacity. Because of their potential to coordinate and improve the productive investment capacity of remittances, hometown associations receive some attention. "HTA" is the predominant reference to diaspora organizations in most industry reports and research.

The physical world organizations reviewed here, as well as the DO reviews to date, suggest significant potential in their contributions to reducing poverty and improving quality of life. And, as argued above, this potential is likely to be increasingly realized as DOs evolve in their sophistication and capacity. This alone, will not lead to increased engagement with official development assistance. The organizations reviewed are highly diverse; they include a formal but volunteer-based nonprofit organization (Afghans4Tomorrow), a formal and highly professional nonprofit (Coptic Orphans), and a transnational business (Thamel.com). I have intentionally labeled all of these under the rubric of "diaspora organization." I argue that the emphasis on HTAs and the persistence of this rhetoric, even when initiatives may be regional or national in scope, undermines the increasing capacity of diaspora organizations, reinforcing perceptions of small scale and limited significance. Furthermore, it is not descriptive of many organizations, which still tend to be subsumed under its moniker. Promoting the notion of DOs as a sector will likely go far in changing mindsets regarding diasporas' potential development contributions and significance.

This leads to my sixth policy recommendation: Diaspora organizations that seek to make socioeconomic contributions to their homelands should retain control over the labels that describe them. Specifically, "diaspora organization" will confer greater perceptions of potential relevance and sophistication than "hometown association."

Recommendation 7: Learning from the experience of the NGO sector more broadly, DOs should selectively contract and receive funding from governments and donors, paying careful attention to maintaining their organization identity.

Beyond the capacity and capacity development lessons discussed above, DOs could benefit from studying more generally the experience of NGOs as they have been integrated into formal development programming. Many of these NGOs began as well-intentioned, often small-scale volunteer efforts. They entered the official development arena with a strong sense of organization identity. The maintenance of organization identity is "the extent to which an organization remains consistent and committed to its mission, core values, and constituency"; and maintains characteristics "reflective of the organizational type from which the organization originates" (Brinkerhoff 2002b, 15, 16). For NGOs (and DOs) the latter component includes maintaining comparative advantages such as flexibility and responsiveness. When NGOs became increasingly integrated into formal development programming (and government contracting), they began to take on the characteristics of their funding organizations, becoming bureaucratic and overly responsive to funding opportunities, rather than remaining true to their own organization identity (mission, values, and constituencies) (see, for example, Bush 1992; Hulme and Edwards 1997; Van der Heijden 1987).

This experience leads to my final recommendation: Learning from the experience of the NGO sector more broadly, DOs should selectively contract and receive funding from governments and donors, paying careful attention to maintaining their organization identity.

CONCLUSION

Independently, the online conversations and even the communities and organizations they create may seem peripheral to the concerns of international affairs. This study underscores just how pertinent they are to primary concerns of integration, security, politics, and socioeconomic development. They are an integral component in a system of diaspora identity and mobilization. With the continuing ease of migration and telecommunications access and development, the world is increasingly interconnected. We ignore these phenomena at our peril and at the risk of neglecting important resources to achieve the peaceful and prosperous world we all aspire to.

The Internet is an invaluable asset to diaspora well-being. It holds significant potential to relieve identity stress and build the bonding and bridging social capital necessary for psychological health among diasporans. The identity negotiation and storytelling the Internet affords is at once fun, necessary, and deadly serious. Identity negotiation processes ideally yield experimentation with and integration of adopted homeland cultural artifacts, such as enhanced faith in and manifestation of liberal values: democracy, pluralism, and human rights, including basic freedoms of speech, assembly, and self-determination. The resulting hybridity can buttress soft assimilation, where diasporans at once self-identify as American (in the case of the diasporas studied here) and embrace their cultural heritage (Portes 2003).

With regard to the physical world, such healthy integration has security implications for both the adopted and ancestral homelands. In the receiving society, the identity resources and support, and the bonding and bridging social capital digital diasporas generate can help to avert marginalization and promote understanding of the structures and social groups of the adopted society. The Internet provides a forum for reinforcing and negotiating diaspora identity (see Brainard and Brinkerhoff 2004; Brinkerhoff 2004), potentially alleviating the need for diasporas to agitate for their own vision of homeland, thus reducing tension in the physical world. And it provides an organizational resource to consider, develop, and mobilize for constructive political and development agendas for the homeland.

The communities and organizations examined in these pages represent a small snapshot of digital diasporas. As we have seen, they are at once unique – defying comparison on many levels, especially with respect to potential physical world impact – and similar in the functions they provide to diasporans. Yet understood as a functional component of a larger system, their significance to international affairs cannot be ignored. As migration continues to expand, particularly from the developing to industrialized countries, policymakers risk misunderstanding challenges and opportunities if they overlook the growing phenomenon of digital diasporas.

Appendix: Methodology

For the CGOs, web pages and their interactive components were analyzed along two dimensions: the nature of the benefit gained from the member's participation and the type of communication involved. The analysis builds on Wilson's (1995) three types of member benefits: purposive, material, and solidary, discussed in Chapter 2. Members generate purposive benefits when they pursue goals directed beyond the boundaries of the organization. These might include the provision of services to nonmembers or advocating for a particular cause. Material benefits include information, referrals, and the tangible outcomes of service delivery. Solidarity (associational advantages that flow from feeling connected to others and belonging to a community) cannot be created without a core membership, so a quantitative analysis (frequency of posts, rates of response to posts, interaction rate within identified subgroups) and qualitative analysis (references to specific members, quality of interaction with members) inform understanding of the core membership of each site. I add a fourth category, cultural identity benefit, or opportunities for members to engage with others to explore and negotiate their individual, as well as community, cultural identities. I identify examples and frequency of each of these benefits through thread and message analyses.

I also investigated messages and threads according to communication type. Drawing on McLaughlin and associates' (1997) study of community in cyberspace, I distinguished among three categories of messages: conventional (everyday communication among strangers);

interpersonal (exchange that recognizes and invokes personal identity among members); and communal (communication that refers directly to community as a whole). I added announcements as another category to signify one-way communication that represents simple information sharing. These categories are not mutually exclusive. I also analyzed message content for references to and demonstration of democratic values. The analysis of these various components informed my selection of threads and posts for citation and discussion in each of the case chapters.

Acronyms

A4T	Afghans4Tommorrow
AFFORD	African Foundation for Development
CGO	Cybergrassroots Organization
CIA	Central Intelligence Agency
CO	Coptic Orphans
CSO	Civil Society Organization
DEA	Drug Enforcement Agency
DfID	Department for International Development
DO	Diaspora Organization
EWB-I	Engineers without Borders International
GOE	Government of Egypt
HMG	His Majesty's Government of Nepal
HTA	Hometown Association
ICC	International Criminal Court
MOF	Ministry of Finance
NGO	Nongovernmental Organization
OCP	Overseas Chinese Professional
PRC	People's Republic of China
RA	Rebuild Afghanistan
TLF	Tibetan Liberation Front (username)
UK	United Kingdom
UNHCR	UN High Commissioner for Refugees
USAID	U.S. Agency for International Development
VOA	Voice of America

Bibliography

Adams Parham, Angel. "Diaspora, Community, and Communication: Internet Use in Transnational Haiti." *Global Networks*, Vol. 4, No. 2 (April 2004): 199–217.

Afghans4Tomorrow. *2005 Newsletter*. Available at: http://www.afghans4 tomorrow.com/pdf/RevisedA4T121305.pdf. Accessed July 21, 2006.

Africast.com. "Poet's Son held by 'Web' Police in Egypt." November 26, 2001. Africast.com.

Anderson, Benedict. *Imagined Communities: Reflections on the Origins and Spread of Nationalism*. London: Verso, 1991.

Anderson, Mary B. *Do No Harm: How Aid Can Support Peace – Or War*. Boulder, CO: Lynne Rienner Publishers, 1999.

Andraws, George. Founder of MyCopticChurch.com. Personal interview by Jennifer M. Brinkerhoff, May 27, 2003.

Anheier, Helmut and Jeremy Kendall. "Interpersonal Trust and Voluntary Associations: Examining Three Approaches." *British Journal of Sociology*, Vol. 53, No. 3 (September 2002): 343–363.

Anonymous. "Diaspora Humanitarian Assistance to Armenia in the Last Decade." Paper prepared for the Armenia Diaspora Conference, Yerevan, September 22–23, 1999. http://www.armeniadiaspora.com/conference99/ humanitarian.html.

Aoki, Kumiko. Virtual Communities in Japan. (ftp://ftp.sunsite,udc.edu/ academic/comms/papers). November 1994.

Appadurai, Arjun. "The Capacity to Aspire: Culture and the Terms of Recognition." In Rao Vijayendra and Michael Walton, eds. *Culture and Public Action*. Stanford, CA: Stanford University Press, 2004.

Appreciative Inquiry Commons. "AI History and Timeline."Available at: http://appreciativeinquiry.case.edu/intro/timeline.cfm. Accessed December 11, 2007.

Armstrong, John A. "Mobilized and Proletarian Diasporas." *American Political Science Review*, Vol. 70, No. 2 (June 1976): 393–408.

Asmallash, Malugetah. Remarks on the Dir Foundation Coffee project in Ethiopia. Policy Seminar on Migration and Development: Diasporas and Policy Dialogue. African Development Policy Centre with support from the Dutch Ministry of Foreign Affairs. Institute of Social Studies, The Hague, October 24, 2007.

Awan, Akil N. "Virtual Jihadist Media: Function, Legitimacy, and Radicalizing Efficacy." *European Journal of Cultural Studies*, Vol. 10, No. 3 (August 2007): 389–408.

Ayón, David R. "Long Road to the *Vota Postal*: Mexican Policy and People of Mexican Origin in the U.S." Policy Paper, No. 6. Berkeley, CA: Center for Latin American Studies, University of California, Berkeley, February 2006. Available at: http://socrates.berkeley.edu:7001/Publications/workingpapers/policypapers/AyonWeb.pdf. Accessed July 26, 2006.

Ayres, Jeffrey M. "From the Streets to the Internet: The Cyber-Diffusion of Contention." *Annals of the American Academy of Political and Social Science*, Vol. 566, No. 1 (November 1999): 132–143.

Bandura, Albert. *Self-Efficacy: The Exercise of Control*. New York: Freeman, 1997.

Baogang He and Barry Sautman. "The Politics of the Dalai Lama's New Initiative for Autonomy." *Pacific Affairs*, Vol. 78, No. 4 (Winter 2005/2006): 601–629.

Barber, Benjamin R. *Jihad vs. McWorld: How Globalism and Tribalism are Reshaping the World*. New York: Ballantine Books, 1995.

Barber, Brian. "Political Violence, Social Integration, and Youth Functioning: Palestinian Youth from the Intifada." *Journal of Community Psychology*, Vol. 29, No. 3 (May 2001): 259–280.

Battera, Frederico. "State- & Democracy-Building in Sub-Saharan Africa: The Case of Somaliland – A Comparative Perspective." *Global Jurist Frontiers*, Vol. 4, No. 1 (January 2004): 1–21.

Baumann, Martin. "Conceptualizing Diaspora: The Preservation of Religious Identity in Foreign Parts, Exemplified by Hindu Communities Outside India." *Temenos*, Vol. 31 (1995): 19–35.

Benhabib, Seyla. *Situating the Self*. Cambridge: Polity Press, 1992.

Bennett Daniel and Pam Fielding. *The Net Effect: How Cyberadvocacy Is Changing the Political Landscape*. Capital Advantage: New York, 1999.

Bernal, Victoria. "Diaspora, Cyberspace, and Political Imagination: The Eritrean Diaspora Online." *Global Networks*, Vol. 6, No. 2 (April-June 2006): 161–179.

Berry, John W. "Immigration, Acculturation, and Adaptation." *Applied Psychology: An International Review*, Vol. 46, No. 1 (January 1997): 5–34.

Bhatia, Sunil and Anjali Ram. "Locating the Dialogical Self in the Age of Transnational Migrations, Border Crossings and Diasporas." *Culture & Psychology*, Vol. 7, No. 3 (September 2001): 297–309.

Biao, Xiang. "Promoting Knowledge Exchange Through Diaspora Networks (The Case of the People's Republic of China)." In Clay Wescott and Jennifer

M. Brinkerhoff, eds. *Converting Migration Drains into Gains: Harnessing the Resources of Overseas Professionals*. Manila: Asian Development Bank, 2006: 33–72.

Birch, Anthony H. "Economic Models in Political Science: The Case of 'Exit, Voice, and Loyalty.'" *British Journal of Political Science*, Vol. 5, No. 1 (January 1975): 69–82.

Bourdieu, Pierre. "The Forms of Capital." In John G. Richardson, ed. *Handbook of Theory and Research for the Sociology of Education*. New York: Greenwood Press, 1986: 241–258.

Brainard, Lori A. "Citizen Organizing in Cyberspace: Illustrations from Health Care and Implications for Public Administration." *American Review of Public Administration*, Vol. 33, No. 4 (December 2003): 384–406.

Brainard, Lori A. and Jennifer M. Brinkerhoff. "Sovereignty Under Siege or a Circuitous Path to Strengthening the State?: Digital Diasporas and Human Rights." *International Journal of Public Administration*, Vol. 9, No. 8 (2006): 595–618.

Brainard, Lori A. and Jennifer M. Brinkerhoff. "Lost in Cyberspace: Shedding Light on the Dark Matter of Grassroots Organizations." *Nonprofit and Voluntary Sector Quarterly*, Vol. 33, No. 3 Supplement (September 2004): 32S–53S.

Brainard, Lori A. and Patricia D. Siplon. "Toward Nonprofit Organization Reform in the Voluntary Spirit: Lessons from the Internet." *Nonprofit and Voluntary Sector Quarterly*, Vol. 33, No. 3 (September 2004): 435–457.

Brainard, Lori and Patricia Siplon. "Cyberspace Challenges to Mainstream Non-Profit Health Organizations." *Administration & Society*, Vol. 34, No. 2 (2002a): 141–175.

Brainard, Lori and Patricia Siplon. "The Internet and NGO-Government Relations: Injecting Chaos into Order." *Public Administration and Development*, Vol. 22, No. 1 (2002b): 63–72.

Brewer, Marilynn B. "Reducing Prejudice Through Cross-Categorization: Effects of Multiple Social Identities." In Stuart Oskamp, ed. *Reducing Prejudice and Discrimination*. Mahwah, NJ: Erlbaum, 2000: 165–84.

Brinkerhoff, Derick W. and Samuel Taddesse. "Recruiting from the Diaspora: The Local Governance Program in Iraq." In Jennifer M. Brinkerhoff, ed. *Diasporas and Development: Exploring the Potential*. Boulder, CO: Lynne Rienner Publishers, Inc., 2008: 67–87.

Brinkerhoff, Jennifer M. "Diaspora Identity and the Potential for Violence: Toward an Identity-Mobilization Framework." *Identity: An International Journal of Theory and Research*, Vol. 8, No. 1 (January 2008a): 67–88.

Brinkerhoff, Jennifer M. "Diaspora Philanthropy in an At-Risk Society: The Case of Coptic Orphans in Egypt." *Nonprofit and Voluntary Sector Quarterly*, Vol. 37, No. 2 (September 2008b): 411–433.

Brinkerhoff, Jennifer M. "Contributions of Digital Diasporas to Governance Reconstruction in Post-Conflict and Fragile States: Potential and Promise." In Derick W. Brinkerhoff, ed. *Governance in Post-Conflict Societies: Rebuilding Fragile States*. London: Routledge, 2007: 185–203.

Brinkerhoff, Jennifer M. "Digital Diasporas and Conflict Prevention: The Case of Somalinet.com." *Review of International Studies*, Vol. 32, No. 1 (January 2006a): 25–47.

Brinkerhoff, Jennifer M. "Diaspora Mobilization Factors and Policy Options." In Clay Wescott and Jennifer M. Brinkerhoff, eds. *Converting Migration Drains into Gains: Harnessing the Resources of Overseas Professionals.* Manila: Asian Development Bank, 2006b: 127–153.

Brinkerhoff, Jennifer M. "Digital Diasporas and Semi-Authoritarian States: The Case of the Egyptian Copts." *Public Administration and Development*, Vol. 25, No. 3 (August 2005): 193–204.

Brinkerhoff, Jennifer M. "Digital Diasporas and International Development: Afghan-Americans and the Reconstruction of Afghanistan." *Public Administration and Development*, Vol. 24, No. 5 (December 2004): 397–413.

Brinkerhoff, Jennifer M. "Global Public Policy, Partnership, and the Case of the World Commission on Dams." *Public Administration Review*, Vol. 62, No. 3 (May/June 2002a): 317–329.

Brinkerhoff, Jennifer M. *Partnership for International Development: Rhetoric or Results?* Boulder, CO: Lynne Rienner Publishers, Inc., 2002b.

Brinkerhoff, Jennifer M. and Derick W. Brinkerhoff. "Government-Nonprofit Relations in Comparative Perspective: Evolution, Themes, and New Directions." *Public Administration and Development*, Vol. 22, No. 1 (February 2002): 3–18.

Brophy, Peter and Edward Halpin. "Through the Net to Freedom: Information, the Internet and Human Rights." *Journal of Information Science*, Vol. 25, No. 5 (October 1999): 351–64.

Brynen, Rex. "Diaspora Populations and Security Issues in Host Countries." Paper presented at the Metropolis Interconference Seminar "Immigrants and the Homeland." Dubrovnik, Croatia, May 9-12, 2002. Available at: http://international.metropolis.net/events/croatia/brynen.pdf. Accessed June 15, 2008.

Burt, Ronald S. "The Network Structure of Social Capital." In Robert I. Sutton and Barry M. Staw, eds. *Research in Organizational Behavior*, Vol. 22. Greenwich, CT: JAI Press, 2000: 345–423.

Bush, Richard. "Survival of the Nonprofit Spirit in a For-Profit World." *Nonprofit and Voluntary Sector Quarterly*, Vol. 12, No. 4 (Winter 1992): 391–410.

Butler, Kim D. "Defining Diaspora, Refining a Discourse." *Diaspora*, Vol. 10, No. 2 (Fall 2001): 189–218.

Byman, Daniel, Peter Chalk, Bruce Hoffman, William Rosenau, and David Brannan. *Trends in Outside Support for Insurgent Movements.* Santa Monica, CA: Rand Corporation, 2001.

Cabras, Alessandra. "Beyond the Internet: Democracy on the Phone?" In Michael J. Mazarr, ed. *Information Technology and World Politics.* New York: Palgrave MacMillan, 2002: 85–99.

Cameron, Maxwell A., ed. *To Walk Without Fear: The Global Movement to Ban Landmines.* Oxford: Oxford University Press, 1998.

Central Intelligence Agency. *Central Intelligence Factbook.* Washington, DC: Author, 2006.

Chaliand, Gérard and Jean-Pierre Rageau. *The Penguin Atlas of Diasporas.* New York: Penguin, 1997.

Chandra, Kanchan. "Ethnic Bargains, Group Instability, and Social Choice Theory." *Politics & Society*, Vol. 29, No. 3 (September 2001): 337–362.

Chung, Jae Ho. "Challenging the State: Falungong and Regulatory Dilemmas in China." In John D. Montgomery and Nathan Glazer, eds. *How Governments Respond: Sovereignty Under Challenge.* New Brunswick and London: Transaction Publishers, 2002: 83–106.

Clifford, James. "Diasporas." *Cultural Anthropology*, Vol. 9, No. 3 (August 1994): 302–338.

Clifford, James. *The Predicament of Culture: Twentieth Century Ethnography, Literature, and Art.* Cambridge, MA: Harvard University Press, 1988.

Coffman, Elesha. "Lost in America: Arab Christians in the US Have a Rich Heritage and a Shaky Future." *Christianity Today*, March 26, 2004. Available at: http://www.christianitytoday.com/ct/2004/004/2.38.html. Accessed July 28, 2006.

Cohen, Robin. *Global Diasporas: An Introduction.* London: UC London Press, 1997.

Cohen, Robin. "Diasporas and the Nation-State: From Victims to Challengers." *International Affairs*, Vol. 72, No. 3 (July 1996): 507–520.

Coleman, James S. *Foundations of Social Theory.* Cambridge, MA: Belknap-Harvard University Press, 1990.

Coleman, James S. "Social Capital in the Creation of Human Capital." Supplement: "Organizations and Institutions: Sociological and Economic Approaches to the Analysis of Social Structure."*American Journal of Sociology*, Vol. 94 (Supplement 1988): S95–S120.

Coll, Steve, and Susan B. Glasser. "Terrorists Turn to the Web as Base of Operations." *The Washington Post*, August 7, 2005, A1.

Collier, Paul, Lani Elliott, Havard Hegre, Anke Hoeffler, Marta Reynol-Querol, and Nicholas Sambanis. *Breaking the Conflict Trap: Civil War and Development Policy.* Washington, DC: The World Bank and Oxford University Press, 2003.

Collier, Paul and Anke Hoeffler. "Greed and Grievances in Civil War." *Policy Research Working Paper* No. 2355. Washington, DC: The World Bank, 2001.

Coptic Orphans. *Building Bridges: 2003 Annual Report.* Merrifield, VA: Coptic Orphans, 2004.

Cortini, Michela, Guiseppe Mininni, and Amelia Manuti. "The Diatextual Construction of the Self in Short Message Systems." *Identity: An International Journal of Theory and Research*, Vol. 4, No. 4 (October 2004): 355–370.

Coston, Jennifer M. "Grassroots Organizations and Influencing Public Policy Processes: Lessons from Around the World." *International Journal of Organization Theory and Behavior*, Vol. 2, Nos. 1 & 2 (January/February 1999): 1–26.

Cramer, Christopher and Jonathan Goodhand. "Try Again, Fail Again, Fail Better? War, the State, and the 'Post Conflict' Challenge in Afghanistan." *Development and Change*, Vol. 33, No. 5 (November 2002): 885–909.

Crescenzi, Antonella, Eva Ketzer, Mark Van Ommeren, Kalsang Phuntsok, Ivan Komproe, and Joop T.V.M de Jong. "Effect of Political Imprisonment and Trauma History on Recent Tibetan Refugees in India." *Journal of Trauma Stress*, Vol. 15, No. 5 (October 2002): 369–375.

Curry, Andrew. "War and Exile." *US News & World Report*, Vol. 131, No. 16 (October 12, 2001): 42–45.

Curtis, James E., Douglas E. Baer, and Edward G. Grabb. "Nations of Joiners: Explaining Voluntary Association Membership in Democratic Societies." *American Sociological Review*, Vol. 66, No. 6 (December 2001): 783–805.

D'Souza, Dinesh. "Ten Great Reasons to Celebrate." *Washington Times*, July 4, 2002, A16.

Dade, Carlo. "Policy Considerations for Working with Diaspora Populations." Keynote speech to "Diasporas as Wealth Creators" Workshop, Jönköping, Sweden, April 6-7, 2006. Available at: http://www.diwec.org/Downloads.htm. Accessed July 23, 2006.

Dahan, Michael and Gabriel Sheffer. "Ethnic Groups and Distance Shrinking Communication Technologies." *Journal of Ethnic and Migration Studies*, Vol. 7, No. 1 (Spring 2001): 85–107.

Dahles, Heidi. "Venturing Across Borders: Investment Strategies of Singapore-Chinese Entrepreneurs in Mainland China." *Asian Journal of Social Science*, Vol. 32, No. 1 (March 2004): 19–41.

Danitz, Tiffany and Warren P. Strobel. "Networking Dissent: Cyber Activists Use the Internet to Promote Democracy in Burma." *Virtual Diplomacy Series*, No. 3. Washington, DC: United States Institute of Peace, February 2000.

Dartnell, Michael. "Information Technology and the Web Activism of the Revolutionary Association of the Women of Afghanistan (RAWA) – Electronic Politics and New Global Conflict." In Robert Latham, ed. *Bombs and Bandwidth: The Emerging Relationship Between Information Technology and Security*. New York and London: The New Press, 2003: 251–267.

Dichter, Thomas W. *Despite Good Intentions: Why Development Assistance to the Third World has Failed*. Amherst and Boston: University of Massachusetts Press, 2003.

Diener, Ed. "Subjective Well-Being." *Psychological Bulletin*, Vol. 95, No. 3 (May 1984): 542–75.

Diener, Ed and Robert Biswas-Diener. "Psychological Empowerment and Subjective Well-Being." In Deepa Narayan, ed. *Measuring Empowerment: Cross-Disciplinary Perspectives*. Washington, DC: The World Bank, 2005: 125–140.

Douglas, James. "Political Theories of Nonprofit Organization." In Walter W. Powell and Elizabeth S. Clemens, eds. *Private Action and the Public Good*. New Haven and London: Yale University Press, 1998: 43–54.

Duffield, Mark. *Global Governance and the New Wars: The Merging of Development and Security*. London and New York: Zed Press, 2001.

Dutton, William H. and Wan-Ying Lin. "Using the Web in the Democratic Process. The Web-Orchestrated 'Stop the Overlay' Cyber-Campaign." *European Review*, Vol. 9, No. 2 (May 2001): 185–199.

Edgerton, Robert B. "Traditional Beliefs and Practices – Are Some Better than Others?" In Lawrence E. Harrison, and Samuel P. Huntington, eds. *Culture Matters: How Values Shape Human Progress*. New York: Basic Books, 2000: 126–140.

Elgindy, Khaled. "Diaspora Troublemakers: Is the Organized Coptic Community in the US Doing more Harm than Good?" *Cairo Times*, Vol. 2, No. 25 (February 4, 1999). Available at: http://www.cairotimes.com/content/issues/copts/expats.html. Accessed July 24, 2002.

Elkins, David. "Globalization, Telecommunication, and Virtual Ethnic Communities." *International Political Science Review*, Vol. 18, No. 2 (April 1997): 139–152.

Elnur, Ibrahim. "11 September and the Widening North-South Gap: Root Causes of Terrorism in the Global Order." *Arab Studies Quarterly*, Vol. 25, Nos. 1 & 2 (Winter 2003): 57–70.

Erikson, Erik H. "'Identity Crisis' in Perspective."In Erik H. Erikson. *Life History and the Historical Moment*. New York: Norton, 1975: 17–18.

Esman, Milton. "The Factors Conducive to Diaspora Investment: Comparing China, Armenia, and Ireland." In Jennifer M. Brinkerhoff, ed. *Diasporas and Development: Exploring the Potential*. Boulder, CO: Lynne Rienner Publishers, Inc., 2008: 99–111.

Esman, Milton J. *Ethnic Politics*. Ithaca, NY: Cornell University Press, 1994.

Esman, Milton J. "Diasporas and International Relations." In Gabriel Sheffer, ed. *Modern Diasporas in International Politics*. London and Sydney: Croom Helm, 1986: 333–349.

Faist, Thomas. "'Extension du Domaine de la Lutte': International Migration and Security Before and After September 11, 2001." *International Migration Review*, Vol. 36, No. 1 (March 2002): 7–14.

Falk, Richard A. *Human Rights and State Sovereignty*. New York: Homes & Meier Publishers, 1981.

Farag, Phoebe. Personal Communication with Jennifer M. Brinkerhoff, December 6, 2007.

Farag, Phoebe. International Program Director, Coptic Orphans. Personal Interview by Jennifer M. Brinkerhoff, January 21, 2004.

Fargues, Philippe. "Demographic Islamization: Non-Muslims in Muslim Countries." *SAIS Review*, Vol. 21, No. 2 (Summer-Fall 2001): 103–116.

Fearon, James D. and David D. Laitin. "Explaining Interethnic Cooperation." *The American Political Science Review*, Vol. 90, No. 4 (December 1996): 715–735.

Florini, Ann, ed. *The Third Force: The Rise of Transnational Civil Society*. Washington, DC: Carnegie Endowment for International Peace, 2000.

Fontaine, Thomson with Jennifer M. Brinkerhoff. "National Development Planning: The Case of Dominica." In Jennifer M. Brinkerhoff, ed. *Diasporas and International Development: Exploring the Potential*. Boulder, CO: Lynne Rienner Publishers, Inc., 2008: 185–203.

Foster, Derek. "Community and Identity in the Electronic Village." In David Porter, ed. *Internet Culture*. New York: Routledge, 1996: 23–37.

Fox, Gregory H. "New Approaches to International Human Rights: The Sovereign State Revisited." In Sohail H. Hashmi, ed. *State Sovereignty: Change and Persistence in International Relations*. University Park, PA: Pennsylvania State University Press, 1997: 105–130.

Franklin, Marianne I. "I Define My Own Identity: Pacific Articulations of 'Race' and 'Culture' on the Internet." *Ethnicities*, Vol. 3, No. 4 (December 2003): 465–490.

Friedman, Jonathan. *Cultural Identity and Global Process*. London and Thousand Oaks, CA: Sage Publications, 1994.

Fuller, Gary A., Alexander B. Murphy, Mark A. Ridgley, and Richard Ulack. "Measuring Potential Ethnic Conflict in Southeast Asia." *Growth and Change*, Vol. 31, No. 2 (Spring 2000): 305–331.

Gajjala, Radhika. "South Asian Digital Diasporas and Cyberfeminist Webs: Negotiating Globalization, Nation, Gender and Information Technology Design." *Contemporary South Asia*, Vol. 12, No. 1 (March 2003): 41–56.

Galston, William A. "The Impact of the Internet on Civic Life: An Early Assessment." In Elaine Ciulla Kamarck and Joseph S. Nye, Jr., eds. *Governance.com: Democracy in the Information Age*. Washington, DC: Brookings Institution Press, 2002: 40–58.

Galtung, Johan. *Peace by Peaceful means: Peace and Conflict, Development and Civilization*. Thousand Oaks, CA: Sage Publications, 1996.

Gamlen, Alan. "The Brain Drain is Dead, Long Live the New Zealand Diaspora." *Working Paper* No. 10. Oxford, UK: University of Oxford, Centre on Migration, Policy and Society, 2005.

Geertz, Clifford. *Islam Observed: Religious Developments in Morocco and Indonesia*. Chicago: University of Chicago Press, 1968.

Gergen, Kenneth J. "Social Understanding and the Inscription of Self." In James W. Stigler, Richard A. Shweder, and Gilbert Herdt, eds. *Cultural Psychology: Essays on Comparative Human Development*. Cambridge: Cambridge University Press, 1990: 233–40.

Giddens, Anthony. *Modernity and Self-Identity: Self and Society in the Late Modern Age*. Stanford, CA: Stanford University Press, 1991.

Gillespie, Kate and Anna Andriasova. "Supporting Business Development: The Experience of Armenia." In Jennifer M. Brinkerhoff, ed. *Diasporas and Development: Exploring the Potential*. Boulder, CO: Lynne Rienner Publishers, 2008: 113–131.

Gillespie, Kate Edward Sayre, and Liesl Riddle. "Palestinian Interest in Homeland Investment." *Middle East Journal*, Vol. 55, No. 2 (Spring 2001): 237–255.

Gillespie, Kate, Liesl Riddle, Edward Sayre, and David Sturges. "Diaspora Homeland Investment." *Journal of International Business Studies*, Vol. 30, No. 3 (Summer 1999): 623–634.

Gilroy, Paul. *The Black Atlantic: Modernity and Double Consciousness*. London: Verso, 1993.

Gilroy, Paul. *There Ain't no Black in the Union Jack*. London: Hutchinson, 1987.

Gissinger, Ranvieg and Nils Petter Gleditch. "Globalization and Conflict: Welfare, Distribution, and Political Unrest." *Journal of World Systems Research*, Vol. 5, No. 2 (Summer 1999): 274–300.

Gittel, Ross and Avis Vidal. *Community Organizing: Building Social Capital as a Development Strategy.* Thousand Oaks, CA: Sage Publications, 1998.

Glasser, Susan B. and Steve Coll. "The Web as Weapon; Zarqawi Intertwines Acts on Ground in Iraq With Propaganda Campaign on the Internet." *The Washington Post*, August 9, 2005, A1.

Global Commission on International Migration. *Migration in an Interconnected World: New Directions for Action.* Geneva: Author, 2005. Available at: http://www.gcim.org/en/. Accessed February 3, 2006.

Goldstein, Melvyn. "Tibet, China, and the United States: Reflections on the Tibet Question." Washington, DC: Atlantic Council of the United States, 1995.

Graham, Mark and Shahram Khosravi. "Reordering Public and Private in Iranian Cyberspace: Identity, Politics, and Mobilization." *Identities: Global Studies in Culture and Power*, Vol. 9, No. 2 (April-June 2002): 219–246.

Granger, Robert. Co-Director of Thamel International. Personal Interview by Jennifer M. Brinkerhoff, September 17, 2004.

Greig, J Michael. "The End of Geography? Globalization, Communications, and Culture in the International System." *Journal of Conflict Resolution*, Vol. 46, No. 2 (April 2002): 225–243.

Griffin, Larry. "Narrative, Event-Structure Analysis, and Causal Interpretation in Historical Sociology." *American Journal of Sociology*, Vol. 98, No. 5 (March 1993): 1094–1133.

Grosfoguel, Ramón and Héctor Cordero-Guzmán. "International Migration in a Global Context: Recent Approaches to Migration Theory." *Diaspora: A Journal of Transnational Studies*, Vol. 7, No. 3 (Winter 1998): 351–368.

Guarnizo, Luis Edwardo and Luz M. Diaz. "Transnational Migration: A View from Colombia." *Ethnic and Racial Studies*, Vol. 22, No. 2 (March 1999): 397–421.

Guarnizo, Luis Edwardo, Alejandro Portes, and William Haller. "Assimilation and Transnationalism: Determinants of Transnational Political Action Among Contemporary Migrants." *American Journal of Sociology*, Vol. 108, No. 6 (May 2003): 1211–1248.

Gunderson, Lee. "Voice of the Teenage Diasporas." *Journal of Adolescent & Adult Literacy*, Vol. 43, No. 8 (May 2000): 692–706.

Gyari, Kasur Lodi Gyaltsen. Special Envoy of His Holiness the Dalai Lama. "Statement by Special Envoy of His Holiness the Dalai Lama, Kasur Lodi Gyaltsen Gyari." *Central Tibetan Administration Press Release*, May 8, 2008. Available at: http://www.tibet.net/en/prelease/2008/080508.html. Accessed June 19, 2008.

Hall, Stuart. "Old and New Identities, Old and New Ethnicities." In Anthony Douglas King, ed. *Culture, Globalization and the World-System.* Houndmills, UK: Macmillan, 1991: 41–68.

Hall, Stuart. "Cultural Identity and Diaspora." In Jonathan Rutherford, ed. *Identity: Community, Culture, Difference*. London: Lawrence, 1990: 222–237.

Hammar, Tomas. *Democracy and the Nation-State: Aliens, Denizens and Citizens in a World of International Migratin*. Aldershot, UK: Avebury, 1990.

Hampton, Keith N. and Barry Wellman. "The Not so Global Village of Netville." In Barry Wellman and Caroline Haythornthwaite, eds. *The Internet and Everyday Life*. Oxford, UK: Blackwell, 2002: 345–371.

Hanafi, Sari. "Reshaping Geography: Palestinian Community Networks in Europe and the New Media." *Journal of Ethnic and Migration Studies*, Vol. 31, No. 3 (May 2005): 581–198.

Hanifi, Shah Mahmoud. "Material and Social Remittances to Afghanistan." In Clay Wescott and Jennifer M. Brinkerhoff, eds. *Converting Migration Drains into Gains: Harnessing the Resources of Overseas Professionals*. Manila: Asian Development Bank, 2006: 72–93.

Hansen, M.L. "The Study of Man: The Third Generation in America. A Classic Essay in Immigrant History." *Commentary*, (1952): 492–500.

Hansmann, Henry. "Economic Theories of Nonprofit Organization." In Walter W. Powell, ed. *The Nonprofit Sector: A Research Handbook*. New Haven, CT: Yale University Press, 1987: 27–42.

Hashmi, Sohail H. "Introduction." In Sohail H. Hashmi, ed. *State Sovereignty: Change and Persistence in International Relations*. University Park, PA: Pennsylvania State University Press, 1997: 1–14.

Haynes, Jeff. "Religion, Secularisation, and Politics: A Postmodern Conspectus." *Third World Quarterly*, Vol. 18, No. 4 (December 1997): 709–728.

Heath, Jennifer and Sheryl Shapiro. "Report from Afghanistan. A Summary of a Humanitarian Journey to Afghanistan, 2003."Available at: http://www.taparts.org/TAPdocs/afghanreport.pdf.Accessed September 13, 2003.

Helland, Christopher. "Diaspora on the Electronic Frontier: Developing Virtual Connections with Sacred Homelands." *Journal of Computer-Mediated Communication*, Vol. 12, No. 3 (April 2007): 956–976.

Henke, Tari. "Stewardship from Afar: An Entrepreneur from Nepal Promotes Community and Creates Jobs – From Half a World Away." Global Envision, Creating Market Opportunities for People Worldwide, an Initiative of Mercy Corps, 2002–2003. Available at: http://www.globalenvision.org/library/14/242/6/. Accessed January 14, 2005.

Henry, Leroi and Giles Mohan. "Making Homes: The Ghanaian Diaspora, Institutions and Development." *Journal of International Development*, Vol. 15, No. 5 (June 2003): 611–622.

Hergnyan, Manuk and Anna Makaryan. "The Role of the Diaspora in Generating Foreign Direct Investments in Armenia." *Armenian Journal of Public Policy*, Vol. 2, No. 2 (January 2007): 259–294.

Hermans, Hubert and Harry Kempen. "Moving Cultures: The Perilous Problems of Cultural Dichotomies in a Globalizing Society." *American Psychologist*, Vol. 53, No. 10 (October 1998): 1111–1120.

Hernandez, Lynn, Marilyn J. Montgomery, and William M. Kurtines. "Identity Distress and Adjustment Problems in At-Risk Adolescents." *Identity: An International Journal of Theory and Research*, Vol. 6, No. 1 (January 2006): 27–33.

Hersant, Jeanne and Alexandre Toumarkine. "Hometown Organisations in Turkey: An Overview." *European Journal of Turkish Studies, Thematic Issue No. 2*, Hometown Organisations in Turkey, 2005. Available at: http://www.ejts.org/document397.html Accessed July 22, 2006.

Hewstone, Miles, Mark Rubin and Hazel Willis. "Intergroup Bias." *Annual Review of Psychology*, Vol. 53 (2002): 575–604.

Hinkle, Steven, Lee Fox-Cardamone, Julia A. Haseleu, Rupert Brown, and Lois M. Irwin. "Grassroots Political Action as an Intergroup Phenomenon." *Journal of Social Issues*, Vol. 52, No. 1 (Spring 1996): 39–51.

Hirschman, Albert O. *Exit, Voice, and Loyalty: Responses to Decline in Firms, Organizations, and States*. Cambridge, MA: Harvard University Press, 1970.

Howeidy, Amira. "Web Cats." *Al-Ahram Weekly Online*, November 29, 2001. Available at: http://weekly.ahram.org.eg/2001/562/eg6.htm. Accessed July 30, 2006.

Hozic, Aida. "Hello. My Name is… : Articulating Loneliness in a Digital Diaspora." *Afterimage*, Vol. 21, January 1, 2001: 1–9. Available at: http://findarticles.com/p/articles/mi_m2479/is_4_28/ai_76560784/pg_1. Accessed December, 1, 2007.

Hulme David and Michael Edwards, eds. *NGOs, States and Donors: Too Close for Comfort?* St. Martin's Press, in association with Save the Children: New York, 1997.

Ibrahim, Youssef M. "US Bill has Egypt's Copts Squirming." *New York Times*, April 12, 1998, I10.

Inglehart, Ronald. "Culture and Democracy." In Lawrence E. Harrison, and Samuel P. Huntington, eds. *Culture Matters: How Values Shape Human Progress*. New York: Basic Books, 2000: 80–97.

International Campaign for Tibet. "US Proposes New Tibetan Refugee Admissions Program." Author, September 7, 2005. Available at: http://www.savetibet.org/news/newsitem.php?id=808. Accessed July 28, 2006.

International Fund for Agricultural Development. *Sending Money Home: Worldwide Remittance Flows to Developing Countries*. Rome: Author, 2007. Available at: http://www.ifad.org/events/remittances/maps/index.htm Accessed November, 30, 2007.

Iskander, Natasha. "Diaspora Networks for Creating National Infrastructure: Rural Morocco, 1985–2005." In Jennifer M. Brinkerhoff, ed. *Diasporas and Development: Exploring the Potential*. Boulder, CO: Lynne Rienner Publishers, Inc., 2008: 163–183.

Jacobsen, Michael and Stephanie Lawson. "Between Globalization and Localization: A Case Study of Human Rights Versus State Sovereignty." *Global Governance*, Vol. 5, No. 2 (April-June 1999): 203–220.

Jiménez, Efraín. "Presentación en Holanda." *NOVIB International Expert Meeting on Bridging the Gap: The Role of Migrants and their Remittances on Development*. Noordwijk, the Netherlands, November 19-20, 2004.

Available at: http://www.federacionzacatecana.org/index.php?sectionName=home&;subSection=news&story_id=238. Accessed July 23, 2006.

Joshi, Bal K. Personal Communication with Jennifer M. Brinkerhoff, December 6, 2007.

Joshi, Bal K. Cofounder and Managing Director of Thamel.com, Codirector of Thamel International. Personal Interview by Jennifer M. Brinkerhoff, September, 17, 2004a.

Joshi, Bal K. "Thamel.com – Serving Diaspora Communities Through ICT." *ICT Connections: Local Ideas, Global Applications.* Center to Bridge the Digital Divide, Washington State University, October 1, 2004b. Available at: http://cbdd.typepad.com/global/2004/10/thamelcom_servi.html. Accessed January 14, 2005.

Joshi, Bal K. and Robert Granger. "THAMEL: Reducing the Social, Cultural, and Economic Cost of Immigration through the Power of ICT." The Global Knowledge Partnership, *ICT Stories*, September 23, 2003. Available at: http://www.iicd.org/stories/articles/Story.import5102/. Accessed January 14, 2005.

Kadende-Kaiser, Rose M. "The Internet's Mediation Potential in Protracted Conflicts: The Case of Burundi." In Robert Latham, ed. *Bombs and Bandwidth: The Emerging Relationship Between Information Technology and Security.* New York and London: The New Press, 2003: 268–278.

Kalathil, Shanthi. "Dot.Com for Dictators." *Foreign Policy*, No. 135 (March/April 2003): 42–49.

Kalathil, Shanthi and Taylor C. Boas. *Open Networks, Closed Regimes: The Impact of the Internet on Authoritarian Rule.* Washington, DC: Carnegie Endowment for International Peace, 2003.

Karim, Karim H. "Mapping Diasporic Mediascapes." In Karim H. Karim, ed. *The Media of Diaspora.* London: Routledge, 2003a: 1–18.

Karim, Karim H., ed. *The Media of Diaspora.* London: Routledge, 2003b.

Kastoryano, Riva. "Muslim Diaspora(s) in Western Europe." *South Atlantic Quarterly*, Vol. 98, Nos. 1 & 2 (Winter/Spring 1999): 191–202.

Katauskas, Ted. "He'll Get Your Goat."*Portland Monthly*, (September, 2004): 36, 42.

Keck, Margaret and Katherine Sikkink. *Activists Beyond Borders: Transnational Advocacy Networks in International Politics.* Ithaca, NY: Cornell University Press, 1998.

Kelly, Caroline and John Kelly. "Who Gets Involved in Collective Action?: Social Psychological Determinants of Individual Participation in Trade Unions."*Human Relations*, Vol. 47, No. 1 (January 1994): 63–88.

Kerlin, Janelle. "Organizational Responses to Homeland Crisis: The US Afghan Diaspora." In Jennifer M. Brinkerhoff, ed. *Diasporas and Development: Exploring the Potential.* Boulder, CO: Lynne Rienner Publishers, 2008: 29–44.

King, Charles and Neil J. Melvin. "Diaspora Politics: Ethnic Linkages, Foreign Policy, and Security in Eurasia."*International Security*, Vol. 24, No. 3 (Winter 1999/2000): 108–138.

King, David and Miles Pomper. "The US Congress and the Contingent Influence of Diaspora Lobbies: Lessons from US Policy Toward Armenia and Azerbaijan." *Journal of Armenian Studies*, Vol. 8, No. 1 (Fall/Winter 2004): 72–98.

King, Tony. "Rhodesians in Hyperspace: The Maintenance of a National and Cultural Identity." In Karim H. Karim, ed. *The Media of Diaspora*. London: Routledge, 2003: 177–188.

Klandermans, Bert. *The Social Psychology of Protest*. Oxford: Blackwell, 1997.

Klandermans, Bert and Dirk Oegema. "Potentials, Networks, Motivations, and Barriers: Steps towards Participation in Social Movements."*American Sociological Review*, Vol. 52, No. 4 (August 1987): 519–531.

Korten, David C. *Getting to the 21st Century: Voluntary Action and the Global Agenda*. West Hartford, CT: Kumarian Press, 1990.

Korten, David C. "Third Generation NGO Strategies: A Key to People-Centered Development." *World Development*, Vol. 15, Supplement (Autumn 1987): 145–159.

Koslowski, Rey. "International Migration and the Globalization of Domestic Politics: A Conceptual Framework." In Rey Koslowski, ed. *International Migration and the Globalization of Domestic Politics*. Oxon, U.K and New York: Routledge, 2005: 5–32.

Krasner, Stephen D. *Sovereignty: Organized Hypocrisy*. Princeton, NJ: Princeton University Press, 1999.

Lake, David A. and Donald Rothchild, eds. *The International Spread of Ethnic Conflict: Fear, Diffusion, and Escalation*. Princeton, NJ: Princeton University Press, 1996.

Lal, Vinay. "Terror and its Networks: Disappearing Trails in Cyberspace." Paper presented at the Virtual Diasporas and Global Problem-Solving Workshop, sponsored by the Nautilus Institute and the World Affairs Council. Berkeley and San Francisco, California, April 25-26, 2002. Available at: http://www.nautilus.org/virtual-diasporas/paper/Lal.html. Accessed March 13, 2004.

Lal, Vinay. "The Politics of History on the Internet: Cyber-Diasporic Hinduism and the North American Hindu Diaspora." *Diaspora: A Journal of Transnational Studies*, Vol. 8, No. 2 (Fall 1999): 137–172.

Lavie, Smadar and Ted Swedenburg, eds. *Displacement, Diaspora, and Geographies of Identity*. Durham and London: Duke University Press, 1996.

Leatherman, Janie, William DeMars, Patrick D. Gaffnew, and Raimo Vayrynen. *Breaking Cycles of Violence: Conflict Prevention in Intrastate Crises*. West Hartford, CT: Kumarian Press, 1999.

Lemarchand, René. *Exclusion, Marginalization and Political Mobilization: The Road to Hell in the Great Lakes*. Bonn: Center for Development Research, 2000.

Levitt, Peggy. "Transnational Migration: Taking Stock and Future Directions." *Global Networks*, Vol. 1, No. 3 (July 2001): 195–216.

Levitt, Peggy and Raphael de la Dehesa. "Transnational Migration and the Redefinition of the State: Variations and Explanations." *Ethnic and Racial Studies*, Vol. 26, No. 4 (July 2004): 587–611.

Lewis and Clark College. "Alumni Profiles: Bal Joshi." Portland, OR: Author, 2004. Available at: http://www.lclark.edu/dept/iso/alumniprofiles.html. Accessed January 14, 2005.

Lewis, I.M. *A Pastoral Democracy. London: International African Institute*, 1961 (Reprinted in 1982 by Africana Publishing Company).

Lindenberg, Marc and Coralie Bryant. *Going Global: Transforming Relief and Development NGOs*. Bloomfield, CT: Kumarian Press, 2001.

Lipsky, Michael and Steven R. Smith. "Nonprofit Organizations, Government, and the Welfare State." *Political Science Quarterly*, Vol. 104, No. 4 (Winter 1989-1990): 625–648.

Livingston, Steven. "Diplomacy in the New Information Environment." *Georgetown Journal of International Affairs*, Vol. 4, No. 2 (Summer/Fall 2003): 111–116.

Louie, Andrea. "Creating Places Through Mobility: Chinese-American 'Roots-Searching' in China." *Identities*, Vol. 8, No. 3 (September 2001): 343–379.

Lowell, B. Lindsay, and Rodolofo O. De la Garza. *The Developmental Role of Remittances in U.S. Latino Communities and in Latin American Countries: A Final Project Report*. Washington, DC: Inter-American Dialogue and the Tomas Rivera Policy Institute, June, 2000.

Lowell, B. Lindsay and Stefka G. Gerova. "Diasporas and Economic Development: State of Knowledge." Washington, DC: Georgetown University Institute for the Study of International Migration, September 13, 2004. Available at: http://siteresources.worldbank.org/INTGEP2006/Resources/LowellDiaspora. doc. Accessed July 14, 2006.

Lowell, B. Lindsay, Allan Findlay, and Emma Stewart. "Brain Strain: Optimising Highly Skilled Migration from Developing Countries."*Asylum and Migration Working Paper 3*. London: Institute for Public Policy Research, August, 2004.

Lubkemann, Stephen. "'Global Locals' and Political Process in War-torn Paper presented at the Nations: The Liberian Diaspora in War-Making and Peace-Building." African Studies Association annual meeting, New Orleans, LA, November 11, 2004.

Mahler, Sarah J. "Migration and Transnational Issues: Recent Trends and Prospects for 2020." Hamburg: Institut für Iberoamerika-Kunde, CA 2020 Working Paper No. 4, 2000.

Manchanda, Rita. "Politics-Nepal: Women Flocking to Ranks of Maoist Rebels." *Global Information Network*. New York: November 3, 2004, 1.

Mansbridge, Jane. "On the Contested Nature of the Public Good." In Walter W. Powell and Elizabeth S. Clemens, eds. *Private Action and the Public Good*. New Haven, CT and London: Yale University Press, 1998: 3–19.

Maphosa, France. " The Impact of Remittances from Zimbabweans Working in South Africa on Rural Livelihoods in the Southern Districts of Zimbabwe."

Forced Migration Working Paper Series, No. 4. Forced Migration Studies Program University of Witswatersrand, South Africa, January 2005. Available at: http://migration.wits.ac.za/Maphosa.pdf. Accessed July 22, 2006.

Marcus, Aliza. "Kurdish TV from Britain is Nationalist Voice." *Reuters World Service*, May 15, 1995.

Margolis, Mac with Sudip Mazumdar, Craig Simons, Kim Gurney, Maureen Chigbo, Liat Radcliffe, and Jaime Cunningham. "Brain Gain; Sending Workers Abroad Doesn't Mean Squandering Minds. For Many Countries, Diaspora Talent is the Key to Success." *Newsweek*, March 8, 2004, 30.

Margulies, Peter. "The Clear and Present Internet: Terrorism, Cyberspace, and The First Amendment." *UCLA Journal of Law and Technology*, Vol. 8, No. 2 (Fall 2004). Available at: http://www.lawtechjournal.com/home/?cat=2. Accessed 15 June, 2008.

Mason, Victoria. "Children of the 'Idea of Palestine': Negotiating Identity, Belonging and Home in the Palestinian Diaspora." *Journal of Intercultural Studies*, Vol. 28, No. 3 (August 2007): 271–285.

Matute-Bianchi, Maria Eugenia. "Situational Ethnicity and Patterns of School Performance among Immigrant and Nonimmigrant Mexican-Descent Students." In Margaret Gibson and John U. Ogbu, eds. *Minority Status and Schooling: A Comparative Study of Immigrant and Involuntary Minorities*. New York: Garland, 1991: 205–247.

Mayel, Tooba (Acting President and Public Relations Director), Ferdous Hakim (Financial Director), and Hassib Amiryar (Information Technology Director). Personal Interview by Lori A. Brainard and Jennifer M. Brinkerhoff, July 28, 2003.

Mbanzendore, Stéfanie. Chairperson of the Netherlands-based Burundian Women for Peace and Development. Focus group meeting on diasporas and development (organized by Oxfam Novib on behalf of Jennifer M. Brinkerhoff). The Hague, October 25, 2007.

McCormick, Glenn M. "Stateless Nations: 'I Pledge Allegiance To...?'" In Michael J. Mazarr, ed. *Information Technology and World Politics*. New York: Palgrave MacMillan, 2002: 11–23.

McFerson, Hazel. "Rethinking Ethnic Conflict: Somalia and Fiji." *American Behavioral Scientist*, Vol. 40, No. 1 (September 1996): 18–32.

McGranahan, Carole. "Truth, Fear, and Lies: Exile Politics and Arrested Histories of the Tibetan Resistance."*Cultural Anthropology*, Vol. 24, No. 4 (November 2005): 570–600.

McLaughlin, Margaret L., Kerry K. Osborne, and Nicole B. Ellison. "Virtual Community in a Telepresence Environment." In Steven G. Jones, ed. *Virtual Culture: Identity and Communication in Cybersociety*. London and Thousand Oaks, CA: Sage Publications, 1997: 146–168.

Mele, Christopher. "Cyberspace and Disadvantaged Communities: The Internet as a Tool for Collective Action." In Marc A. Smith and Peter Kollock, eds. *Communities in Cyberspace*. London: Routledge, 1999: 290–310.

Meraj, Abdul. Personal Communication, September 12, 2003.

Meraj, Abdul. Personal Interview by Lori A. Brainard and Jennifer M. Brinkerhoff, October 2, 2002.

Merz, Barbara Jean, Lincoln C. Chen, and Peter F. Geithner, eds. *Diasporas and Development*. Boston: Harvard University Press, 2007.

Meunier, Michael. *President and CEO, US Copts Association*. Personal Interview by Lori A. Brainard and Jennifer M. Brinkerhoff, December 17, 2002a.

Meunier, Michael. President and CEO U.S. Copts Association. Personal Interview by Jennifer Brinkerhoff, November 25, 2002b.

Meyer, John-Baptiste and Mercy Brown. "Scientific Diasporas: A New Approach to the Brain Drain." Prepared for the World Conference on Science, UNESCO-ICSU. Budapest, Hungary, 26 June-1 July, 1999.

Meyer, John-Baptiste, Jorge Charum, Dora Bernal, Jacques Gaillard, José Granés, John Leon, Alvaro Montenegro, Alvaro Morales, Carlos Murcia, Nora Narvaez-Berthelemot, Luz Stella Parrado, and Bernard Schlemmer. "Turning Brain Drain into Brain Gain: The Colombian Experience of the Diaspora Option." *Science Technology and Society*, Vol. 2, No. 2 (September 1997).

Montgomery, John D. "Sovereignty in Transition." In John D. Montgomery and Nathan Glazer, eds. *How Governments Respond: Sovereignty Under Challenge*. New Brunswick and London: Transaction Publishers, 2002: 3–30.

Montgomery, John D. and Dennis A. Rondinelli, eds. *Beyond Reconstruction in Afghanistan: Lessons from Development Experience*. New York: Palgrave MacMillan, 2004.

Moya, Jose C. "Immigrants and Associations: A Global and Historical Perspective." *Journal of Ethnic and Migration Studies*, Vol. 31, No. 5 (September 2005): 833–864.

Nafie, Ibrahim. "Domestic Threats to Peace: Sectarian Cashes in Alexandria Sound an Alarm it is Perilous to Ignore." *Al-Ahram Weekly*, April 24, 2006. Available at: http://weekly.ahram.org.eg/2006/791/op1.htm. Accessed May 26, 2006.

Navarro, Sharon. "Border Narratives: The Politics of Identity and Mobilization." *Latin American Politics and Society*, Vol. 45, No. 3 (Fall 2003): 129–139.

Ndofor-Tah, Carolyne. *Diaspora and Development: Contributions by African Organisations in the UK to Africa's Development*. Report Commissioned by the African Foundation for Development (AFFORD). London: Author, September 2000.

Nelson-Jones, Richard. "Diverse Goals for Multicultural Counselling and Therapy." *Counselling Psychology Quarterly*, Vol. 15, No. 2 (June 2002): 133–143.

Nenova, Tatiana and Tim Harford. "Anarchy and Invention: How Does Somalia's Private Sector Cope without Government?" *Public Policy for the Private Sector, Note Number 280*. Washington, DC: World Bank Group Private Sector Development Vice Presidency, November, 2004.

Northrup, Terrell. "The Dynamics of Identity in Personal and Social Conflict." In Louis Kriesberg, Terrell Northrop and Stuart Thorson, eds. *Intractable*

Conflicts and their Transformation. Syracuse, NY: Syracuse University Press, 1989: 55–82.

Nudup, Dorjee. Founder, TibetBoard. Personal Interview by Jennifer M. Brinkerhoff, October 12, 2003.

Nyberg-Sorensen, Ninna. "The Development Dimension of Migrant Remittances." *Migration Policy Research Working Paper Series, 1,* 2004. Available at http://www.iom.int//DOCUMENTS/PUBLICATION/EN/mpr1.pdf. Accessed January 14, 2005.

Nyberg-Sorensen, Ninna, Nicholas Van Hear, and Poul Engberg-Pedersen. "The Migration-Development Nexus: Evidence and Policy Options." *IOM Migration Research Series*, No. 8. International Organization for Migration, July 2002.

Olad Hassan, Mohamed. "20 Members of Somalia's Parliament Resign." *Washington Post*. The Associated Press, July 27, 2006. Available at: http://www.washingtonpost.com/wp-dyn/content/article/2006/07/27/AR2006072700392_pf.html. Accessed July 28, 2006.

Oleson, Asta. *Islam and Politics in Afghanistan*. London: Curzon Press, 1995.

Omar, Wahid. (Director of Education Department, Afghans4Tommorow). Afghans4Tomorrow, Department of Education: Report for the months of March/April, 2003. Available at: http://www.afghans4tomorrow.com. Accessed September 12, 2003.

OMB Watch. "Senate Report on Homegrown Terrorism and the Internet Generates Criticism." *OMB Watch*, Vol. 9, No. 11, May 28, 2008. Available at: http://www.ombwatch.org/article/articleview/4260/1/538. Accessed June 16, 2008.

Orozco, Manuel. "Conceptualizing Diasporas: Remarks about the Latino and Caribbean Experience." Unpublished manuscript, 2005.

Orozco, Manuel. *Hometown Associations and their Present and Future Partnerships: New Development Opportunities?* Report commissioned by the U.S. Agency for International Development. Washington, DC: Inter-American Dialogue, September, 2003.

Orozco, Manuel with Michelle Lapointe. "Mexican Hometown Associations and Development Opportunities." *Journal of International Affairs*, Vol. 57, No. 2 (Spring 2004): 31–49.

Osman, Abdi. Founder, Somalinet.com. Personal Interview by Jennifer M. Brinkerhoff, October 2, 2003.

Ostrom, Elinor. *Governing the Commons: The Evolution of Institutions for Collective Action*. New York: Cambridge University Press, 1990.

Ostrom, Elinor, Roy Gardner, and James Walker. *Rules, Games, and Common-Pool Resources*. Ann Arbor: University of Michigan Press, 1994.

Özerdem, Alpaslan. "The Mountain Tsunami: Afterthoughts on the Kashmir Earthquake." *Third World Quarterly*, Vol. 27, No. 3 (2006): 397–419.

Panagakos, Anastasia N. "Downloading New Identities: Ethnicity, Technology, and Media in the Global Greek Village." *Identities: Global Studies in Culture and Power*, Vol. 10, No. 2 (April-June 2003): 201–219.

Panagakos, Anastasia and Heather A. Horst, eds."Return to Cyberia: Technology and the Social Worlds of Transnational Migrants." Special Journal Issue of *Global Networks*, Vol. 6, No. 2 (April 2006).

Parker, David and Miri Song. "Inclusion, Participation and the Emergence of British Chinese Websites." *Journal of Ethnic and Migration Studies*, Vol. 33, No. 7 (September 2007): 1043–1061.

Parker, David and Miri Song. "New Ethnicities Online: Reflexive Racialisation and the Internet." *Sociological Review*, Vol. 54, No. 3 (August 2006): 575–594.

Pew Research Center. *Muslim Americans: Middle Class and Mostly Mainstream*. Washington, DC: Author, 2007. Available at: http://pewresearch.org/assets/pdf/muslim-americans.pdf. Accessed June 16, 2008.

Phillips, Tommy M. and Joe F. Pittman. "Identity Processes in Poor Adolescents: Exploring the Linkages Between Economic Disadvantage and the Primary Task of Adolescence." *Identity: An International Journal of Theory and Research*, Vol. 3, No. 2 (April 2003): 115–129.

Philpott, Daniel. "Ideas and the Evolution of Sovereignty." In Sohail H. Hashmi, ed. *State Sovereignty: Change and Persistence in International Relations*. University Park, PA: Pennsylvania State University Press, 1997: 15–47.

Pires-Hester, Laura. "The Emergence of Bilateral Diaspora Ethnicity Among Cape Verdean-Americans." In Isidore Okpewho, Carole Boyce Davies, and Ali A. Mazrui, eds. *The African Diaspora: African Origins and New World Identities*. Bloomington: Indiana University Press, 1999: 485–503.

Popkin, Eric. "Transnational Migration and Development in Post-War Peripheral States: An Examination of Guatemalan and Salvadoran State Linkages with Their Migrant Populations in Los Angeles."*Current Sociology*, Vol. 51, Nos. 3–4 (May 2003): 347–374.

Portes, Alejandro. Remarks at the Bellagio Dialogue on Migration, Closing Conference. Bellagio, Italy: The German Marshall Fund and The Rockefeller Foundation, July 14–15, 2006.

Portes, Alejandro. "Conclusion: Theoretical Convergencies and Empirical Evidence in the Study of Immigrant Transnationalism." *International Migration Review*, Vol. 37, No. 3 (Fall 2003): 874–892.

Portes, Alejandro and Mi Zhou. "The New Second Generation: Segmented Assimilation and Its Variants (Interminority Affairs in the U.S.: Pluralism at the Crossroads)." *The Annals of the American Academy of Political and Social Science*, Vol. 30 (November 1993): 74–97.

Portes, Alejandro, Cristina Escobar, and Alexandria Walton Radford. "Immigrant Transnational Organizations and Development: A Comparative Study." *International Migration Review*, Vol. 41, No. 1 (March 2007): 242–281.

Prahalad, C.K. and Ramaswamy, Venkatram. *The Future of Competition: Co-Creating Unique Value with Customers*. Boston, MA: Harvard Business School Press, 2004.

Prahalad, C.K. and Stuart L. Hart. "The Fortune at the Bottom of the Pyramid." *Strategy+Business*, Vol. 26 (First Quarter 2002): 1–14.

Pratkanis, Anthony R. and Marlene E. Turner. "Persuasion and Democracy: Strategies for Increasing Deliberative Participation and Enacting Social Change." *Journal of Social Issues*, Vol. 52, No. 1 (Spring 1996): 187–205.

Putnam, Robert. *Making Democracy Work*. Princeton, NJ: Princeton University Press, 1993.

Qazi, Abdullah. Founder, AfghanistanOnline. Personal Interview by Lori A. Brainard and Jennifer M. Brinkerhoff, October, 2, 2002.

Rai, Amit S. "India On-Line: Electronic Bulletin Boards and the Construction of Diasporic Hindu Identity." *Diaspora: A Journal of Transnational Studies*, Vol. 4, No. 1 (Spring 1995): 31–57.

Rao, Aparna. "Debating Religious Practice in Cyberspace: Lived Islam and Antinomian Identities in a Kashmiri Muslim Community." In Imtiaz Ahmad and Helmut Reifeld, eds. *Lived Islam in South Asia: Adaptation, Accommodation, and Conflict*. Oxford: Berghahn Books, 2004: 83–106.

Raz, Joseph. "Multiculturalism: A Liberal Perspective." *Dissent* (1994): 67–79.

Redeker Hepner, Tricia. "Transnational Governance and the Centralization of State Power in Eritrea and Exile." *Ethnic and Racial Studies*, Vol. 31, No. 3 (March 2008): 476–502.

Renshon, Stanley A. "Dual Citizens in America: An Issue of Vast Proportions and Broad Signficance." Center for Immigration Studies Backgrounder, July 2000. Available at: http://www.cis.org/articles/2000/back700.html#20. Accessed November 28, 2007.

Rheingold, Howard. *The Virtual Community: Homesteading on the Electronic Frontier*. Reading, MA: Addison-Wesley, 1993.

Riad, Nermien. Executive Director and founder, Coptic Orphans. Personal Interview by Jennifer M. Brinkerhoff, May 11, 2007.

Riad, Nermien. Executive Director and founder, Coptic Orphans. Personal Interview by Jennifer M. Brinkerhoff, January 21, 2004.

Riddle, Liesl and Valentina Marano. "Homeland Export and Investment Promotion Agencies: The Case of Afghanistan." In Jennifer M. Brinkerhoff, ed. *Diasporas and Development: Exploring the Potential*. Boulder, CO: Lynne Rienner Publishers, Inc., 2008: 133–149.

Riddle, Liesl, Jennifer M. Brinkerhoff, and Tjai Nielsen. "Partnering to Beckon them Home: Public Sector Innovation for Diaspora Homeland Investment." *Public Administration and Development*, Vol. 28, No. 1 (February 2008): 54–66.

Rosenau, James N. *Distant Proximities: Dynamics Beyond Globalization*. Princeton, NJ and Oxford: Princeton University Press, 2003.

Ross, Jack C. *An Assembly of Good Fellows: Voluntary Associations in History*. Westport, CT: Greenwood Press, 1976.

Ross, Marc Howard. *The Culture of Conflict. Interpretations and Interests in Comparative Perspective*. New Haven, CT: Yale University Press, 1993.

Rowe, Paul S. "Four Guys and a Fax Machine? Diasporas, New Information Technologies, and the Internationalization of Religion in Egypt." *Journal of Church and State*, Vol. 43, No. 1 (Winter 2001): 81–92.

Rubin, Jeffrey A., Dean G. Pruitt, and Sung Hee Kim. *Social Conflict: Escalation, Stalemate and Settlement*, 2nd ed. New York: McGraw-Hill, 1994.

Rude, John C. "Birth of a Nation in Cyberspace." *The Humanist*, Vol. 56, No. 2 (March-April 1996): 17–22.

Rudmin, Floyd W. "Critical History of the Acculturation Psychology of Assimilation, Separation, Integration, and Marginalization." *Review of General Psychology*, Vol. 7, No. 1 (March 2003): 3–37.

Rumbaut, Rubén and Alejandro Portes, eds. *Ethnicities: Children of Immigrants in America*. Berkeley: University of California Press, 2001.

Safe Democracy Foundation. "Democracy, Terrorism and the Internet." Panel transcription. International Summit on Democracy Terrorism and Security. March 8–11, 2005, Madrid. Available at: http://english.safe-democracy.org/keynotes/democracy-terrorism-and-the-internet.html. Accessed June 17, 2008.

Safran, William. "Comparing Diasporas: A Review Essay." *Diaspora: A Journal of Transnational Studies*, Vol. 8, No. 3 (Winter 1999): 255–291.

Safran, William. "Diasporas in Modern Societies: Myths of Homeland and Return."*Diaspora: A Journal of Transnational Studies*, Vol. 1, No. 1 (1991): 83–99.

Salamon, Lester M. "Of Market Failure, Voluntary Failure, and Third-Party Government: Toward a Theory of Government-Nonprofit Relations in the Modern Welfare State." *Journal of Voluntary Action Research*, Vol. 16, Nos. 1 & 2 (January–June 1987): 29–49.

Samatar, Said. *Oral Poetry and Somali Nationalism: The Case of Sayyid Mahammad "Abdille" Hassan*. Cambridge: Cambridge University Press, 1982.

Sánchez Gibau, Gina. "Contested Identities: Narratives of Race and Ethnicity in the Cape Verdean Diaspora." *Identities: Global Studies in Culture and Power*, Vol. 12, No. 3 (July–September 2005): 405–438.

Santianni, Michael. "The Movement for a Free Tibet: Cyberspace and the Ambivalence of Cultural Translation." In Karim H. Karim, ed. *The Media of Diaspora*. London: Routledge, 2003: 189–202.

Sapienza, Filipp. "Nurturing Translocal Communication: Russian Immigrants on the World Wide Web." *Technical Communication*, Vol. 48, No. 4 (November 2001): 435–448.

Sato, Noriko. "Selective Amnesia: Memory and History of the Urfalli Syrian Orthodox Christians." *Identities*, Vol. 12, No. 3 (July–September 2005): 315–333.

Saunders, Richard A. "Nationality: Cyber-Russian." *Russia in Global Affairs*, No. 4 (October–November 2004). Available at: http://eng.globalaffairs.ru/numbers/9/716.html. Accessed December 1, 2007.

Sautman, Barry. "'Cultural Genocide' and Tibet." *Texas International Law Journal*, Vol. 38, No. 2 (Spring 2003): 173–247.

Saxenian, AnnaLee. *The New Argonauts: Regional Advantage in a Global Economy*. Boston: Harvard University Press, 2006.

Saxenian Anna Lee. "Brain Circulation: How High-skill Immigration Makes Everyone Better Off. *The Brookings Review*, Vol. 20, No. 1 (Winter 2002a): 28–31.

Saxenian, AnnaLee. "Transnational Communities and the Evolution of Global Production Networks." *Industry & Innovation*, Vol. 9, No. 2 (December 2002b): 183–202.

Seddon, David. "Nepal's Dependence on Exporting Labor." *Migration Policy Institute Country Profiles*. Washington, DC: Migration Policy Institute, 2005. Available at: http://www.migrationinformation.org/Profiles/display.cfm?ID=277. Accessed January 14, 2005.

Seddon, David with Jagannath Adhikari, and Ganesh Gurung. "Foreign Labor Migration and the Remittance Economy in Nepal." *Critical Asian Studies*, Vol. 34, No. 1 (March 2002): 19–40.

Seelye, H. Ned and Marilynn B. Brewer. "Ethnocentrism and Acculturation of North Americans in Guatemala." *Journal of Social Psychology*, Vol. 80, No. 2 (April 1970): 147–155.

Sen, Amartya. *Identity and Violence: The Illusion of Destiny*. New York: W.W. Norton, 2006.

Shain, Yossi. *Marketing the American Creed Abroad: Diasporas in the U.S. and Their Homelands*. Cambridge, UK: Cambridge University Press, 1999.

Shain, Yossi. "Multicultural Foreign Policy." *Foreign Policy*, Vol. 100 (Fall 1995): 69–88.

Shain, Yossi. "Ethnic Diasporas and US Foreign Policy." *Political Science Quarterly*, Vol. 109, No. 10 (Winter 1994–1995): 811–841.

Shain, Yossi and Aharon Barth. "Diasporas and International Relations Theory." *International Organization*, Vol. 57, No. 3 (July 2003): 449–479.

Sharma, A. "Muckraking Mullahs." *Foreign Policy*, Vol. 130 (May–June 2002): 99.

Sheffer, Gabriel. *Diaspora Politics: At Home Abroad*. Cambridge: Cambridge University Press, 2006.

Sheffer, Gabriel. "A New Field of Study: Modern Diasporas in International Politics." In Gabriel Sheffer, ed. *Modern Diasporas in International Politics*. London and Sydney: Croom Helm, 1986a: 1–15.

Sheffer, Gabriel, ed. *Modern Diasporas in International Politics*. London and Sydney: Croom Helm, 1986b.

Siapera, Eugenia. "Minority Activism on the Web: Between Deliberative Democracy and Multiculturalism." *Journal of Ethnic and Migration Studies*, Vol. 31, No. 3 (May 2005): 499–519.

Singh, Simboonath. "Cultures of Exile: Diasporic Identities and the 'Imaginations' of Africa and India in the Caribbean." *Identity: An International Journal of Theory and Research*, Vol. 1, No. 3 (July 2001): 289–305.

Singh, Sonal. "Tears from the Land of Snow: Health and Human Rights in Tibet." *The Lancet*, Vol. 364, No. 9438 (September 11–17, 2004): 1009.

Smith, David Horton. *Grassroots Organizations*. Thousand Oaks, CA: Sage Publications, Inc., 2000.

Smith, Constance E. and Anne E. Freedman. *Voluntary Associations: Perspectives on the Literature*. Cambridge, MA: Harvard University Press, 1972.

Snow, David A. and Robert D. Benford. "Framing Processes and Social Movements: An Overview and Assessment." *Annual Review of Sociology*, Vol. 26 (2000): 611–39.

Snow, David A., E. Burke Rochford, Jr., Steven K. Worden, and Robert D. Benford. "Frame Alignment Processes, Micro-Mobilization, and Movement Participation." *American Sociological Review*, Vol. 51, No. 4 (August 1986): 464–481.

Sökefeld, Martin. "Alevism Online: Re-Imagining a Community in Virtual Space." *Diaspora: A Journal of Transnational Studies*, Vol. 11, No. 1 (Spring 2002): 85–123.

Sorial, Wafaa. Egypt Director, Coptic Orphans. Personal Interview by Jennifer M. Brinkerhoff, January 15, 2004.

Spinner, Jeff. *The Boundaries of Citizenship*. Baltimore, MD: Johns Hopkins University Press, 1994.

Suarez-Orozco, Marcelo M. "Becoming Somebody: Central American Immigrants in U.S. Inner-City Schools." *Anthropology and Education Quarterly*, Vol. 18, No. 4 (December 1987): 287–299.

Taylor, Donald M. and Winnifred Louis. "Terrorism and the Quest for Identity." In Fathali M. Moghaddam and Anthony J. Marsella, eds. *Understanding Terrorism: Psychosocial Roots, Consequences, and Interventions*. Washington, DC: American Psychological Association, 2004: 169–185.

Tekwani, Shyam. "The Tamil Diaspora, Tamil Militancy, and the Internet." In Kong-Chong Ho, Randy Kluver, and Kenneth C.C. Yang, eds. *Asia.com: Asia Encounters the Internet*. London: RoutledgeCurzon, 2003: 175–192.

Teufel Dreyer, June. "Economic Development in Tibet Under the People's Republic of China." *Journal of Contemporary China*, Vol. 12, No. 36 (August 2003): 411.

Thieme, Susan, Raju Bhattrai, Ganesh Gurung, and Michael Kollmair et al. "Addressing the Needs of Nepalese Migrant Workers in Nepal and in Delhi, India." *Mountain Research and Development*, Vol. 25, No. 2 (May 2005): 109–114.

Thomson, Mark and Maurice Crul. "The Second Generation in Europe and the United States: How is the Transatlantic Debate Relevant for Further Research on the European Second Generation?" *Journal of Ethnic and Migration Studies*, Vol. 33, No. 7 (September 2007): 1025–1041.

Tölölyan, Khachig. "Diasporama." *Diaspora: A Journal of Transnational Studies*, Vol. 3, No. 3 (Winter 1994): 235.

Tsaliki, Liza. "Globalisation and Hybridity: The Construction of Greekness on the Internet." In Karim H. Karim, ed. *The Media of Diaspora*. London: Routledge, 2003: 162–176.

Tsfati, Yariv and Gabriel Weimann. "www.terrorism.com: Terror on the Internet." *Studies in Conflict and Terrorism*, Vol. 25, No. 5 (September 2002): 316–332.

Turkish Daily News. "Limits on Kurdish Movies and Music Lifted." *Turkish Daily News*. June 13, 2006. Available at: http://www.turkishdailynews. com.tr/article.php?enewsid=46049&;mailtofriend=1. Accessed July 23, 2006.

Tynes, Robert. "Nation-Building and the Diaspora on Leonenet: A Case of Sierra Leone in Cyberspace." *New Media & Society*, Vol. 9, No. 3 (June 2007): 497–518.

United Nations Development Programme. *Human Development Report 2005. International Cooperation at a Crossroads: Aid, Trade and Security in an Unequal World*. New York: Author, 2005. Available at: http://hdr.undp.org/ reports/global/2005/. Accessed July 28, 2006.

United Nations Development Programme. *Nepal Human Development Report 2004. Empowerment and Poverty Reduction*. New York: Author, 2004. Available at: http://www.undp.org.np/publication/html/nhdr2004/index.php. Accessed July 28, 2006.

U.S. Census Bureau. *United States Census 2000*. Washington, DC: Author, 2001. Available at: http://www.census.gov/main/www/cen2000.html Accessed January 16, 2006.

U.S. Central Intelligence Agency. *The World Factbook*. Washington, DC: Author, July 20, 2006. Available at: https://www.cia.gov/cia/publications/ factbook/geos/np.html#Intro. Accessed July 28, 2006.

U.S. Committee for Refugees. *World Refugee Survey 2005*. Washington, DC: Author, 2006. Available at: http://www.refugees.org/data/wrs/06/docs/ principal_sources_of_refugees.pdf. Accessed July 28, 2006.

U.S. Committee for Refugees. *World Refugee Survey 2003*. Washington, DC: Author, 2003. Available at: http://www.refugees.org/WRS/2003.cfm#statistics. Accessed March 18, 2004.

U.S. Copts Association. *Copt Digest*, January 9, 2003a.

U.S. Copts Association. Website. http://www.Copts.com. Accessed May 24, 2003b.

U.S. Department of State. *Country Reports on Human Rights Practices for 2005*. "China/Tibet." Washington, DC: Bureau of Democracy, Human Rights, and Labor, March 8, 2006a. Available at: http://www.state.gov/g/ drl/rls/hrrpt/2005/61605.htm#tibet. Accessed July 28, 2006.

U.S. Department of State. *Country Reports on Human Rights Practices*. "Egypt – 2005." Washington, DC: Bureau of Democracy, Human Rights, and Labor, March 8, 2006b. Available at: http://www.state.gov/g/drl/rls/hrrpt/2005/ 61687.htm. Accessed May 26, 2006.

U.S. Department of State. *Country Reports on Human Rights Practices for 2001*. "Nepal." Washington, DC: Bureau of Democracy, Human Rights, and Labor, March 8, 2006c. Available at: http://www.state.gov/g/drl/rls/ hrrpt/2005/61709.htm. Accessed July 28, 2006.

U.S. Department of State. *Egypt: International Religious Freedom Report*. Washington, DC: Bureau of Democracy, Human Rights, and Labor, October 7, 2002a. Available from: http://www.state.gov/g/drl/rls/irf/2002/ 13994.htm. Accessed October 7, 2002.

U.S. Department of State. *Egypt: Country Reports on Human Rights Practices 2001*. Washington, DC: Bureau of Democracy, Human Rights, and Labor, March 4, 2002b. Available from: http://www.state.gov/g/drl/rls/hrrpt/2001/nea/8248.htm. Accessed March 4, 2002.

U.S. Office of Immigration Statistics. *2005 Yearbook of Immigration Statistics*. Washington, DC: Author, 2006. Available at: http://www.uscis.gov/graphics/shared/statistics/yearbook/index.htm. Accessed July 28, 2006.

U.S. Senate, Committee on Homeland Security and Governmental Affairs. *Violent Islamist Extremism, the Internet, and the Homegrown Terrorist Threat. Majority and Minority Staff Report*. Washington, DC: Author, May 8, 2008.

Uphoff, Norman. "Analytical Issues in Measuring Empowerment at the Community and Local Levels." In Deepa Narayan, ed. *Measuring Empowerment: Cross-Disciplinary Perspectives*. Washington, DC: The World Bank, 2005: 219–246.

Uphoff, Norman. "Understanding Social Capital: Learning from the Analysis and Experience of Participation." In Partha Dasgupta and Ismail Seregeldin, eds. *Social Capital: A Multifaceted Perspective*. Washington, DC: The World Bank, 2000: 215–52.

Uphoff, Norman. "Distinguishing Power, Authority, and Legitimacy: Taking Max Weber at His Word Using Resource Exchange Analysis." *Polity*, Vol. 22, No. 2 (Winter 1989): 295–322.

Van den Bos, Matthijs. "Hyperlinked Dutch-Iranian Cyberspace." *International Sociology*, Vol. 21, No. 1 (January 2006): 83–99.

Van den Bos, Matthijs and Liza Nell. "Territorial Bounds to Virtual Space: Transnational Online and Offline Networks of Iranian and Turkish-Kurdish Immigrants in the Netherlands." *Global Networks*, Vol. 6, No. 2 (April–June 2006): 201–220.

Van der Heijden, Hendrik. "The Reconciliation of NGO Autonomy, Program Integrity, and Operational Effectiveness with Accountability to Donors." *World Development*, No. 15, Supplement (1987): 103–112.

Van Hear, Nicholas, Frank Pieke, and Steven Vertovec (with assistance from Anna Lindley, Barbara Jettinger, and Meera Balarajan). *The Contribution of UK-Based Diasporas to Development and Poverty Reduction*. A Report by the ESRC Center on Migration, Policy, and Society (COMPAS), University of Oxford, for the Department for International Development. Oxford: COMPAS, April 2004.

Varshney, Ashutosh. "Ethnic Conflict and Civil Society: India and Beyond." *World Politics*, Vol. 53, No. 3 (April 2001): 362–398.

Vayrynen, Tarja. *Culture and International Conflict Resolution: A Critical Analysis of the Work of John Burton*. Manchester and New York: Manchester University Press, 2001.

Verrier, Michel. "From the Bush to the Television Studio: A Trump Card for Turkey's Kurdish Geurillas." *Le Monde Diplomatique*. December 1997. Available at: http://mondediplo.com/1997/12/pkk. Accessed July 23, 2006.

Vertovec, Steven. "Migrant Transnationalism and Modes of Transformation." *The International Migration Review*, Vol. 38, No. 3 (Fall 2004): 970–1001.

Vertovec, Steven. "Three Meanings of 'Diaspora,' Exemplified among South Asian Religions." *Diaspora: A Journal of Transnational Studies*, Vol. 6, No. 3 (Winter 1997): 277–299.

Vertovec, Steven and A. Rogers, eds. *Muslim European Youth: Re-producing Religion, Ethnicity, Culture*. Aldershot, UK: Ashgate, 1998.

Waldinger, Roger and Cynthia Feliciano. "Will the New Second Generation Experience 'Downward Assimilation'? Segmented Assimilation Re-Assessed." *Ethnic and Racial Studies*, Vol. 27, No. 3 (May 2004): 376–402.

Wallis, Roy and Steve Bruce. "Secularization: The Orthodox Model." In Steve Bruce, ed. *Religion and Modernization: Sociologists and Historians Debate the Secularization Thesis*. Oxford: Clarendon Press, 1992: 8–30.

Walther, Joseph B. "Relational Aspects of Computer-Mediated Communication: Experimental Observations Over Time." *Organization Science*, Vol. 6, No. 2 (March–April 1995): 186–203.

Warkentin, Craig and Karen Mingst. "International Institutions, the State, and Global Civil Society in the Age of the World Wide Web." *Global Governance*, Vol. 6, No. 2 (April–June 2000): 237–256.

Waters, Mary C. *Black Identities: West Indian Immigrant Dreams and American Realities*. Cambridge, MA: Harvard University Press, 1999.

Watts, Jonathan. "Tibetan Health Care Takes Back Seat to Infrastructure." *The Lancet*, Vol. 362, No. 9386 (September 6, 2003): 810.

Weick, Karl. *Sensemaking in Organizations*. Thousand Oaks, CA: Sage Publications, 1995.

Weick, Karl. *The Social Psychology of Organizing*. New York: McGraw Hill, 1979.

Weimann, Gabriel. *Terror on the Internet: The New Arena, The New Challenges*. Washington, DC: U.S. Institute of Peace, 2006.

Weiner, Myron. *The Global Migration Crisis: Challenge to States and Human Rights*. New York: Harper Collins, 1995.

Weisbrod, Burton A. "Toward A Theory of The Voluntary Non-Profit Sector in a Three-Sector Economy." In Edmund S. Phelps, ed. *Altruism, Morality, and Economic Theory*. New York: Russell Sage Foundation, 1975: 197–223.

Weisner, Thomas S. "Culture, Childhood, and Progress in Sub-Saharan Africa." In Lawrence E. Harrison, and Samuel P. Huntington, eds. *Culture Matters: How Values Shape Human Progress*. New York: Basic Books, 2000: 141–157.

Wellman, Barry and Milena Gulia. "Virtual Communities as Communities: Net Surfers Don't Ride Alone." In Marc A. Smith and Peter Kollock, eds. *Communities in Cyberspace*. London: Routledge, 1999: 167–194.

Wellman, Barry, Annabel Quan Haase, James Witte and Keith N. Hampton. "Does the Internet Increase, Decrease, or Supplement Social Capital: Social Networks, Participation, and Community Commitment." *American Behavioral Scientist*, Vol. 45, No. 3 (November 2001): 436–455.

Wescott, Clay and Jennifer M. Brinkerhoff, eds. *Converting Migration Drains into Gains: Harnessing the Resources of Overseas Professionals.* Manila: Asian Development Bank, 2006. Available online at: http://www.adb.org/Documents/Books/Converting-Migration-Drains-Gains. Accessed November, 28, 2007.

Whine, Michael. "Cyberspace – A New Medium for Communication, Command and Control by Extremists." *Studies in Conflict & Terrorism*, Vol. 22, No. 3 (January 1999): 231–245.

Whitlock, Craig. "Briton Used Internet As His Bully Pulpit." *The Washington Post*, August 8, 2005, A1.

Wilson III, EJ. "Globalization, Information Technology and Conflict in the Second and Third Worlds: A Critical Review of the Literature." Project on World Security. New York: Rockefeller Brothers Foundation, 1998.

Wilson, James Q. *Political Organizations.* Princeton, NJ: Princeton University Press. Originally published 1974. Basic Books: New York, 1995.

Wittig, Michelle Andrisin, and Joseph Schmitz. "Electronic Grassroots Organizing." *Journal of Social Issues*, Vol. 52, No. 1 (March 1996): 53–69.

World Bank. *Global Economic Prospects (GEP): Economic Implications of Remittances and Migration.* Washington, DC: Author, 2006.

World Bank. *World Development Indicators 2005.* Washington, DC: Author, 2005.

World Bank. *World Development Indicators 2004.* Washington, DC: Author, 2004.

Xinhua News. "President Hu: Next Contact with Dalai Lama To Be Held at Appropriate Time." *Xinhua News*, May 7, 2008. Available at: http://news.xinhuanet.com/english/2008-05/07/content_8122950.htm. Accessed June 19, 2008.

Zan, Samuel. *"One Nation, One People, One Destiny"? The Ghanaian Diasporas Contribution to National Development Using Diverse Channels.* Report prepared as part of the "Hello Africa: Shifting Power, Tackling Poverty by Connecting Africa and the African Diaspora." Project funded by Comic Relief. Accra, Ghana: SEND Foundation of West Africa, May 2004.

Zartman, I. William. "Negotiations and Prenegotiations in Ethnic Conflict: The Beginning, the Middle, and the Ends." In Joseph Montville, ed. *Conflict and Peacemaking in Multiethnic Societies.* New York: D.C. Heath, 1991: 511–534.

Zupp, Adrian. "Why Won't the Dalai Lama Pick a Fight?" *The Humanist*, Vol. 64, No. 1 (January-February 2004): 5.

Index